ALL THINGS ARE POSSIBLE

SAINT FRANCES CABRINI

All Things Are Possible

The Selected Writings of Mother Cabrini

Edited by Dawn Beutner

IGNATIUS PRESS SAN FRANCISCO

Excerpts in all chapters but "The Mystic" are taken with permission from *The Letters of Saint Frances Xavier Cabrini* and *Travels of Mother Frances Cabrini*, copyright © 1970 and 1944, Missionary Sisters of the Sacred Heart of Jesus. The text has been emended for accuracy and idiom.

Excerpts in the chapter titled "The Mystic" are translated from *Pensieri e propositi*, published by Centro Cabriniano. Translated by Thomas Jacobi, Ignatius Press.

Cover photos from the digital archives of Cabrini University

Cover design by Enrique J. Aguilar

ISBN 978-1-62164-785-0 (PB)
ISBN 978-1-64229-352-4 (eBook)
Library of Congress Control Number 2025930860
Printed in the United States of America ♾

CONTENTS

FOREWORD

by Sister Nancy Usselmann, F.S.P.

Every canonized saint of the Catholic Church exemplifies some ordinary talent, gift, or virtue to such a degree that it becomes extraordinary. Saint Frances Xavier Cabrini's gift, which saw her through many trials, was tenacity, or the virtue of perseverance. Her ability to not give up in the face of difficulty, which she experienced continuously throughout her life, came not from natural talent, but rather from her intimate, mystical relationship with Christ. This quality is effectively expressed in her letters to her religious sisters.

Her tenacity displayed itself before governors, archbishops, and even the pope, but always with respect for their authority. Though she desired to be a missionary to China, Pope Leo XIII challenged the then thirty-seven-year-old Mother Cabrini to take care of the poor Italian immigrants in America. Unfortunately, she arrived in New York only to find that the archbishop hadn't gotten the memo. He told her to go back to Italy. Strengthened by her love for

Sister Nancy Usselmann, F.S.P., is the Director of Pauline Media Studies in Los Angeles. She is a media literacy educator, theologian, international speaker, and film and TV reviewer. She is the author of *Media Fasting: Six Weeks to Recharge in Christ* and *A Sacred Look: Becoming Cultural Mystics*, a theology of popular culture. She has an M.A. in Theology from Fuller Theological Seminary and certificates in Catechetics and Media Literacy Education.

Christ and her tenacity, she insisted on her mandate from the pope and persevered in her mission.

My affinity with Saint Frances Xavier Cabrini comes from this moment in her life when she felt the most misunderstood. Her tenacity is echoed in a young Italian sister of twenty-four who felt the call to evangelize America forty-three years after Mother Cabrini arrived in New York. The first Daughter of Saint Paul to set foot on American soil in 1932 was Mother Paula Cordero. She received the same greeting from the archdiocese: "Go back to Italy!" Starting an Italian order dedicated to media evangelization, the Daughters of Saint Paul's founder, Blessed James Alberione, believed the sisters needed to be present in the largest cities of the world to communicate the gospel through the fastest, most efficacious means. New York qualified, but the timing was less than ideal. Amid the Great Depression, the Archdiocese of New York was already inundated with the arrival of many religious communities.

As Mother Cabrini followed the pope's directive, Mother Paula obeyed Father Alberione's inspirations. She persevered despite having in her pocket what would be the equivalent of seventeen cents today. She went on to establish Catholic media institutions and faced bishops, politicians, businessmen, and attorneys with the tenacity of the great Mother Cabrini. These women have supported me in my religious vocation and given me the desire to *live Christ* as they did, to the point that Saint Paul says, "It is no longer I who live, but Christ who lives in me" (Gal 2:20).

This beautiful volume of Saint Frances Cabrini's writings brims over with the conviction that with Christ all things are possible (cf. Mt 19:26). In a letter written from Nicaragua on December 12, 1891, she tells her sisters, "So, my daughters, let us learn to lift up our eyes immediately when we face difficulties, because the grace to carry out our duty and practice every virtue will come from above." No one can have such an influence for good unless imbued with God.

Mother Cabrini's letters show a woman who lived a practical mysticism. On a trip through the American West, she offers extensive descriptive details of the natural and man-made beauty she saw, especially in California. Her words to her sisters were like a film reel bringing the images to life.

Her mysticism, a transformative experience of God, witnessed to a soul enthralled by the beauty of Christ who alone captured her heart. Her tenacity of spirit became the virtue of perseverance in the face of challenges through the power of Christ. May Saint Frances Cabrini intercede for all those who lack hope when life's troubles abound. May her letters be a source of strength for those who feel the burden of disappointment, leading them instead on the path of tenacious surrender to God, who knows our needs before we ask (cf. Mt 6:8).

INTRODUCTION

Frances Xavier Cabrini (1850–1917) was a religious sister, the founder of a religious institute, and the first American citizen to be canonized. But hundreds of religious sisters have been declared saints throughout the history of the Church. What sets her apart? What makes the letters of Frances Cabrini worth reading today, over a century after her death?

Like all saints, Frances loved God with her whole heart, mind, and soul. But the Holy Spirit moves in each soul in a unique way, leading it on its own path of holiness. God particularly called Frances to become a teacher, a missionary, and a spiritual guide.

Frances was inspired by Saints Rose of Lima and Mariana of Quito, two women who consecrated their lives to Christ and served the poor. Perhaps that is why Frances also dedicated her life to helping the needy, particularly by teaching children and serving immigrants.

From the time she was a girl, Frances yearned to become a missionary and wanted to bring the Gospel to people all over the world. She played with dolls, but she dressed her dolls as nuns. She made paper boats and floated them in a nearby stream, but her boats carried violets which she dreamed were missionaries heading to faraway countries. When, as a young sister, she changed her middle name to Saverio—or "Xavier"—it was to honor the famous Jesuit evangelist, Saint Francis Xavier, who baptized so many people at one time that his arm grew tired.

Frances was apparently an extrovert by nature, but she spent hours each day alone in prayer. Although she lived in crowded cities and her time was often filled with administrative details and business meetings, she didn't fill her life with noise and chatter. Instead, she carefully poured the spiritual fruits she received from prayer into the lives of her spiritual daughters and those she served.

Frances' personal devotion to the Sacred Heart of Jesus was so important to her that she incorporated it into the name of her order: the Missionary Sisters of the Sacred Heart. Just like her beloved Saint Margaret Mary Alacoque, Frances often shared her love of the Sacred Heart with her sisters. The original name of Frances' order included the word *Salesian*, pointing to her affection for Saint Francis de Sales, the gentle bishop and wise spiritual advisor. Frances was also devoted to Saint John Berchmans, a young man who died while still a Jesuit novice. Frances, like Saint John, demonstrated unwavering cheerfulness, purity of heart, and a desire for spiritual perfection.

The letters and journals of Saint Frances Cabrini do more than help us learn about her favorite saints and how she tried to emulate them. They also teach us how she understood her mission as a religious sister and a founder of a religious order of women. They offer us a window into the life of a modern saint as she met with popes, handled business deals, and trained her spiritual daughters from the other side of the world. They reveal her brushes with death, the persecution she received for serving poor Italians, and her caution in avoiding swindlers in business. They show us her love of nature, her insights into different cultures, and her seemingly supernatural ability to remain hopeful in the face of apparent calamities. Her letters also demonstrate how she managed to encourage and correct her sisters and what kind of spiritual guidance she gave to help *them* become saints.

Frances Cabrini crossed oceans to bring souls to Jesus Christ. Her letters show us how she did it.

Frances' Childhood

Frances—or, in Italian, Francesca—was the tenth of eleven children born to Agostino and Stella Cabrini in 1850 in the small town of Sant'Angelo Lodigiano, Italy.[1] Agostino was a frugal farmer who was so upright that his neighbors nicknamed him "Agostino the Good". He and Stella had known each other all their lives before they married, and they were devout Catholics.

Frances' parents taught her the doctrines of the faith, but they also showed her how to trust in God even during times of suffering. Only four of the eleven Cabrini children reached adulthood, with the others dying either immediately after birth or later from childhood illnesses. Frances' surviving siblings, all of whom were older than she was, were Rosa, Giovanni, and Maddalena, who was born with disabilities.[2]

Frances—called "Cecchina" by her family—was born two months earlier than expected. At the time, her mother, Stella, had a houseful of young children to take care of and chores to do. Stella asked her fifteen-year-old daughter

[1] Some biographies say that Stella had thirteen children. *Mother Cabrini: "Italian Immigrant of the Century"* states that the parish records in her hometown list only eleven children. Stella may have suffered two miscarriages or stillbirths, leading to the confusion.

[2] Some sources state that Maddalena was brain damaged, and others imply that she could not walk.

Rosa to set aside her own desires of becoming a nun to care for the delicate and premature baby Frances instead.

Rosa dutifully gave up her hopes for religious life and devoted herself to raising Frances, along with performing other household duties. But Rosa certainly did not spoil her younger sister. Perhaps out of resentment, she set very high standards for Frances' behavior. Frances later attributed her survival of smallpox to Rosa's careful nursing and her excellent grades to Rosa's tutoring from home. But the stern and critical Rosa also taught Frances about patience and humility, albeit the hard way.

When Frances was twenty years old, both Agostino and Stella died. Her brother had already left their hometown for university. Rosa and Frances were left alone to care for their disabled sister just as the political situation in Italy became increasingly volatile. (After Maddalena's death in 1895, Rosa moved to Argentina, where her brother had emigrated; she died soon afterward.) But Frances had studied hard at a school run by the Daughters of the Sacred Heart, despite repeated health problems and a near-drowning incident. In obedience to her parents' wishes, she earned a teacher's certificate, just like Rosa, and got a temporary job as a teacher in the city of Vidardo.

Like all teachers, Frances had to learn how to earn the respect of her students. She was also pressured to refrain from teaching the Catholic faith in the classroom because of the progressivist anti-Catholic sentiment that was sweeping through Italy at the time. But Frances could not imagine teaching children about any subject without first teaching them about the love of God. She taught her young students through gentleness, never through force or corporal punishment, and won their hearts, an approach she taught to her religious sisters years later. She also brought the anti-Catholic mayor of Vidardo back to the Church through her kindness, generosity, and persistent faith.

Frances' First Religious Community

Frances had become such a beloved teacher in her "temporary" position at Vidardo that no one wanted her to leave. However, she knew she had a religious vocation and tried to enter two different orders. One order refused to accept her because of her poor health, while the other order politely demurred because local clergy had strongly suggested to them that Frances could not be spared from her teaching position at Vidardo.

Frances Cabrini, however, was not easily deterred. She prayed, fasted, practiced physical mortifications, and continued to speak of her desire to become a religious sister to the priests of Vidardo and Sant'Angelo. Eventually, they gave in and recommended that she talk to their bishop. The bishop himself asked this remarkable young woman to become a sister at a new orphanage called the House of Providence.

The House of Providence in Codogno had been founded by Antonia Tondini, a wealthy widow. When the bishop had sent some religious sisters to assist Tondini in the new orphanage, the sisters left the house almost immediately. Tondini convinced the bishop that she should train her own order of religious sisters instead, and the bishop sent Frances to become a new member of that order, directly under Tondini.

Unfortunately, Tondini's leadership was a disaster. For example, when she was given donations to run the orphanage, she often spent the money on herself or secretly gave it to her relatives and friends. It is not clear whether Tondini was merely erratic and dishonest or was mentally unbalanced. Since Frances was famously unwilling to speak ill of others, particularly those who caused her trouble, the precise details have been lost. But the scandal caused by Tondini's behavior eventually brought matters to a crisis.

Frances had imperturbably and charitably responded to Tondini's odd, cruel treatment of her for six years. During that time, she had, once again, shown herself to be an excellent teacher. As she earned the love and respect of her students, she also communicated to them the beauty of God's call to become a religious sister. Frances' missionary spirit was contagious, and some of her students wanted to enter religious life.

Just as Tondini's reputation and orphanage were falling apart, twenty young women had become part of the new order under Frances' direction. After a messy legal battle between Tondini and the bishop, Frances was finally released from her obligation to the House of Providence and encouraged by the bishop to start her own order. And, taking with her the aspirants, postulants, novices, and professed sisters[3] who had been captivated by her personal witness, she did.

Frances' New Religious Order

Frances had already impressed her bishop and several priests, but they underestimated her vision. They merely hoped that this diminutive woman would form a religious

[3] A woman who successfully entered the Missionary Sisters would pass through three stages of formation—aspirant, postulant, and novice—before becoming a professed sister.

order to serve their own diocese. They were aghast when she talked about going to faraway China, particularly since her order had only existed for a short time.

Other Church leaders balked when she called her new order the Institute of the Salesian Missionaries of the Sacred Heart.[4] Although religious sisters had followed missionaries into the field many times in the history of the Church, to them it seemed unsuitable for women themselves to be called missionaries and to lead the way into mission countries. Frances simply pointed out that Saint Mary Magdalene, a woman, could be justly called the first missionary of the Church.

In the meantime, Frances and her sisters uncomplainingly moved into their first house, a deserted friary in Codogno, Italy, with so few possessions that they ate their first meal sitting on a bench and had to go to bed in the dark because they did not even own a lamp. Frances, who had learned the value of suffering in her own life, showed her sisters how to make sacrifices cheerfully out of love for God and even to expect Him to work miracles. Soon, other young women, mostly from poor peasant families in the area, began to see holiness in Frances and her companions and asked to join them. The new order began to grow.

But Frances was Italian, and she knew that a religious order must have a community in Rome, not just in the little town of Codogno. She wanted to obtain papal approval for her order and wrote a rule of life for herself and her sisters to follow. However, obtaining Church approval for a new order is never a trivial matter.

Frances showed up in Rome at the age of thirty-seven, without letters of recommendation, without friends in high

[4] The term *Salesian* was later dropped from the official name of the Institute to avoid confusion with the Salesian orders.

places, and without financial backing. She carefully avoided ever becoming involved in secular politics, even though a cousin was a prominent liberal leader in Italy. When it came to the matter of money, Frances always trusted in Divine Providence. When she found out that letters of recommendation were important, however, she quickly wrote to her bishop to get them. Finally, after many meetings, setbacks, and negotiations, she was granted permission for her sisters to operate two schools for children in Rome.

After developing relationships with several influential Church leaders in the Eternal City, she was also granted a private audience with Pope Leo XIII. Frances had the greatest respect for the papacy and for Leo himself. Only the pope could have redirected her from her long-held dream of traveling as a missionary to China.

The Holy Father knew that, because of political and financial instability in Italy, tens of thousands of Italians were emigrating to America every year.[5] America had already absorbed many waves of immigrants by the late 1800s, and the latest Italian arrivals were willing to perform the dangerous, low-paying jobs that no one else wanted. But these Italian transplants were also treated as subhuman, verbally insulted with racial slurs, and forced to live and work in unsafe, unhealthy environments.

Spiritually, the situation was even worse. There were not enough Italian-speaking priests in America to care for the immigrants' spiritual needs. In American churches at the time, it was also a common practice for people to pay in order to have a seat during a church service. Most Italians, who were struggling just to feed themselves, refused to pay. They were often forced to worship in dingy basements

[5] A few decades later, the number reached a peak of more than two hundred thousand Italian immigrants entering America in one year.

and made to feel inferior because of their poverty. For all these reasons, many Italians simply stopped attending Mass after they arrived in America, while some Protestant churches attracted poor Italians by providing the social services they needed.

With these concerns in mind, Pope Leo XIII challenged Frances to go west, not east, and to serve the Italian immigrants in America rather than seek conversions in China. After listening to the Holy Father and praying about it, she agreed.

Frances Leads Her Sisters to the New World

Frances and her sisters arrived in New York City in 1889 at the invitation of the archbishop of New York, who had invited them to run a Catholic school. A wealthy Italian countess in America had even offered to provide the funds for the project.

But while Frances and her sisters were still on the steamship from Europe to the New World, the archbishop and the countess had gotten into a disagreement over the location of the school. The address proposed by the countess was in a wealthy neighborhood; the archbishop thought the establishment of a school for poor children there would attract negative attention and could result in anti-Catholic persecution. The countess disagreed with him and, as a result, completely retracted her offer. Frances and her sisters were forced to sleep in a filthy slum, worrying about bedbugs and much worse dangers, during their first night in America.

When Frances met with the archbishop, he explained the difficult situation and told her to return to Italy. But Frances serenely replied that since the pope himself had sent her to America, in America she would stay.

In his 1945 biography of Frances Cabrini, *Too Small a World*, Theodore Maynard repeatedly used two words to describe her: *charming* and *shrewd*. Frances possessed both those characteristics in a holy, not worldly, manner.

Within a few weeks of her arrival in New York, Frances had charmed the countess, mended the disagreement, and located a new home for her sisters. When the archbishop refused to let Frances solicit donations from Americans—out of concerns that it would spark anti-Catholic mobs, which he remembered from his own childhood—she and her sisters went begging. They slowly gathered the funds they needed by walking through the slums and asking the poor to contribute their pennies and dimes to support orphanages and schools. But this humbling activity eventually became a part of another common practice of her sisters. Missionary Sisters went door to door in Italian neighborhoods, personally spoke to Catholic families, extended a friendly invitation to return to Mass and the sacraments, and offered to connect them to priests or other help that they might need.

Frances was a farmer's daughter, and she knew how to stretch a lira. While she was always looking for ways to surprise the children in her homes—she often gave them small treats on feast days—she was extremely careful with the money she was given. When funds were tight, she and her sisters economized at their own expense, sacrificing their own food, heat, and clothing.

Frances also possessed a remarkable business sense. She thoroughly evaluated potential properties to find the best location and building conditions, always tried to get a lower price, and read all the fine print on a contract before signing anything. Decades later, people remarked about her uncanny ability to identify properties that would eventually become prime real estate.

Bishops, unsurprisingly, both loved and feared Frances. They appreciated the blessings that the sisters brought to the poor through wholehearted service. But they could not fathom her willingness to throw herself and her sisters into new projects even when she had no money to support them. As long as she believed that God was leading the way, Frances would follow, no matter what others thought or the size of her bank account. Frances' trust in Divine Providence was heroic, but it was certainly not what diocesan accountants would advise.

Frances was, to use Jesus' terms, as wise as a serpent and as innocent as a dove.

Frances was a teacher, not a medical professional, and she initially shied away from establishing hospitals to be administered by her sisters. But when she realized that Italian immigrants were being refused medical care and that the free clinics available were wholly inadequate to the needs of the poor, she changed her mind.

Then there was another dilemma: What name for the New York hospital would not antagonize American Protestants? Frances' choice, Columbus Hospital, was an inspired title that was immediately respected by both Italians and Americans. Frances always insisted on providing the best possible service in her hospitals—health care so excellent that people of other faiths would seek it out.

Frances' Order Spreads

Frances Cabrini and the Missionary Sisters of the Sacred Heart developed such a reputation for dedication and devotion that Catholics in other cities and countries invited them to come and establish new communities. In the late nineteenth century, airplanes had not yet been invented, so Frances generally traveled by steamship or train.

When Frances was about eight years old, she fell into a stream when she was playing and almost drowned. She never learned to swim and had a very reasonable fear of water. But that fear disappeared when she was doing God's work. She seemed completely at home traveling on a steamship and was able to reassure her sisters—most of the time—when the boat seemed to be in danger.

She also had the advantage of being Italian. That apparently helped her obtain relics of Italian saints, and she carried forty-two of those relics with her when she traveled, asking those saints to intercede for her and her sisters from Heaven when the ocean got rough. Frances also took comfort in being able to receive Communion while on board ship, always hoping that a priest would be among the passengers and would celebrate Mass for her and her sisters. When that did not happen and she was deprived of the Eucharist during a voyage, she felt the loss deeply and would take advantage of any reasonable opportunity to find a church when the ship docked. Sometimes she and her sisters attended multiple Masses in a day, one right after another, if the ship spent long enough in port to make it possible.

With each new foundation, Frances arrived in the location with a small group of sisters, evaluated the needs of the area, made crucial decisions, developed a good relationship with several local leaders, personally served at the new community (sweeping floors herself, if necessary), and ensured that it was on a solid footing. Then she would leave for a new location and a new foundation. This pattern was repeated in North American cities such as Chicago, Denver, Los Angeles, New Orleans, New York, and Seattle, as well as Central and South American cities (in Nicaragua, Panama, and Argentina) and European cities (in England, France, Italy, and Spain).

From the time she was small, Frances had loved history and geography above all other school subjects. When she traveled as a missionary to see the places she had only read about in books, she delighted in writing to her sisters about the natural wonders, cultural practices, languages, climate, and other differences she encountered. Unfortunately, she often had to describe political unrest, threats of violence, bandits, epidemics, and dangers due to war.

Frances' letters also describe her encounters with Protestant believers. Coming from a strongly Catholic country, it was difficult for her to understand non-Catholic Christians. Frances had a profound love for the sacraments, and like the true missionary that she was, she saw these encounters with Protestants as opportunities to spread the truths of the Catholic faith.

The Missionary Sisters began their international mission by teaching students, caring for orphans, and administering hospitals. As they became more involved in each community, they found other ways to serve the needy. For example, they visited prisoners, particularly those on death row, to reconcile them to the Church and to their own families. They cared for the sick during epidemics and natural disasters. They ran dispensaries to provide medicines for the needy sick. These were, of course, natural ways for the sisters to expand their mission in different lands.

Her Final Years

Frances decided to become an American citizen in 1909, and she also learned to speak other languages as she traveled. She always struggled with English, finding it easier to learn languages more closely related to her native Italian.

Throughout her life, Frances suffered from poor health. She was often considered close to death, yet did not begin to slow down until her late sixties.

The sisters who knew her best noticed her decline. By the 1910s, the Missionary Sisters, which had begun with just Frances and her original companions, whom she considered co-foundresses,[6] now numbered over a thousand sisters, living in sixty-seven houses all over the world.

Frances' brother Giovanni, who lived for many years in Argentina, always spoke proudly of his younger sister. But she puzzled him as well, since, as he put it, she seemed to travel from country to country with the ease of someone merely passing from the house to the backyard.

Frances contracted malaria during one of her voyages, and it recurred periodically. This may have contributed to her chronic endocarditis, a condition involving an inflammation of the heart, which finally caused her death on December 22, 1917. It was a fitting end for a woman who loved so much and so well.

After her death, Frances was beatified and canonized on the strength of two thoroughly researched and inexplicable healings. After her sisters prayed for Frances to intercede from Heaven, a baby boy was cured of permanent blindness overnight, and on another occasion, one of her religious sisters was miraculously cured of a terminal illness.

But, as is described in many of the biographies of Frances, her religious sisters had witnessed inexplicable events throughout Frances' lifetime. She sometimes seemed able to read the souls of her sisters and instinctively knew when they were troubled, discouraged, or far from God. On multiple occasions when the sisters were seriously lacking in food, drink, or money, Frances merely laughed and told them to "go look again" in the pantry, cellar, or

[6] Frances was so humble that she refused to let herself be called the foundress of her order, even when it was clear to everyone that she was.

drawer. The lacking item would suddenly be discovered in abundance.

Frances lived a busy, active life, but, unknown to many people, she was also a mystic. For example, she sometimes had vivid dreams that helped her make difficult decisions, and she would share them with her sisters.

Early in the life of her community, Frances shared a bedroom with another sister. When that sister awoke in the morning, she told Frances that she had seen her praying in the middle of the night and that she had seemed to be surrounded by light. The sister innocently asked Frances where the light had come from. Frances replied that she was merely imagining things—and never permitted a sister to share a bedroom with her again.

Frances Cabrini did not tell others about the favors that she received from the Sacred Heart of Jesus in prayer. Fortunately for us, though, she quietly kept a personal journal, and it reveals a great deal about her spiritual experiences. While her many letters help us understand her personality, her trials, and her relationships, her journal entries show us the mystical gifts she received during prayer.

Her Ocean of Letters

Even when there were a thousand Missionary Sisters in her order, Frances tried to be a spiritual mother to all of her spiritual daughters. In the early twentieth century, letters were the best way to do that, so she wrote hundreds of them, and she encouraged all her sisters to write to her regularly as well.

The selection of writings in this book has been culled from her letters and journals and arranged according to different aspects of her life. After all, Frances was many things at once: the founder of an international religious institute, a religious superior who trained her sisters to be Christ-centered teachers, an intrepid missionary who described her travels to inspire them in their vocations, a spiritual guide who advised individual sisters about how to face their own challenges, and a saint with her own unique spiritual insights.

Saint Frances Cabrini's gifts to the world are not limited to the religious institute she founded or the many people whom her sisters have served. Her letters and journal entries reveal her love for the Sacred Heart of Jesus, as well as her life of virtue, common sense, and heroic trust in God. Her insights can inspire us, particularly when our trials seem overwhelming, to remain faithful to Him. In the words of the Scripture verse Frances used more frequently than any other: "I can do all things in him who strengthens me" (Phil 4:13).

TIMELINE OF SAINT FRANCES CABRINI'S LIFE

1850	Frances Cabrini is born on July 15 in Sant'Angelo Lodigiano, Italy.
1870	Her father dies in February, and her mother dies in December.
1871	Frances obtains a teacher's diploma.
1872	She accepts a position as teacher in Vidardo, Italy.
1874	She becomes a religious sister at a new institution, the House of Providence, in Codogno, Italy.
1880	She founds her own religious institute in Codogno with six companions.
1882	A second house of the new institute is opened in Grumello, Italy.
1884	A new house and school are opened in Milan, Italy.
1885	A new house and school are opened in Borghetto Lodigiano, Italy.
1887	Frances travels to Rome, secures papal approval of her new order, and opens two schools there.
1888	She opens an academy and accepts directorship of a hospital in Castel San Giovanni, Italy.
1889	She travels with six Sisters to New York City, opens an orphanage and a free school, and returns to Italy.

1890 She returns to New York, relocates her orphanage, establishes a novitiate for her Sisters in the United States, and returns to Italy.

1891 She travels from Le Havre, France, to New York City. Later, she travels to Granada, Nicaragua, to open a new school.

1892 She travels from Nicaragua, passing through La Mosquitia, Honduras, to New Orleans, where she founds a house. On returning to New York, she establishes a mission house with a chapel and school, plus a hospital. She travels from New York to Le Havre, returns to Italy, and opens a house in Monte Compatri.

1893 She establishes a college for women in Rome and an academy in Genoa, Italy.

1894 She organizes the relocation of a college and travels from Genoa to New York with fifteen Sisters.

1895 She relocates her hospital to a larger building, travels to Panama and founds an academy, travels from Balboa, Panama, to Buenos Aires, Argentina, and makes a pilgrimage to Lima, Peru, the birthplace of Saint Rose of Lima. She also makes a dangerous crossing of the Andes mountains to reach Buenos Aires, Argentina, and establishes an academy.

1896–1897 She remains in Italy because of a lawsuit, which is finally settled in her favor.

1898 She founds a house in Paris and returns to New York.

1899 She founds schools in New York City; Scranton, Pennsylvania; Newark, New Jersey; and Chicago. She establishes a summer home for orphaned girls in Long Beach, Mississippi. She returns to Le Havre, France, and founds an academy in Madrid before returning to Italy.

1900 In Italy, she founds houses in Turin, establishes an academy in Città della Pieve, transfers a school to a new location in Rome, and begins building a church. She founds a house in Balboa, Panama, and another in Marsciano, Italy. She travels to Argentina.

1901 She establishes a school and orphanage in Buenos Aires, Argentina, a college in Rosario de Santa Fe, and an academy in Villa Mercedes.

1902 She travels from Paris to London and founds a school. She returns to New York and travels to Denver to found one school and take the directorship of another. She sends Sisters to found a school in São Paulo, Brazil.

1903 She travels to Chicago to found a hospital. In Seattle, she founds an orphanage and a chapel.

1904 She travels to New Orleans to build an orphanage and open another school. She is forced to return to Chicago when the planned hospital runs into serious financial difficulties.

1905 Frances rescues Columbus Hospital in Chicago from its financial difficulties and is present for its opening. She travels to Denver to found an orphanage and to Los Angeles to found another one. She also establishes a country home for her orphans in Burbank, California.

1906 Frances is present at the opening of a New Orleans orphanage, returns to Italy, and visits her homes in Paris, London, and Rome.

1907 Frances' order is officially approved. Later, she makes her nineteenth sea voyage, this one from Barcelona to Buenos Aires.

1908 She visits houses in Argentina and Brazil, and she founds an academy and school in Rio de Janeiro.

1909 She returns to New York and visits all the houses in the United States. She returns to Chicago to found a second hospital.

1910 On her twenty-third sea journey, she returns to Rome. She tries to hand over the leadership of the order, but her Sisters refuse to allow it. She visits her houses in Paris and London and founds an academy in London.

1911 An extension hospital is founded in Chicago.

1912 She travels to New York to organize a reconstruction of her hospital there, but the outbreak of war interferes with her plans. She founds a school and orphanage in Philadelphia.

1913 She visits her houses in Chicago, Denver, Los Angeles, and Seattle. She relocates her orphanage in Seattle to a better site and returns to New York.

1914 She founds a school in Dobbs Ferry, New York. A donor helps the order acquire a newer, better home for the orphanage in Paris.

1915 Because of World War I, she opens a military hospital in her house in Milan, with a similar hospital at the house in Castel San Giovanni.

1916 Despite a gradual decline in her health, she visits all the order's houses in the American West and founds a sanatorium in Seattle.

1917 As her health continues to decline, Frances travels to Chicago. There she continues to attend to her many duties and is remarkably active the day before her death. She dies peacefully—and so unexpectedly that she is alone in her room—around noon on December 22, of a heart condition.

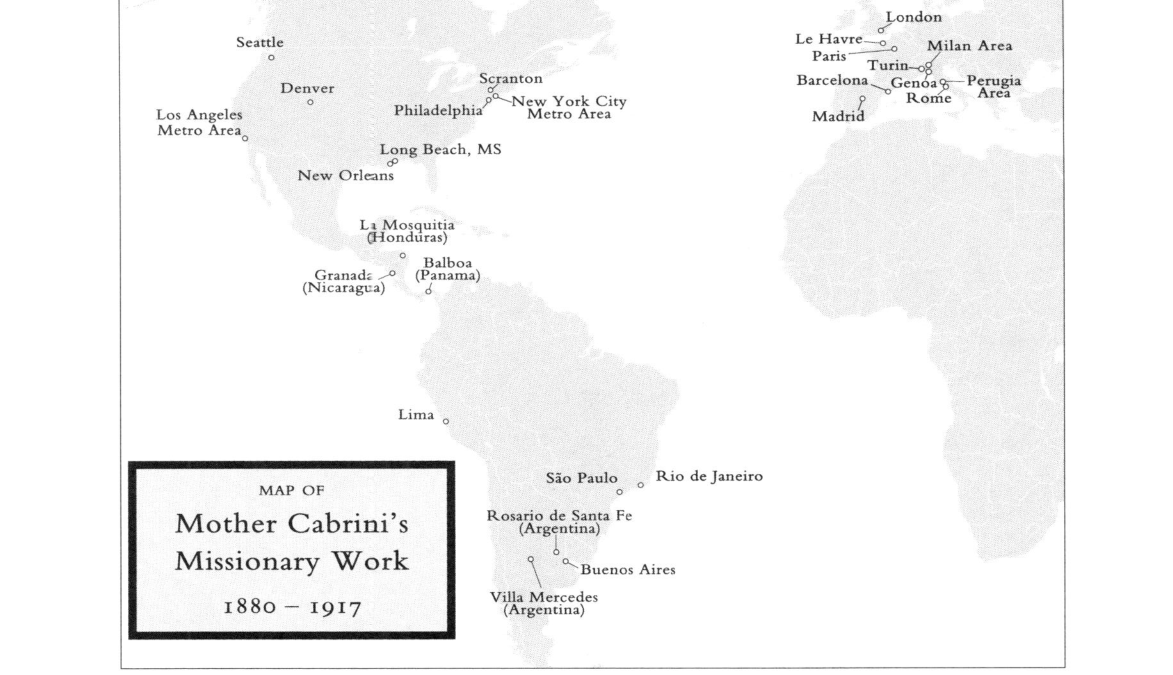
MAP OF
Mother Cabrini's
Missionary Work
1880 – 1917
Seattle
Denver
Los Angeles
Metro Area
Scranton
Philadelphia
New York City
Metro Area
Long Beach, MS
New Orleans
La Mosquitia
(Honduras)
Granada
(Nicaragua)
Balboa
(Panama)
Lima
São Paulo
Rio de Janeiro
Rosario de Santa Fe
(Argentina)
Buenos Aires
Villa Mercedes
(Argentina)
London
Le Havre
Paris
Milan Area
Turin
Barcelona
Genoa
Perugia
Area
Rome
Madrid

1. The Foundress

From the founding of the Missionary Sisters of the Sacred Heart in 1880 until her death in 1917, Frances Cabrini served as the superior general of her religious institute. The following letters highlight some important events in the life of her order.

* * *

January 10, 1888, Rome

This letter describes one of Mother Cabrini's early private audiences with Pope Leo XIII.

J.M.J.F.[1]
My Beloved Daughters,

Today is a day to be remembered! It is the day on which I had a special audience with the Holy Father. I was presented together with Sister Maddalena, Sister Michelina, and Sister Concetta, who carried a gift for the Holy Father. He deeply appreciated the gift and praised the workmanship, saying, "I cherish this because you have made it with your own hands, and I shall keep it in memory of you."

[1] "Jesus, Mary, Joseph, Francis," namely Saint Francis Xavier, the patron of the Missionaries of the Sacred Heart of Jesus. It is a common custom for religious and priests to inscribe their letters with such initials, partly as a blessing on their communication and partly as a reminder that the kingdom of God comes first.

I told him that it had been embroidered at our motherhouse, but he insisted that I had made it.

He asked many things, such as if you faithfully observe the Holy Rule. He begged me to be very strong in demanding of everyone the true spirit of the Institute, so that you will be able to work for the salvation of souls as real missionaries. He wanted to know about all our houses, but he kept on referring to the motherhouse, upon which, he said, he bestowed a special blessing.

He blessed all of us and greatly encouraged us to grow in virtue in order to make ourselves more useful. I had a nice discourse that I wanted to read, but since there were other people awaiting his presence, he said: "Leave it with me and I shall gladly read it." I told him there was a letter from the cardinal vicar in it, and he seemed even happier to have it; he was really like the father of a family. When we entered, we made a genuflection in the middle of the room and then knelt before him and kissed his foot, but in parting he offered us his hand.

So then, my daughters, we have a greater obligation to observe our Holy Rule and endeavor to become, in fact, real missionaries; that is, we should be holy and truly edifying. Our Holy Father, God's representative, has spoken, and we, his daughters, must obey. "He who hears him, hears Me," said Our Lord Jesus Christ [see Luke 10:16]. Thus we shall have the grace one day to find ourselves intimately united to God, to that Divine Heart Who now should be the center of all our affections and aspirations.

I have to leave you now, since I am pressed for time. Pray fervently for me and my intentions. Be kind and courageously virtuous, especially in those [difficult] situations that alone will prove to me your virtue—the only thing I desire of you.

Yours affectionately in the Most Sacred Heart of Jesus,
M. FRANC. SAVERIO CABRINI

September 9, 1889, Codogno, Italy

Mother Cabrini tells one of her Sisters about a serious fire that had just occurred at the community in Codogno. Note that the horarium she mentions in this and other letters is the schedule of prayer and daily life that was established for all the Missionary Sisters.

J.M.J.F.
My Dearest Daughter,

After having made you wait quite some time, I am writing to you now. Very serious affairs caused by a big fire here at Codogno on the night of August 26 prevented me from writing before this.

At nine P.M. the fire broke out in the storeroom, which contained a large quantity of wood, which had just been stored there, and all the laundry. There was a loss of 5,000 lire, which will be reimbursed by the insurance company. At the first sign of fire, all the men of Codogno came and stayed with us all night to extinguish it and to save as much as we could. A few of them were scorched and a few burned their clothes, but they were all happy to have been of service to the nuns. The flames were very high at times and threatened to engulf our chapel and the dormitory, but we were able to avert that disaster with wet blankets. By a special grace of the Sacred Heart of Jesus, no one panicked; but it took me three days to get over the shock and realize what had really happened.

We worked tirelessly to put the house in order for the retreat of the laity that began yesterday. We have about sixty externs.[2]

[2] Mother Cabrini and her Sisters organized retreats for young laywomen living in the area. One of the purposes of these retreats was to identify and attract vocations; some participants ultimately became Sisters themselves.

I do not understand your question about the sick nuns. To me it seems to suggest that up until now, you have not taken care of them properly, and that is not right. You certainly don't wait for the permission of the superior general when a nun is in need of care. It seems to me that you have written without reflection, and I believe that you have not neglected any sick nun as your letter seems to indicate.

As for changing the horarium, I say no, because the horarium has the blessing of Heaven and is not harmful to anyone. Someone who needs to eat can do so at any hour; that does not necessitate changing the horarium. Some Sisters have always taken snacks and, if I am not mistaken, I have seen you doing this also—so we shall not discuss the matter any further. Do what a good mother would do, and that will be enough. Tell all the Sisters to recover quickly because I don't want them to be ill when there is so much to be done.

I was happy to hear that Fr. Aurelio was your retreat master. About our Sisters being young, you should have answered him that twenty years from now, he will find quite a number of old nuns, but not now, when the Institute is in its infancy.

On Saturday the spiritual exercises for the laity will end, and on the 19th ours will begin; these will be followed by the retreat in Milan for externs. Pray that we may obtain many good prospects. The postulants now number twenty, but by next month I want their number increased to thirty. Pray! Five postulants are on retreat in preparation for investiture on Monday or Tuesday. They are excellent prospects for the Institute.

Go to Aspra as soon as you can. I shall send Sister Maria Luigia as soon as possible, and she can evaluate the prospective Sisters; in the meantime pray fervently for my intention.

I am waiting to hear whether the pastor has decided to come. Tell him that I am waiting to see him, and to pray for our retreat so that all may be converted.

Bon voyage to the sisters going to Aspra; I, too, would like to visit the mountains if I could.

Greet the students for me; tell them I would like to be there to enjoy their excellent behavior. Did you find a suitable house in a nice location? If not, we shall search together when I come.

May the Heart of Jesus bless you and make you holy.

Affectionately yours in the Heart of Jesus,

M. FRANC. SAVERIO CABRINI

December 12, 1891, Granada, Nicaragua

In this letter, Mother Cabrini tells another Sister about the progress of their new house in Nicaragua. Leaders in Nicaragua had invited Mother Cabrini to come and establish a school for children from wealthy families. She agreed, hoping this school would open the door for future schools for needy children, and traveled to Granada. But she soon discovered that Catholics there had developed a very lax attitude with respect to the sins of adultery and fornication. It had become a common practice for many Nicaraguan Catholics, even leading citizens, to live together without marrying and for wealthy men to keep mistresses. Mother Cabrini recognized that she could not ignore a widespread acceptance of sinful behavior by Catholics, and she believed that to do so would encourage that sin to continue. She therefore refused to allow illegitimate children to attend her school. The public reaction was so violent that she feared for her life, but she did not back down. Eventually, a remarkable number of leading citizens decided to marry in the Church, and there was at least a temporary improvement in moral standards in the city.

J.M.J.F.
To Mother Superior, Mother Candida,
and Mother Assunta,

Your letters consoled me immensely, and they were a real relief in the midst of the labor and difficulty I experienced in establishing this school. For six or seven nights, at the least noise I imagined they were coming to take my life, but before I was overcome by fear, my soul was filled with the longed-for joy of becoming a martyr for the same cause as Saint John the Baptist; but through your prayers and your efforts to become real missionaries, or because Jesus treats me like a child, the fact is that those who threatened me at first not only came to admit I was right but even became good friends of the Institute and supporters of my principles based on the commandments of God and the Church.

So, my daughters, let us learn to lift up our eyes immediately when we face difficulties, because the grace to carry out our duty and practice every virtue will come from above.

Always be united as one soul. Be profoundly humble: see who among you can humble herself the most. Have great charity for one another, especially for the most difficult personalities. Do not tolerate an unhappy face or low spirits, whether caused by self-love or something else, for very long, but seek out the poor soul and try to correct her. Help her to overcome the fiction she thinks is real.

Always have this charity—it is your duty, and it is charity that will incline the Heart of Jesus toward you. On my return I hope to find you holy; this will be the cup of refreshing water that will restore me after a long journey.

The Sisters and I are well; we are gradually adjusting to this great heat that keeps us perspiring all day and every day and rarely drops to 105 degrees by night. I did not want to believe it, but I had to convince myself it was true when

I saw the thermometer. So you can imagine how we are enveloped by this feverish heat; however, the air is light, refreshing, and very easy to breathe. When I can breathe properly, I feel I have everything.

I beg you to do what you can to increase the number of postulants; make sure that they are good and suitable. Let everyone who can take piano lessons and study French, for we have a great need for these two subjects here, and it seems as though our school will expand. This looks like a real mission, and I am delighted.

Tell Sister Carmela that I answered her letter in my other letter addressed to all the Sisters; therefore, let her study each word I wrote there. With humility all problems can be remedied because this blessed child of God, humility, has infinite power. It is a great grace of God because our very defects can serve as stepping stones to reach it.

May Jesus bless you and inflame your souls as much as the heat of the nearby volcano inflames us. After your small miseries have been burned up, you may be able to inflame the souls of everyone around you.

When you write to the bishop, greet him for me and tell him that I hope he will help me cure the fever of my pride, this disease that is insufferable to the Heart of Jesus.

Pray and have others pray for me.

Yours aff. in the Sacred Heart,

M. FRANCESCA SAVERIO CABRINI

March 12, 1895, New York

Mother Cabrini writes from America to Sisters back in Codogno about the death of Msgr. Serrati, a priest who had supported her and her order from its beginning and who apparently provided Mother with a spiritual warning to be watchful about protecting the order from danger.

A.M.G.SS.C.J.[3]
My Dearest Daughter,

I am glad that Msgr. Serrati left his estate to his parents and his annuities to Teresa; otherwise, God knows what we would have seen and heard. May God be praised! ... Let us ask God to keep His hand over our heads, for if He should ever remove it, I don't know what we would do.

Pray constantly for our deceased pastor and do not cease until he comes to tell you that he is in Paradise; perhaps he is already there. Beware of those who go around mentioning his defects. If we should not complain about or criticize the living, much less should we criticize the dead. Instead, look for his good works, which you will find in abundance; in this way you will imitate Sacred Scripture, which remembers the dead by begging God to look upon their good works and give them the kiss of peace for all eternity. This is the sacred duty of religious. And you have the additional motive of gratitude for what he has done for the Institute. He was instrumental in helping us across the sea, and even his last letters were those of a father. If you call to mind his good works, you will find enough of them to make you think of him as a saint.

Ask Jesus to give him glory in Heaven commensurate with his good works. Beware of those who delight in recalling his bad moments and the offenses he committed through self-love, because such people not only harm themselves but are also a disgrace to the Institute.

If you did not bother to resent the things Teresa said before, why do so now when you have nothing to do with her? She is a poor peasant; have compassion on her and

[3] "Ad maiorem gloriam sacratissimi cordis Jesu" ("To the greater glory of the Most Sacred Heart of Jesus").

pray for her, for it is also written that evil will befall those who wish evil on persons consecrated to God. So you see how you should have pity on her and pray for her. If I were there, I would comfort her.

It is all right for a Jesuit to give the children's retreat, but it would be good to let the preacher say a few words. You know the story of the disturbance Teresa usually causes every year.... Through Mr. Castelli, let the preacher come, even if he preaches badly. Even if all he says is "Be humble", he will have given you a large share of divine wisdom.

I do not like the way you treat the young Swiss lady. She is a teacher, and if we open a house in Switzerland, she will be of great help to us. Let Sister Bonaventure come to Codogno during Sister Magdalen's absence and keep her under discipline. If she converts, well and good; otherwise, a tree will have to be removed from the Master's vineyard.

Please remind the Sisters to add their family name and their country to their religious name when they write to me. Between the old and the new Sisters, it is quite confusing to figure out who's who without a family name. I like their compositions in Portuguese because this exercise is of great help in mastering the language.

So you enjoyed reading the news about the hospital. Blessings are being poured upon it. I have other good news to give you: in New Orleans, about an hour's distance from the city, they want to give us a villa, a sugar plantation with a furnished house, six donkeys, a horse, two carriages, carts of tools for working the soil, and a hundred chickens—all because they want us to take care of the poor Negroes who have come in huge numbers from Jamaica and Africa.

What a lovely mission! Do you like it? Be good and pray because they are waiting for me to accept this offer. Try to obtain associates for the Negroes because that is really a mission among the unbelievers and means are necessary. We will have to prepare them for baptism and then the rest.... Some are already baptized as Baptists. Your Sisters will work hard, and you help them like Moses.

The other night, Monsignor came to see me and asked me to advise all the Sisters to keep their doors and windows closed, since a revolution had broken out. I replied that I would and invited him to sit down. With great calm he said, "But if you don't hurry, the enemy will come in."

I hurriedly called the Sisters, shutting the windows as I went along, when from a distance I saw a great crowd running toward us. A guard of ten or twelve policemen surrounded our house, and I asked them if there was any trouble. "No, no, remain calm; we are here to defend you."

These words reassured me, and I ran to tell Monsignor, but he was nowhere to be found. When I asked the doorkeeper where he had gone, she said simply, "He is gone."

"But where?" I asked.

She again replied, "He is gone."[4]

Then I understood it was a spiritual warning. A great crowd of enemies, visible and invisible, are always ready to attack us, but we shall be safe if we keep our doors and windows closed: that is, our mouth, eyes, ears, mind, and heart. The administrators of our Institute are the guards who will protect and defend us.

Faith, my daughters, great faith: see that all your works are the kind of works produced by souls illumined by the light of faith. If you are humble, if you have faith, the robust will become stronger and you will no longer fear the enemy; so pray for the soul of our good Msgr. Serrati, who came to warn us.

[4] Mother Cabrini apparently experienced a vision of the late Msgr. Serrati reminding her of spiritual dangers.

Mother Cecilia and [Sister] Scalvini will leave for Panama and no one else. Let them take the bobbin for making lace and some thread for that purpose. I hope you have not forgotten anything I told you in my previous letters. Give them a dozen pairs of flannels, which they can use in Panama; it is not as warm as in Nicaragua.

With all my heart I greet you all. May Jesus give you His blessing.

Affectionately yours in the Most Sacred Heart of Jesus,
M. FRANC. SAVERIO CABRINI

May 7, 1895, New Orleans

Mother Cabrini describes the progress of her new community in New Orleans.

A.M.G.SS.C.J.
My Dearest Daughter,

I have been in New Orleans since the first of May, and I have been able to start the beautiful month of Our Lady in a city dotted with flowers. I'll leave here for Panama on the twenty-fourth, and, thanks to Divine Providence, I have found a boat that leaves every Friday for Puerto Limón, which is only sixteen hours away from Colón. The captain, who is a good man, told me he is happy to give me free passage, suggesting that I leave on the twenty-fourth because there will be another holy captain on board. I hope you receive this in time to begin praying to the Sacred Heart and to Mary Star of the Sea so that they may accompany me as they have done so far.

We will have to stop at Puerto Limón for a few days and wait for the other boats. Perhaps we shall receive the Holy

Spirit on Pentecost Sunday in the land of La Mosquitia. This is very consoling for me because the Holy Spirit will not descend for the two of us only, but for all those souls who have not received the light of the Gospel, and we shall have the chance to do a little missionary work where we hope to open a mission later on.

Pray and accompany me in spirit so that through your prayers some good may be done. I found a mission here that brought me much consolation. Our house is in an Italian parish, and the Sisters are doing a great deal of work that is progressing very nicely; it has such simplicity that it reminds me of an antechamber of Paradise. I wish your house were like this one, but then I would be too happy. The archbishop is like a father to us, and he is studying ways and means of helping us expand our apostolate.

I did not accept the plantation I spoke about because they proposed several, and I am trying to find out which one is best before making a choice. No matter where we open the mission, we shall have Negroes because they come here in large numbers. If we had a hundred Sisters, we could open at least twelve missions among the Baptists.

Multiply yourselves like the sons of Abraham, and then, oh daughters, we can reap the harvest, which is great.

I will write again from Panama if not from here. On the journey I will devote my writing to the Sisters to give them an account of everything that happens. Pray that the sea may not be too calm but that the waves will allow my pen to move along; only then will I be able to tell you something.

Plan the spiritual exercises for laywomen so that you will have good attendance and obtain some good vocations. Only twelve vocations since I left; it is really too few. The nine who will arrive in New York will be like a drop of water in the ocean, as you can imagine.

I will bring this to a close because I have so much to do. I greet you all and offer my respects to everyone I should remember. May Jesus bless you, and may He make you holy. Be observant, humble, and charitable; in this way you will see the wonders of the Lord.

Affectionately in the Most Sacred Heart of Jesus,
M. FRANC. SAVERIO CABRINI

January 6, 1896, Buenos Aires

Several months later, Mother Cabrini is now in Argentina to establish her first home in that country, with many of the usual difficulties.

A.M.G.SS.C.J.
My Dearest Daughter,

Everyone is complaining about my long silence, and you, along with the others, seem to say: "What is the matter? What can it be?"

Well, what happened is that as soon as I arrived in Buenos Aires, at the insistence of the archbishop and other members of the Curia, I had to go up and down the long streets of the city in order to find a suitable house. I did it in such haste that within three weeks a new pair of shoes was rendered unserviceable. At night I was dead tired, but in the morning I started all over again.

Finally I found a house, but now there is a language barrier, since I don't have anyone who can translate for me. Plus, there is the chore of keeping the house clean while Mother Chiara attends to the kitchen; but the house is nice and reminds me of the foundation of the Institute, when we lacked almost everything. It also recalls the foundation in Rome, when poor Mother Serafina was ill and I had to be "priest, doorkeeper, and altar boy", as they say, until the Sisters came to give me a little respite.

Here the matter is a little more serious, since the Sisters whom I have summoned by cablegram will not arrive until next month. Patience! So this particular foundation will have its own story, which we shall read together some day.

The people are very good here, too. Someone always accompanies me to my destination in the city, while a young lady remains with Mother Chiara at home to receive visitors, who have already begun to come. They gave us a beautiful, costly statue of the Sacred Heart. Another woman gave us a statue of Saint Rose that is so beautiful that it seems to come from Heaven. This is a most appropriate gift, since the school will be named after Saint Rose—who, being the patroness of South America, is much beloved here.

Every day we receive gifts of money: the new archbishop wasn't able to give me as much as the deceased archbishop had promised, so he asked families to make a contribution. He has also asked a religious congregation to lend us everything we need for the chapel and to provide a chaplain until we can meet the expense. See how many blessings I have received in coming here accompanied by Saint Rose. Try to introduce her devotion there among the youth.

The recommendation of Bishop Peralta pleased the archbishop and the Curia greatly, and they praised him as a good and zealous pastor; this pleased me to no end since he was a good father to us. Msgr. Espinosa never stops talking about Msgr. Peralta, with whom he studied in Rome. Msgr. Espinosa is so good to us that he gave me several of his calling cards, asking me to write on them whatever I needed. I think Msgr. Peralta will be pleased to hear these things, and after what you tell him, he will forgive me for not having written to him, not even for the new year.

Imagine, on Christmas Eve I returned home at nine P.M., just in time to have some refreshments and then begin our devotions to the Christ Child and Midnight Mass. Meanwhile, I had prepared everything we needed in the house that I wanted to inhabit on the very day of Christmas, wanting the new foundation to have the Christ Child as its founder—He who was such a good friend of Saint Rose. The nuns with whom we were staying sent us dinner and we prepared supper.

Some distinguished Panamanians made connections for me in Chile, who made connections for me in Buenos Aires. To these I am indebted for all the care I am surrounded with—particularly Don Adolfo della Guardia. Moved by his generosity, many people have followed his example. Thank him and everyone for me.

The governor was also most kind on the day of my departure. I enclose one of the cards that I sent to about five hundred families in Buenos Aires either to thank them or to ask for their charity. Now I am preparing the program, and you are not here to help me. I have to do these things, which I really don't know how to do, and I don't have any of your programs on hand because the trunks that they have sent by sea from Valparaíso have not yet arrived and I have to do everything from memory.

On the other hand, it is wonderful to encounter difficulties. It is the only way to induce our good Jesus to lead us by the hand or let Him do everything. How wonderful! Repeat it with me with devotion and try to be very generous, for perfection is not attained by keeping our arms folded but by fighting valorously like brave missionaries during the few days Divine Providence grants us.

If Mother Pauline really does not want to imitate her saint, leave her alone. You and Mother Egidia should try your very best, with confidence that you will have more success in teaching about our good Jesus than one who really knows the language.

I am sending this letter because I do not want to enslave anyone who wants to be free; neither can I permit anyone to remain in the community who does not live the life of an observant religious. If you pray, I may be able to find vocations here, where there are many young women who are well educated and even teachers. Pray without interruption. I greet you all, and I send you a blessing that I implore from the Sacred Heart of Jesus. Become holy, in charity; I feel the need of charity more every day.

You may have heard of the angelic death of our Sister Alfonsina in New York. Blessed is she who was observant and holy! Death comes, my daughters. Don't lose another minute, but give yourselves to perfection by enclosing yourselves in the heart of Jesus.

My best to Fr. Byron, and tell him that his relics made for excellent company and brought me graces; also remember me to Fr. Junguito, telling him how much I appreciate his doing what I asked him to do.

I leave you; accompany me with prayer and sacrifices, and I will do the same for you.

Affectionately in the Most Sacred Heart of Jesus,
M. FRANC. SAVERIO CABRINI

July 9, 1897, Codogno, Italy

Mother Cabrini describes a very encouraging meeting she had with Pope Leo XIII. Although she was initially hesitant to involve her Sisters in running hospitals, she explains how she believes this could work well.

A.M.G.SS.C.J.
My Dearest Daughter,

I was very pleased with the report from the hospital and even more so because it pleased the doctors and others. I hope the hospital will benefit from this report; I would like you to send me a few copies that I can present to other people. You can give the package to one of the captains or someone going on the boat. Please address it as follows: Via Luccoli, No. 30, Genoa, Italy.

I don't know whether I already told you that I had a private audience with the Holy Father without even asking for it. I wanted to give him the large, beautiful bird that you had stuffed for me, but since he has been so busy with all the canonizations that he did not even give an audience to the three hundred bishops who came for the occasion, I asked his chamberlain to present it to him. When he asked the Holy Father if he could do this, His Holiness answered: "Let Mother Cabrini present it herself; I want to see her." So I had a half-hour audience. As soon as I was close to him, he took my face between his hands and said: "You are finally here after a long absence and after so much work." He continued to question me like a loving father about the missions, repeating his words of three years ago, saying that he always remembers me. I had the superior of Rome, Mother Gesuina Diotti, with me. He looked at her intently as if to read her soul. Then turning to me, he said: "Are you pleased with this daughter?"

"Yes," I answered, "very pleased."

Then he took her by the hand, saying: "Always remember to do what Mother tells you in the way she tells you to do it and how she wants it from you, and then you will become saints. This is what I want from all the Sisters of the Institute."

Then he told me many other nice things, among them that he blessed not only the Sisters but their missions and all the people who assist them. Repeat these words to all our benefactors because I had them in mind when I asked for his blessing. The Holy Father wants you to become saints, so obey with generosity because he represents Christ; therefore, it is Christ who makes this request.

When I gave an account of the affairs of our Institute to the Congregation of Religious in Rome, I was asked who takes care of the sick in our hospital. I answered that the doctors and nurses take care of the sick and that the religious tend to the spiritual needs of the patient, as well as the organization and administration of the hospital. They approved, saying that if I had said that the nuns provided medical care to the patients, they would have rejected our Institute's status and categorized it as a non-religious institute run by charitable women. This is the answer to your question about assisting at the operation of those two Franciscan sisters. Make this your norm for the future, to ensure that the Sisters are not exposed to risk and do not take certain liberties.

I stress this strongly because we must work within the scope of our Institute. There are those who are watching you and sending reports to Rome. If some religious should come to the hospital and ask for a sister instead of a nurse to assist in the operating room, they may use some of their own sisters for that purpose, as you would assist one of our own Sisters but not others. Focus your attention on the spiritual so that no soul who comes to our hospital is lost; this will happen when you are all saints through your perfect observance.

In his generosity, the Holy Father has granted us the Pardon of Assisi for all the houses for which I requested it; so you, the patients, and everyone connected with the hospital can gain the indulgence in your chapel as many times as you please.[5] This is also true for Manresa, Brooklyn, and New Orleans. Let these houses know in time. I have not asked for 14th Street since I am not sure we will remain in that house; the Sisters can come to your chapel.

I again suggest you take care of that "uncle" affair; don't rest until you have obtained the $20,000 that Karle wanted to leave me. Poor thing, I always remember him and pray for him. If they give us the money, we will have a hundred Masses said for the repose of his soul. You make the promise and send the money here, where I will have the Masses offered at a special altar.

Yes, it is really Bovier, the head of that committee, who is trying to harm us. Keep your eyes open and pray to the Sacred Heart, Who can overthrow our enemies with one finger.

[5] The Pardon of Assisi is plenary indulgence granted by the Roman Catholic Church on the evening of August 1 and the day of August 2. Pope Benedict XVI gives a neat summary of its history: "St Francis obtained [the Pardon of Assisi] from Pope Honorius III in the year 1216, after having a vision while he was praying in the little church of the Portiuncula. Jesus appeared to him in his glory, with the Virgin Mary on his right and surrounded by many Angels. They asked him to express a wish and Francis implored a 'full and generous pardon' for all those who would visit that church who 'repented and confessed their sins'. Having received papal approval, the Saint did not wait for any written document but hastened to Assisi and when he reached the Portiuncula announced the good news: 'Friends, the Lord wants to have us all in Heaven!' Since then, from noon on 1 August to midnight on the second, it has been possible to obtain, on the usual conditions, a Plenary Indulgence, also for the dead, on visiting a parish church or a Franciscan one." Benedict XVI, Angelus (August 2, 2009).

If Levy wishes to return, accept her and let me know, and I will send my instructions for her. I would like her to return, so as to make reparation for the manner in which she left.

I bless all and pray for all.

Affectionately in the Most Sacred Heart of Jesus,

M. FRANCESCA S. CABRINI

March 11, 1898, Rome

Mother Cabrini meets again with Pope Leo XIII, who continues to encourage her.

A.M.G.SS.C.J.
My Dearest Daughter,

I am sending a lovely gift to our candidates for investiture: nothing less than the blessing of the Holy Father. The other evening, when I least expected it, I received tickets for an audience with the pope with a Mexican pilgrimage that is on its way to the Holy Land. There were about eighty in the group. After he had spoken to each one individually, he sat in the middle of Clementine Hall while a bishop read an address to him. The pope responded with a beautiful discourse. It was a true family gathering at the Vatican. In going around the room, when the Holy Father reached me, he smiled and took my hands in his. I asked if he remembered me, and he replied, "Of course I know you. What are you doing?" I asked him for all the blessings I desired and he seemed to pour them on my head in abundance. I then introduced our two American nuns, and he asked if I was pleased with them. Later he spoke to them and asked them to conform themselves to the spirit of their mother. He also said many other nice things. The special paternal affection that the Holy Father showed for the Institute astonished the spectators.

Have faith, my daughters, for the blessing of the Holy Father brings good fortune; trust in it as a guarantee of the blessing of the Sacred Heart of Jesus, and we shall see an outpouring of graces on our Institute. Tell Monsignor that I also asked for a blessing for him.

The other day the mayor of Caltagirone came to visit us. He had come to Rome for some celebration. He thought we should leave in a hurry, but among the forty members of the committee, there are still a few who oppose this. I am not making any decisions while the situation is like this. We shall see now what to do.

I greet all the Sisters and ask them to become saints; this time I ask in the name of the Holy Father, who expects this consolation from you. Give my respects to the bishop and to Msgr. Vigo. I hope the postulants are preparing for the reception of the holy habit with great fervor. I would like them to obtain some very special graces for the Institute from the Sacred Heart.

And you? I hope you have done your part, and done it in a spirit that marks you as a good daughter of the Institute—don't make me pine for this. Is pride playing with you again? No, I don't believe it is possible, because you promised to do away with pride, so I am expecting good results in everything else.

May Jesus bless you and keep you in His Sacred Heart.

Affectionately in the Most Sacred Heart of Jesus,

M. FRANCESCA S. CABRINI

56

July 22, 1898, Rome

Pope Leo invites Mother Cabrini to a last-minute meeting and gives her a blessing.

A.M.G.SS.C.J.
My Dearest Daughter,

The Holy Father made me miss my train. I had already decided to leave the city tonight because I despaired of seeing him. He had already sent me his blessing through the Brazilian legate, and also, the pope has been so burdened during these days that I lost all hope, but today at three o'clock he sent word for me to see him; in fact he granted me a thirty-minute audience, during which he showed great interest in our missions, in my itinerary, and in our means of support. He told me his troubles and accepted my comfort. His household was really surprised to see him so serene at the end of my audience.

I gave him a picture of our miraculous Infant Jesus, and he wanted to know about its particular graces. I promised him that you would pray to the Holy Missionary Infant for a grace he needs now. I promised this in your name, so pray with all your heart.

He gave me an indulgence for all my Spiritual Communions during my voyages and said many nice things for me to tell everyone. Trust then, for you have proof of the power of the Holy Father's blessing. He rejoiced over our victory, and I told him it was the effect of the blessing that he had sent the previous evening. I will take the train Sunday night at eleven o'clock and be there on Monday.

Two cardinals and many prelates attended our program; it was so well done that we are still receiving congratulations. Among other things, we had an oration given by a child of seven, about forty cantos of Dante recited with admirable understanding, etc. This is a little of the rainbow that comes after a storm. Let us prepare to suffer again, for Jesus suffered before us, and whatever happens to us has been endured by the heart of Christ.

May Jesus bless you. Greetings to all.

Affectionately in the Most Sacred Heart of Jesus,

M. FRANCESCA S. CABRINI

June 6, 1903, Chicago

Mother Cabrini discusses her ideas about opening new houses in America.

A.M.G.SS.C.J.
My Dearest Daughter,

When you have found the house furnished like a convent, let me know so I can send some Sisters. Write to the people who you think can send something. I am enclosing a check for you.

Do not expect anything from Chicago, since they are worried about getting what they need for the chapel of the new house. The archbishop will give us the altar. I am tied up here by something stronger than a chain since I have to clarify a number of misunderstandings that occurred before the contract was signed. I am sorry that time is slipping away, but it is the will of God.

When we are well established here, I shall go to start a house in Colombia. You have not told me anything about that country—whether it is high or low, cold or hot. I want to know everything. Is Seattle high or low? I picture it as at the foot of very high mountains but, if the sea is before us, I don't mind. Is it easy to climb the mountains from Seattle? It seems to me that we should have a house in Los Angeles whose climate contrasts with that of Seattle so that if a Sister is ill, she would have temporary relief.

I am glad that the mission comprising a variety of nationalities has been assigned to us. I shall try to have a Slav come from Italy. You advise me to go to Denver first. Then what? Do you not know that one goes to the sea first and then to the mountains?

Before coming there, I want to see Los Angeles. Try to raise a good sum of money among the people because if the house isn't large, we shall have to build one. A wooden one would not cost much, but for us it would be a large sum. See if you can get the land donated to us so that we can build a nice mission from which the Sisters can go to convert all sorts of people, even the Indians.

I hope you are now filled with the Holy Spirit and that everything will be facilitated for you just as it was for the Apostles. In this manner you will honor the Sacred Heart of Jesus with the virtues of humility and simplicity, the mother virtues of all the others. If they are called mother virtues, you understand that you cannot have the others without these.

Pray much for this and study it deeply, but do even this with simplicity. I forgive everything from my heart, but I want you to have a new life, the one that Jesus wants from you. Greet the Sisters for me. Live in peace and charity, and graces shall abound. When they do, keep humble.

May the good Jesus bless you.

Affectionately in the Most Sacred Heart of Jesus,

M. FRANCESCA S. CABRINI

July 24, 1903, Chicago

With the death of Pope Leo XIII, Mother Cabrini loses her beloved protector.

A.M.G.SS.C.J.
My Dearest Daughter,

You were not able to keep him alive until my return. Well, may God's will be done! If he protected us on earth, he will do more than that from Heaven. The holy old man had worked enough and was called home in the middle of the battle. Blessed is he who was prepared, and fortunate are we to have such a powerful patron. Even though I think he is in possession of his reward, we are nevertheless obliged as dutiful children, and out of a sense of gratitude, to pray for the venerable pontiff by saying the Office of the Dead for eight consecutive days, and also on the thirtieth day to offer all our works of piety. Have a High Mass for the deceased celebrated in our chapel.

Pray fervently for him and you will be repaid. You know how he loved the Institute and how he favored us. There is no need for me to enumerate all his benefits, because you know them better than I do. I felt his death keenly, but a calmness settled over me upon realizing that we have a new patron in Heaven. He was pure and holy and very dear to God.

Pray also to the Holy Spirit for the election of the new pope so that God will give the Church a leader like Jesus Christ who will maintain the Church without blemish. Do not comment on this or that candidate; keep silent on this matter. When we have a new pope, go to the chapel immediately and pray for him, inserting his name in the prayer we say.

Write to me immediately informing me of the posts assigned to the various cardinals so I will know how to proceed. I'll know the name of the new pontiff immediately or within two hours because cablegrams arrive here swiftly. I knew about his death about an hour after it occurred. I must have the news from you. I won't get the newspapers unless you roll them up because they are stolen at sea. I hope you will have your retreat soon and also one for externs, from which I pray you get some vocations. Please look for vocations, for we need them.

I greet you all. Pray for me. I have almost finished with the contract in Chicago and by the middle of August will be in New York for the retreat. May Jesus bless you and all.

Affectionately in the Most Sacred Heart of Jesus,
M. FRANCESCA S. CABRINI

July 29, 1903, Chicago

Mother Cabrini gives thanks for the late Pope Leo's support of the order.

A.M.G.SS.C.J.
My Dearest Daughter,

The sickness and death of the venerable pontiff would almost crush me if it were not for the fact that we must adore the holy will of the Most High, Who has wished to reward the merits of His vicar. I hope you have prayed for the repose of his soul. If you have not, do it now with the recitation of the Office of the Dead for eight days, and during that period of time offer all your works of piety and sacrifices for the repose of his soul.

We are indebted to the holy memory of Leo XIII, not only as the simple faithful to the representative of Jesus Christ, but as to a beloved father who dearly loved our Institute. It was he who approved it on March 12, 1888. It was he who encouraged me to undertake the missions to the United States and who kept on telling me to go to all parts of the world. It was he who gave me various gifts:

sometimes he paid for my voyages; at other times he gave me money—for instance, to purchase the two houses in Rome. It was he who gave me the means for building the Church of Our Redeemer close to our house in Rome. If I were to count all the benevolent acts of that holy man, my list would never end, so you see how we are obliged to pray for him with all our hearts.

Pray also for the election of the new pope without discussing any of the possible candidates. Pray and sacrifice in silence, and when you hear the name of the new pope, go to the chapel and sing the "Te Deum". Also insert his name in our prayer for the Holy Father.

I hope Mother Clement has arrived there. She can be the superior until further orders. Work hard and in a hurry, because I don't think I can leave you there for long.

The Immigrant Bank of New York does not have offices outside of the state. I could not find any in Newark. You have to raise $10,000 in order to spend $20,000. Now that there are six of you, get going and you will see that Divine Providence will lead you to the money. There are good deposits in Montana; go and get them while it is still warm. Try to obtain a nice forest, a good piece of land, because we can make use of everything. I will come when you have collected enough; before that it would be useless.

Your trunks have been sent, but I do not know by what express company. They will arrive eventually, and in the meantime, you are gaining experience. Something like that happened to me in Argentina, where I waited three months for my baggage. I have not received anything from the bishop; I wonder if he has even received my letters.

On the sixth, the house will be consigned to us, and on the twelfth, I will go to New York; on the twentieth, I will make the retreat. Please pray that I make a good one.

You will make it later, as soon as you collect $10,000. Work fast! With six Sisters in the house, you are entitled to have the Blessed Sacrament, so please ask the bishop.

May the good Jesus bless you and help you always.

Affectionately in the Most Sacred Heart of Jesus,

M. FRANCESCA S. CABRINI

August 11, 1903, Chicago

With the election of Pope Pius X, Mother Cabrini makes plans to introduce her order to him.

A.M.G.SS.C.J.
My Dearest Daughter,

I sent you the letter for the Holy Father, but I did not tell you to whom you must deliver it. It is his personal secretary, Bressan, who has replaced Msgr. Angeli.

I have already written to Msgr. Giustini to thank him for his concern in sending me the document that serves me in place of the blessing of Leo XIII that you were unable to obtain for me; but I feel that he has blessed me from Heaven because the contract of the newly acquired house, which gave me an immense amount of trouble, was signed on the day Pius X was made pope. On that day Leo must have been greatly consoled by seeing that the Church has been provided with the successor he must have desired.

Our dear Jesus is good, and He does not abandon the Church He has founded. We who are consecrated to His Sacred Heart must have great faith that as long as we are good religious, His support will not fail us. Tribulations will come, but the thorns pierced His heart before reaching us, so they will be less painful and sweeter.

When you can, please get me a blessing from Pius X, by means of which I hope to see miracles among these poor people who are in extreme need.

You have not spoken to me yet about the retreats, and vacation is coming to an end. I want all of you to make them in the best possible manner.

I greet you all and beg you to pray for my intentions. I want you to have three Masses offered for the souls in Purgatory. May the good Jesus bless you and all.

Affectionately in the Most Sacred Heart of Jesus,
M. FRANCESCA S. CABRINI

November 3, 1903, Seattle

Mother Cabrini explains the progress of her efforts to establish a house in Seattle.

A.M.G.SS.C.J.
My Dearest Daughter,

It would be better to send me the Holy Father's blessing in a letter. It's difficult to get mail here. After the letter reaches New York, a long time goes by before it reaches my hands, as I am far from there. I'll keep on yearning for it as I did for the medals. I am so happy about the blessing of the Holy Father; with it, I believe I will see miracles. I have great faith in it, and I am very grateful to you for this favor.

I find myself here on top of the world with a nine-hour difference between Seattle and Italy. When you are getting up in the morning, we have finished our evening prayers, and when we discuss the points of a meditation, you are making it; but we are always in the company of Jesus, Who never sleeps so that He can watch over His beloved spouses.

This is a new city that is growing beneath our very eyes, and little by little, it will become like New York because of its location, its port, and its transportation system, which connects directly with Alaska. Although it is far up north, it is not cold; instead, it has a mild climate like Nervi in Genoa. It is built on twenty-two hills, and our house is located on one of the highest ones, overlooking the lake and half the city. It has three lakes, which makes it a health resort. People with lung and stomach trouble come here to recover, so when I come here for the foundation, I also take advantage of the air for my health.

The bishop of Seattle is so good to us. His name is O'Dea, and he is delighted to have nuns here who bear the title of Missionary Sisters of the Sacred Heart, since he is very devoted to the Heart of Jesus and tries to spread this devotion. In the valleys between these hills, there are about five thousand Italians, who follow us like chicks follow a hen. We hope to help them, because they have been neglected, although faith is not dead in their hearts. They love Our Lady, and she has protected them; now she is giving them our mission.

Now I see that my business here will take the greater part of two months, although I thought I would finish it in two weeks. I have to purchase a house, and the interest rates are very high everywhere, yet I cannot leave until the business is completed. The Sisters have no knowledge of finances, and there are many swindlers around, although the majority of people are good. It seems as if bandits have assembled in this region of the country. In a few days, a number of trains have been wrecked. To come here I had to go a roundabout way because I knew they were on the trains. When I leave Seattle for Denver, the bandits will not be around, because the Sacred Heart is watching over us, and I have such great faith in Him that even on the train I will sleep peacefully; so, my dear daughters, trust Him especially when you are in difficulty, and realize that those disturbances that we term *difficulties* are child's play for our dear Jesus.

Tell Piccioni that I know he is intelligent enough to understand that a girl who knows someone is in love with her cannot stay long in a community of young women. He should be happy to have removed her; he loves the Institute and should be glad to have helped it. He will have the merit of the good that is done and the blessing of God. Write my words for Piccioni, and you will see that he will calm down.

Tell Mother Maria Teresa to be calm but willing to make a trip to Madrid if the Sacred Heart wants it. Express my gratitude to the Holy Father's personal secretary for the precious gift of the pope's blessing. Tell him I will say some special prayers for his intentions.

I hope Mother Augustine has taken care of that gentleman Cucco. Tell her to be kind to him until the end—otherwise we will have trouble and we shall be the losers.

If you want to try asking the Holy Father, go ahead, but it would be better to feel around a bit first. I don't know if the cardinal vicar is as confidential with him as he was with Leo and his secretary of state. Try to approach Msgr. Bressan. He can do it if he wants to, but don't make any requests in my name. Before I do that, I will have to see and speak to him, and it will be some time before I can. I cannot leave my business unfinished, especially after the disturbances I have had with Sisters who were not really daughters of the Institute. Patience!

Gradually we become accustomed to all things. With Jesus the burden becomes light. May He bless you and help you in all things.

Affectionately in the Most Sacred Heart of Jesus,

M. FRANCESCA S. CABRINI

66

November 8, 1903, Seattle

Mother Cabrini shares good news about the flourishing mission in Seattle and considers sending Sisters to Alaska.

A.M.G.SS.C.J.
My Dearest Daughter,

The holy days that are making so much work for you have occupied me too, and that is the reason why I delayed writing to you. I am sorry that this will not reach you by your feast day, but on that day I will tell Jesus to overwhelm you with His graces so you will become a holy religious, a worthy missionary of His Sacred Heart who sanctifies all the souls she approaches and spreads peace throughout the house—that sweet peace, that charity that ignites all souls and inspires them to walk the way of our sublime vocation.

You did very well to advise Msgr. Giustini, but I wish you would succeed in getting her to return. I hope things will change when the English one leaves; meanwhile you can find out something from Boanca, who writes to Codogno. We must pray much because with prayer we can obtain all things that serve for God's glory. I'll willingly endure any pain, but I have not yet learned to resign myself to the thought of unfaithful daughters. That thought simply unnerves me, and the pain is indescribable; so pray wholeheartedly to obtain the conversion of all the Sisters, for when all are holy, I shall be very happy and desire nothing more on this earth.

When I received Cardinal Rampolla's letter, I thanked him immediately for his kind words, but it seems that he has not received my letter. I regret this very much. Now I am wondering if he received my Christmas greetings. Let me know. In the meantime, tell him that I regret his absence from the usual place very much and will feel it much more keenly on my return, just as I will feel the absence of Leo XIII, but it will be a comfort for me to see him and hear his holy words.

As the work on the church is progressing, it would be wise to prepare the designs you want for the paintings and not wait until the last minute. Cucco said that any design will be all right with him. Prepare something symbolic. Mother Maria Teresa has seen the church in Madrid of Our Lady Help of Christians. Get some of those designs, because they are beautiful and at the same time devotional.

What is the pastor of our Church of the Redeemer doing? I hope he will adorn it in a way that is worthy of the Redeemer; later we can procure many assistants to make it a great mission. He should also help us purchase the Macchi house, and then we could have the adoration chapel there. Tell him that this is my fondest dream and that I would be happy if he made it a reality. What merit he would gain! May you succeed in this.

If only you could see what a flourishing mission this is! How many Italians we are able to draw! They come by the hundreds and are moved by the ceremonies we have for them. Here in Seattle we are celebrating the feast of Our Lady of Montevergine, who is venerated in Caserta, Italy. I have asked the bishop of Cosenza to send me a nice picture of that Madonna. Certainly I would like a big one, but who knows if he received my letter. I wish you would write and plead with him too, because the people of Caserta are greatly moved by the devotions to Our Lady of Montevergine and will abstain on Wednesday in her honor. Get in touch with the rector of the Sanctuary of Montevergine or whoever is able to furnish you with a quantity of holy pictures and medals of this Madonna; get the price too, because we will soon need about a thousand.

Our mission here will function as a parish, and we will have baptisms, weddings, funerals, etc., as we have already begun to do. We started building the church and are going much faster than in Rome. It will be finished in a month. It is made of wood, with the sacristy on one side and the confessional on the other. I am here to direct the work and make the Sisters go around asking for donations and gifts.

The wood alone costs 15,000 lire, but it was donated. We shall only have to pay for the nails and the labor, about 3,000 lire. These are hard times, but we have the consolation of seeing many Italians coming to church. We are really touched by the great faith of some of them who have been absent from church for twenty-eight, thirty, forty, or fifty years.

I enclose my request for the Propagation of the Faith and the bishop's letter that he wanted to write in Italian. (He thinks it is well written.) I imagine Rome will get the drift of his thought, and that suffices. I guess they will have a good laugh. Prepare the answer for me and for the bishop. I urge you to write a nice letter for the bishop so that he will be encouraged to favor our work, but do it soon, please!

You know that we are only one circle away from the North Pole here and that Alaska is the last circle that awaits us, as a mission not only for the Italians who are there, but also for the Eskimos. We will go there as soon as possible; first I need to know how many mortified Sisters we have who would like to go.[6] It is a land of intense cold with few or no means of heating the homes, not to mention other privations. I already have forty Sisters from New York and other missions who are volunteering. See how many you can get from there. Certainly one who sacrifices much

[6] Mother Cabrini means "mortified" in the sense of being ready to give one's life for the gospel.

enjoys more, but many do not want to have that experience; there are only a few lovers of the Cross of Jesus. Send out my call and I shall await the applications. Out of the forty who applied, I would select five, but I need at least twelve. If it is necessary to arouse the zeal of some, tell them that the Protestants are already there working enthusiastically with these poor people; it is something that brings me to tears.

Accompany me everywhere with your prayers and rest assured that I am always with you in spirit. My regards to everyone. May the good Jesus bless you and all, and may Jesus be Jesus to you on your feast day and always.

Affectionately in the Most Sacred Heart of Jesus,
M. FRANCESCA S. CABRINI

May 24, 1904, New Orleans

She narrowly escapes death from bandits while traveling from Denver.

A.M.G.SS.C.J.
My Dearest Daughter,

Didn't I write and tell you that I am miraculously still alive? Coming from Denver, as soon as we passed Dallas one night at ten-thirty P.M., the enemies of the railroad who had been hiding in the woods fired at the train. A bullet aimed at my head fell to my side, although it should have pierced my skull. My companion was terribly frightened. She looked to see what had happened to me; but calm and unharmed, I asked what was happening.

Sister was doubly scared because she had been dreaming of the devil, who was chiding her for telling everything to her mother. In her dream the devil had been telling her that it was not necessary to tell her everything "because Mother makes decisions and gives orders that make me suffer very much." Then grinding his teeth, the devil said: "Oh, if I only had that old Mother in my hands! I would break her to pieces."

I am not afraid of the devil. The fear of the Lord is enough for me, and I ask the Holy Spirit for it daily. Learn not to give in to the devil by withholding what should be said, because your welfare and that of the Institute require that you tell me everything with simplicity.

The railroad personnel kept on coming to see us because they could hardly believe that I was unharmed and thought that I had someone watching over me. When I told them that it was the Sacred Heart, to Whom I had entrusted the journey, being Protestants, they did not understand.

Cardinal Satolli leaves Naples on the SS *Princess Irene* on May 27. Find out the time of his arrival and go to meet him and the countess. Give one of the enclosed letters to the cardinal and the other to the countess. Try to invite him to Manresa. If he accepts, prepare a big reception for him; invite the archbishop, the bishop, the vicar general, General Cesnola, and other distinguished people. Do not invite me, because I am too busy and I would lose a month's time; besides, I cannot possibly leave the work now at hand; otherwise I will lose it.

Give my greetings to all. Tell them to become saints by means of recollection and silence, especially now that they are filled with the Holy Spirit. I would be glad if you kept Mother Bernardina because you can give her more attention.

May the good Jesus bless you and all.

Affectionately in the Most Sacred Heart of Jesus,

M. FRANCESCA S. CABRINI

July 1, 1904, New Orleans

Mother Cabrini describes her conversation with a wealthy donor about building a new orphanage.

A.M.G.SS.C.J.
My Dearest Daughter,

Two months ago today I came to New Orleans. Ever since then, the temperature has been so high that we have been bathed in perspiration day and night, but I am glad that it has not been in vain. After spending all this time with Captain Salvatore Pizzati, I have succeeded in getting him to build a house for our orphans, who are in such close quarters that they were all getting sick.

When he finally decided, he said: "Well, I will give you $10,000."

I answered: "I can't build a house with $10,000. I need much more."

Then he came up to $20,000, which he wanted to give me over a ten-year period, and he wanted to see the house erected first. I told him that we could not possibly put the money down, and that it would be better if he built it. He replied: "Prepare the ground for me, and I will have it built."

He already has the plans, and they are wonderful. We shall have a convent, a chapel, and a large auditorium at the cost of $75,000. This is a grace of the Sacred Heart granted to this house, where the spirit of simplicity, obedience, and observance has always been preserved. I enclose two newspaper articles that an English Sister can translate to inspire the Sisters to thank the Sacred Heart and pray for Captain Pizzati. We do not come by a gift of 375,000 francs every day. I am now working on the contract for the land, and that will keep me busy throughout July. I feel well and sufficiently strong.

Greet everyone for me and have them imitate the virtues of this house. I hope to receive better news about Mother Julia. Kindly give my regards to Monsignor. May the good Jesus bless you and help you in all things.

Affectionately in the Most Sacred Heart of Jesus,
M. FRANCESCA S. CABRINI

December 7, 1908, Rio de Janeiro

Mother Cabrini discovers a beautiful property for a foundation in Rio de Janeiro.

A.M.G.SS.C.J.
My Dearest Daughter,

I don't think Msgr. Sabatucci is going to do anything; nevertheless, I am enclosing a letter for you to hand to him after keeping a copy of it in the house. If necessary, you may show him the statistics to verify what I have said.

After many tribulations in Rio, the Sacred Heart has favored us by making me come across a beautiful seventy-acre estate on a hill with waterfalls and a lake and a furnished house, and all for a hundred contos.[7] Others cost much more, almost double the price, and are small by comparison. You will learn everything from the letter I sent to Cardinal Arcoverde. We are now staying at the villa, and I am writing to you from the room I have been confined to for the last three days on account of the malaria I contracted in São Paulo last week. The medication I am taking

[7] A conto was a unit of Portuguese currency at the time.

is good, and I hope to be up and about in a few days. In Rio I have already regained my strength and health.

The window of my room overlooks the mountain range known as Serra dos Órgãos, and the Finger of God dominates the center. To me it seems to say, "This is the place I have found for you; be grateful and faithful." Let Cardinal Arcoverde explain the beauty of the Finger of God.

Mother Savaré tells me that she has to make Mother Augustine keep quiet because she is the one who is speaking against me. If this is true, whose duty is it to make her keep still and stop talking against her mother? Don't mention this, for I will write to her; I just wanted you to know what was going on.

Try to keep well. Tell all the Sisters I appreciated their greetings and greet them with all my heart. Give my regards to everyone. I have written to Cardinal Vives. May Jesus bless, help, and console you.

Affectionately in the Most Sacred Heart of Jesus,
M. FRANCESCA S. CABRINI

November 24, 1910, London

Mother Cabrini offers practical advice to a Sister about new and existing foundations.

A.M.G.SS.C.J.
My Dearest Daughter,

If a Sister told you what you are telling me, you would respond: "Oh, what nonsense! It isn't right to give importance to such matters." I think I even heard you saying something of the kind to a Sister. Well, today is the day to apply it to yourself.

You say that you don't know anything about hospitals; as a matter of fact, none of us knew anything about hospitals until obedience asked us to open hospitals, and then we did everything we had to do to the best of our ability. Be careful about making excuses if everything does not proceed properly for the patients, administration, and maintenance. Practice economy in all things so as to provide the means of making our hospital an ideal one.

I wish we could begin in the spring, but if you haven't saved a sufficient sum, it will be impossible. Send letters asking for aid for the construction and have the newspapers publicize our project. If you are ready in the spring, I will come there to inaugurate it.

When it is time for the renewal of vows, let the Sisters renew them in their own house, if they are ready, and I shall delegate the superior to receive them in my name.

If Mother Estella's sister is good and happy, leave her with the girls and have her do two years' study in one if possible. For investiture, wait until Eastertime because in winter many of the Sisters are sick. It is better to keep March and September for these functions.

A habit for postulants is suitable in orphanages where some have to be tried for a longer period, so see what is most convenient.

I think you paid too much for the coal—six dollars a ton—so be careful when you shop. The number of boarders is too small. Look around for some more; I would like ninety at least.

See what Mother Antonietta has to say about Frengoni. If the novices have no spirit, we shall have to let them go out the window at the end of the year and come in the door; otherwise in a short time they will give us trouble and leave.

See that Manresa is clean and orderly. Mother Luigina was not too particular in Denver and New Orleans, and you may have an unexpected inspection. Be firm with those who have the bad habit of hitting the children. They must stop it.

I am enclosing a program for the new school I am opening here. Have the Sisters show it to good families who often send their children to London for an education; also let the Spanish and Portuguese families know about it.

Greet everyone and pray for me. May Jesus bless you and help you in all things, especially to become as simple as you were when I first accepted you, and then you will be a little saint.

Affectionately in the Most Sacred Heart of Jesus,
M. FRANCESCA S. CABRINI

June 15, 1914, New York

Mother Cabrini advises a Sister regarding the renting of an apartment, and shares news about the new house at Dobbs Ferry. She also provides advice for difficult times.

My Dearest Daughter,

It seems advisable to me to rent that apartment, since there are so many students. Regarding the question of whether to pay a lower sum in rent and be responsible for the other expenses yourselves, or pay more and have them covered, you can decide what seems best.

As for your black-black-black days, endeavor to make them a triple rose with perfect abandonment and great confidence in the Sacred Heart of Jesus. To abandon yourself as a child in that Divine Heart and to be helped immediately are one and the same thing. Try it at once. Your eyes are spiritually blurred. Ask Jesus for new ones, and you will see everything as sweet and easy, especially in difficult times.

Don't you have any vocations? Why aren't you productive in your work? Refresh yourselves in the love of God, and with generosity rob the world of beautiful souls to give them to Jesus.

I am enclosing a postcard of the new house [Dobbs Ferry], which will be inaugurated on July 4 by the apostolic delegate. On that occasion we shall celebrate the silver jubilee of our missions.

Greet everyone for me and pray for me. Pay my respects to the bishop for whom I have so much veneration and gratitude. May Jesus bless you and help you in all things by granting you peace, as a true child of God.

Affectionately in the Most Sacred Heart of Jesus,
M. FRANCESCA S. CABRINI

September 14, 1914, New York

Mother Cabrini discusses the death of Pope Pius X and the news of a new pope, Benedict XV, during wartime.

A.M.G.SS.C.J.
My Dearest Daughter,

I would complain that you have not written to me for so long if I had not found out that you have been on retreat.

This is the first time that you have spoken to me about the death of Pius X. I learned of the death of Msgr. Tedeschi from the newspapers, but I did not want to believe it. I believed it only after reading your letters, and I will begin to pray for the repose of so good and noble a person. You never even told me that he was ill. I would like to know all the details about a person who was so good to us.

I have already written to you about the new pope, saying how glad I was about the choice and what a blessing he will be for the universal Church. I think he will be as good as Leo XIII, especially if he is helped by Cardinal [name illegible, likely Gasparri] as secretary of state. I think he will be a blessing for us too even though we are so small that such lofty things do not touch us; however, the need arises occasionally even for us, and then it is good to know that a friendly person with a paternal heart is seated on the throne.

Here we had magnificent services for the funeral of Pius X and for the coronation of Benedict XV. I would like to be free to kneel at his feet but—patience, especially since you don't want me there during wartime.

You know it is not true to say that moving from one place to another is a hardship. I hope that in your fear, you will not squander what God has entrusted to us.

All is well in Paris. The military officials wanted the Sisters to take in some of the injured, but the Directress convinced them to send instead the daughters of fallen soldiers to be our students. They were satisfied and left the Sisters in peace. Mother Giuseppina, courageous as she is, told them that she couldn't care for the girls if she couldn't go out asking for money. The Ambassador told her that he would pay for everything as long as the war lasts. See what blessings come from the Sacred Heart of Montmartre. We must have confidence in God, always.

Affectionately in the Most Sacred Heart of Jesus,
M. FRANCESCA S. CABRINI

September 24, 1914, New York

Mother Cabrini talks about the new pope, who had been very supportive of the order before his election. She also explains a proposal from the Nicaraguan government, which might pay restitution to the order for the government's past decision to forcibly remove the Sisters from the country during a time of unrest.

A.M.G.SS.C.J.
My Dearest Daughter,

Here we are with a new pontiff. Who would have ever guessed that Della Chiesa would be elected! Yet God predestined him even though he never imagined it; in fact, he was not prepared for it and had to come up with his papal name right there and then. With his election I seem to be reliving my first days in Rome, especially the beginning of our missions. He was the first to work for us with Leo XIII and Rampolla.

We should make him recall this and ask him to say a good word on our behalf because just now, Nicaragua is deciding to indemnify us for the bad treatment they accorded our Institute twenty years ago when they expelled us on two hours' notice.

Now they say the government of Nicaragua has decided to give us $14,000, although I had asked for $30,000. As long as they give us the money soon, I will even accept $14,000, provided there are no strings attached. They would like to include a clause stating that we shall return and open a school there with the $14,000. I am insisting that the money be handed over freely. With the passage of time, we may return to Nicaragua and open a school, but not now, when the country is unstable.

Now watch and see who will be secretary of state. If you are unable to speak with the Holy Father, communicate with the secretary, who will pass the word along to the Nicaraguan minister; in this way the Holy Father will continue the work he himself initiated.

Tell the Holy Father that I am most happy about his election and that I feel at peace about the welfare of the Church and our Institute. He is fearless and holy and therefore will never be without heavenly assistance.

I heard that there are soldiers in our house in Paris. This pleases me because I remember that we had some military officials in my home in 1859, and for that reason we were respected and protected. Let us hope that something good will come from so many evils.

I hope that the two Sisters have left London, since it is not safe. I think it is best to leave only a few Sisters there, as we have done in Paris. Suggest that they all prepare secular clothes to use in case of necessity.

Matters will be more serious if Italy enters the European conflagration, but you know that I have room for all of you here. I feel like preparing a place for the Holy Father also. Tell him that I offer him our house, especially the one in Dobbs Ferry. That would be a little more worthy of his presence, for, as the apostolic delegate said when he came on July 4, "This is a Vatican." It is really nice.

I wish I could be there during these awful days of war, but at the same time I am sufficiently at peace knowing that you are hidden and that you truly plan to do all that has to be done as circumstances arise. I would like to have the first medal that is made of the Holy Father. Send me all the medals to keep them in a secure place. Now I will send my congratulations to the Holy Father, and you obtain his blessing. Send me all the clippings on the Holy Father because I am deeply interested in him.

I greet all of you. May Jesus bless you and help you in a special way.

Affectionately in the Most Sacred Heart of Jesus,
M. FRANCESCA S. CABRINI

June 15, 1915, New York

World War I affects the entire world, including Mother Cabrini's Sisters. Mother suggests a spiritual remedy.

A.M.G.SS.C.J.
My Dearest Daughter,

Your long descriptive letter filled me with consolation. I felt sure that the Sacred Heart of Montmartre would help you in all things and save you, but the graces and assistance that He has given you fill my heart with wonder and immense appreciation. Always have great faith in that Heart Who looks down upon you, my dearest daughters, from the height of that holy mountain. And you, by a holy, observant, and truly religious life, continue to merit this mark of predilection.

Don't get accustomed to zeppelins, please, but beware of them and stay on guard. Our dear Lord says, "Help yourselves and I will help you." Keep on being as brave as you have been in the past. Strength must be a characteristic of the Missionary Sisters of the Sacred Heart.

Mother Umilia and the other sick Sisters offer their pains daily to placate the anger of God so that He will suspend the terrible chastisement that we have deserved. The world has become too evil; the infinite purity of God was sickened, and so His hand has weighed upon mankind. Once He sent a deluge of water; now it is a deluge of blood because He has seen the hardness of His creatures in persisting in their evil ways as if they wanted to win against God. The defect lies there, but it seems that people don't want to understand that you cannot toy with God. It is necessary to change our lives.

Pray and have the children pray to obtain the conversion of all nations. This is the only way to placate the anger of God. You, as loving spouses of Jesus, can obtain everything from Him when you are observant, humble, and mortified. Innocent children, pure and simple, are always heard by the Almighty, so let them raise their hands in prayer to obtain pardon and mercy.

It would be a good thing if you obtained the cancellation of taxes, but don't insist on it, because it also has its evil effects. What you must do is obtain greater help, as you did on other occasions. Now is the time to obtain from the civil authorities the permits needed to collect alms, and then no one will disturb you.

War is a punishment of God, but people seem to be so blind as to think that war is in fashion, and everybody wants it; so don't be surprised if war breaks out here too. Then what will happen to Mother?

Don't think about it, for Providence—which has always surrounded me in a thousand and one difficulties—will take care of me. We are in the hands of God. Let us abandon ourselves to Him, and He will always defend us. I have no fear for myself or my daughters. Naturally I think about how to provide for necessities, and have always advised our houses to think about it as well; but help is certain to come from above even during this calamity, so don't worry about me, and live in security.

Greet all the Sisters for me. Remember me especially to Mother Umilia. Tell her not to eat too much, and her stomach will feel better. I want her to get well. Ask her to recall the Lent I made her fast and how she came to thank me at the end because she felt so much better. Even if she is very sick, the doctor could cure her by means of abstinence, and I would be very happy.

May the good Jesus bless you and grant you all the special help you need while this war lasts.

Affectionately in the Most Sacred Heart of Jesus,

M. FRANCESCA S. CABRINI

August 15, 1916, Seattle

In this long letter, Mother Cabrini explains events surrounding a difficult foundation in Seattle.

A.M.G.SS.C.J.
My Dearest Daughter,

Now you have reason to complain, since I have not written in four months. It can't be true that all the others have gone down with the submarines. Enough! You have remained all alone and I am very sorry. I have faced some unusual dangers here.

While looking for a house for poor children, I came across a nice, sturdy, richly furnished building: the Perry Hotel, which they would give me for one-third of the cost.

The Sisters encouraged me to take it. I was not too inclined to make this purchase, but in trying to determine the will of God, I went to see the bishop of Seattle. When he heard the cost of the furnished building, he exclaimed: "Oh, Mother, this is a grace that Heaven is sending you; accept it while the Lord gives it to you." He said that he had seen it being erected, that it cost half a million dollars without the furniture, and that if they were really giving it away for $200,000 ... "Go immediately to deposit $100,000 or others will take it."

I replied that I could not deposit more than $10,000. Seeing he was well disposed to the idea, I told him that even if the hotel was given away at that low price, it was still too expensive for us, and that if I took it, I would have to set aside the front rooms for rich patients; otherwise I would be unable to maintain the building.

"Very well," he said, "make it self-supporting."

I answered, "I will move forward with courage." After six months I had to sign the contract, and I was able to get the building for $190,000.

No sooner was the contract signed than the newspapers publicized the fact and a fierce storm arose. All the agents of the city and various lawyers tried to annul the contract. I worked day and night with the owners in New York and with friends so as not to lose this building. Would you believe it? Even the bishop's lawyer and the cathedral priests began to work so that we would not acquire the property. Since the first contract expired on May 1, they hatched a few plots to act on that day. But I always managed to find out everything ahead of time and had the right to the title according to the agreement made, so I tried to have the new contract signed four days early; so on April 26 I sent four Sisters to the Perry Hotel to take an inventory, although the managers of the hotel would not leave until May 1. I begged the newspapers to be silent, but the news spread, and people came to the glass doors to see if the Sisters were really occupying the hotel.

They gave vent to their fury by circulating a petition to the effect that they did not want a children's home in this beautiful section of Seattle. Even the people who had subscribed to this charitable work canceled their donations. When the bishop came to bless the house, I told him that since the people had failed to keep their word, it would be impossible for me to carry on a charitable work without money, so I had decided that the entire building would be used as a sanitarium, as he had requested in the beginning. In this way the house would be self-supporting.

"Very well," he said, "I bless your great undertaking." He advised me not to take psychiatric patients because they require specialized care and would ruin the building. He said this in front of the audience that had come for the blessing of the house.

After this we began to set the house in order for the designated purpose. Two months were required for this, and meanwhile, the angry mob, which did not succeed in taking the property away from us, tried to turn the bishop against us.

He said that he did not want any trouble with hospital nuns and that we should go back to our original plan of running a home for children. I told him frankly that it was now too late, that he had encouraged me to buy the house and had suggested making it self-supporting, that I had done everything with his permission and his blessing, and that now it was impossible to withdraw. In the end he wrote me a letter in which he said, "Do anything you want as long as you don't make it into a hospital." So we proceeded with the sanitarium, which is now coming along nicely, and the people are enthusiastic about it as something that was really needed on the Pacific Coast.

Mother Savaré is writing to me about the Vezzani affair. I have told her so many times to modify it in some way and finish it. Tell her I will write soon, but I am telling you so you will let her know. You will always have unruly children. Maintain discipline, but when one makes a mistake, be quick to pardon, realizing that a bad upbringing, whether in school or in the family, excuses much.

So many Sisters speak to me of their jubilees, but the amount of work we have at hand makes the days go by unobserved. It means that we are soldiers of Christ and run to the front lines, forgetting everything else and leaving the care of the wounded to our good Physician, Spouse, and Father. Oh, the Heart of Jesus truly knows how to alleviate every pain.

I hear that our two military hospitals are doing excellently and I am more than happy. When shall I return? When the submarines have left the sea, the way will be free. Pray for peace. Greet all for me and pray for me. May Jesus bless you and help you in all things.

Affectionately in the Most Sacred Heart of Jesus,
M. FRANCESCA S. CABRINI

P.S.—When you see the Holy Father, ask him for a big blessing for me and for the work I have at hand. Tell him that he lives in our midst, that we always speak of him and of his great pontificate.

Buenos Aires (undated)

In another long letter, Mother Cabrini describes the difficulties of founding a new school in Buenos Aires, including a lack of financial support.

A.M.G.SS.C.J.
My Dearest Daughter,

Complaints about my silence reach me from all our houses, and soon I expect to receive them from laypeople also. During the past three months, there has been neither Christmas nor New Year's for me, but only travel and work such as I have never endured before.

I had to stop in Chile for over a month because of the heavy snow on the Andes. Then the archbishop of

Santiago asked me to look around the city so that I might be enticed to open a mission there. In less than a month I saw a great deal. I was so warmly received by the people and so strongly pressed to stay that I almost decided to open a mission there before going to Buenos Aires.

When I arrived in Buenos Aires, instead of the archbishop who had sent for us, I found a newly installed prelate who, like a good father, welcomed me extravagantly, and I began to work. Since God wanted us here, the devil began tormenting us by causing great fear in the nuns of the aristocracy that we had come to harm their work. This was a foolish fear in a city of over a million people.

Here our habit impressed people as being rich and dignified, and they were enchanted with our title of Missionary Sisters of the Sacred Heart. Seeing that the devil was at work, I begged our good Jesus to chain the poor beast for a while. Then I quickly set out to look for a house before the devil started more trouble. In compliance with the archbishop's request, I visited several pastors of the city to consult with them about the proper location for a school. At night, Mother Chiara and I would return home dead tired but ready to start again the next day.

Three pastors did all they could to have us establish a school in their parish, but the buildings were not suitable for that purpose. Finally, after seeing about sixty buildings in three weeks, when my shoes were worn out and we could no longer continue, we found a house in the center of the city. It was so nice and adaptable that it seemed to have been made just for us to meet the needs of the city. The owner, a good lawyer, had been about to rent it out for a good price but canceled his contract with the other person and gave it to us for very little.

The archbishop was very pleased and began to help us. He also asked others to give us assistance until we were firmly established. So we started a school for young ladies, and the best part of it all was that I had to transact all the business without knowing the language. I had to prepare notices, programs, schedules, etc., which I never did before without your help.

A holy and erudite priest to whom the archbishop referred us does the translations, and since he has a printing press, he prints them for us at no cost. We are in the parish of Saint Ignatius, but since the Dominican church is the nearest to us, we go there for our devotions. The sacristan there offered to help with our chapel and is getting people to donate vestments, candelabras, etc.

The boarders will pay forty-five dollars monthly; the day students, ten to twenty dollars according to their class. This will be the center from which all other missions will spring, for there is great need and I have had several requests. I would need about a thousand good Sisters, and then we would be able to do a great deal of work. This good priest has many of the same ideas as the late archbishop and wishes us to establish a teacher's college. In the school program I have stated that the higher courses would be comparable to those of a teacher's college.

Since I do not know when the Sisters will arrive, I will have to remain here for four months. I have sent for only four this time, but in a month or less I will send for another four or six. Have Mother Rosario Marchesi study Castilian Spanish—likewise Sister Catherine, who will come as procurator, and the others who do not yet know that they are coming. Since Mother Frances and Mother Margaret left, you no longer have the instructors there, so send them to Milan and call in the professor who taught Mother Cherubina. Let Mother Cristina learn it well, because she will have to help out in the school.

I will also need a Sister of the second class who is strong and robust and presents herself well. I will need her among the group I shall call by telegram; in the list of names, I will indicate her by "other". Do you understand? I hope the Sisters are on their way and will soon be here to help us. It is impossible to go on.

I am lucky to have a good lady who comes daily to help us. I go out with her for necessities while Mother Chiara remains alone at home to receive people, cook, and keep the house in order. When I am home, I act as doorkeeper and Mother Chiara attends to the rest. The house is so large that we cannot call to each other for help.

With the exception of Rome, this is the only house where I have experienced this difficulty, but I am pleased, and I recall the privations and hardships of the first foundation of our Institute in 1880, when I had to accompany each Sister to her bedroom at night without a light after we had finished eating on a bench with little or no silverware. But all this gives us joy and peace and holy hope, which increases our strength every day. The first day, I swept the long halls and got blisters on my hands, but now the skin is hardened and I see that the poor are really blessed if they appreciate their fortunate situation.

I just heard that a pastor is giving us a nice big altar and another confessional. Soon we shall have Jesus with us, and I hope that with the arrival of the Sisters, everything will be ready to alleviate the sufferings of their long journey.

A licensed teacher from Buenos Aires who knows French, piano, and painting is asking to join us. I shall have to get information on her. Pray that God will send us many of this caliber, because we have real need.

Write to all the houses to remove any false ideas they may have about my silence, and to other persons who may have been surprised that I did not remember them at Christmastime. Tell them that I have never been such a missionary as I am now. Write immediately to Cardinal Rampolla, the cardinal vicar, Fr. Granello, Msgr. Montegazza, the bishop of Lodi, the one of Piacenza, and others. Tell Don Giovanni and Professor Castelli in person.

This letter has been written at intervals. I can now report that a lady has come to take measurements for the Sacred Heart statue and of other saints we want, and she will pay for them. Another woman has sent us a golden table with a marble top; still another has sent us stations of the Cross. All are pleased with our lovely house, which looks like a real convent and presents a nice appearance, so they are all helping willingly. Pray for everyone.

The school will be called the College of Saint Rose in accordance with the promise I made in Lima. The school's address is Calle Belgrano 660, Buenos Aires, Argentina. It is located right in the center of the city, where there is no other school.

I greet you with all my heart. Become holy, lead the life of true religious, and enjoy the peace of the Lord, which I invoke upon you.

Affectionately in the Most Sacred Heart of Jesus,

M. FRANCESCA S. CABRINI

2. The Religious Superior

Mother Cabrini often addressed her letters to an entire community of Sisters. After all, she personally helped establish every foundation, so she knew some or all of the Sisters in each community, as well as the challenges they were facing. These letters show how she guided her Sisters even though she was far away from them.

* * *

December 1, 1887, Rome

Her Sisters miss her presence, particularly at Christmas, so Mother tries to encourage them with suggestions for spiritual preparation during the season.

J.M.J.F.
My Dearest Daughters,

I have heard that some of you say you have forgotten what I look like. By contrast, I have each one of you engraved in my mind, and neither time nor distance will ever efface your image. Often during prayer I think of each one of you individually, and then I see you spiritually—a sight that either gives me joy or saddens me, according to the joy or rancor I witness. I beg you, then, to be kind to me, so that when I look at you, I will always find reasons for rejoicing. This will be the greatest comfort I can have to compensate for my sorrow at being away from you because of the needs of the Institute.

Now we are in Advent, a time of penance. Be mortified in the manner commanded by our Holy Rule; meditate on the eternal truths in your hearts as the Church commands. In the meditation on the Judgment, reflect that perhaps in a short time, sooner than we think, we shall have to present ourselves to Jesus, Who is now our Spouse but Whom we shall meet then as a severe and inexorable Judge. I myself, who now excuse and willingly cover your defects, will be obliged on that day to condemn you if you have not been faithful. You, for your part, will condemn me for my faults because justice will demand it.

Prepare yourselves for the feast of the Immaculate Conception with special prayers so that this most pure Mother will take you under her mantle and make you her true imitators by the purity of your manners and the generosity of your spirit, especially in difficult encounters.

During the octave of Saint Francis Xavier, make the meditations on his life and compare it with your own in order to inspire yourselves to imitate it so that you will bear the name of missionary less unworthily. I shall go to the saint's altar to receive Holy Communion for you at the Church of the Gesù, where his arm, which baptized thousands of unbelievers, is venerated. Be good, my daughters, be holy for the few days of life that still remain.

Write your Christmas letters and do all that is necessary to be recollected as the solemnity approaches. Think of the manger, and make a day's retreat if possible before the novena begins. Write to the bishop for Christmas, to the bishop of Pavia, to Don Angelo Nolli, to Mantegazza, Don Giovanni Denali, the bishop of Piacenza, of Mantua, etc. Think of all the others to whom we are obliged to write.

Sister Carmelina, for the dancing teacher, do as you had intended to do last year with the one from Pietrasanta; also consult Monsignor and everything will be done well.

I give Sister Salesia the obedience to get well. Let her make a fervent novena and drink Saint Ignatius' water three times a day and she will be cured.

May the Heart of Jesus bless you and make you holy.

Yours affectionately in the Most Sacred Heart of Jesus,

M. FRANC. SAVERIO CABRINI

December 20, 1887, Rome

Mother Cabrini writes to a community of Sisters, offering them spiritual advice, encouragement in virtue, and a description of the difficulties she and the Sisters in Rome are facing.

J.M.J.F.
My Dearest Daughters,

Here I am in your midst, but just for a moment, because I must turn quickly to the serious affairs of the Institute in Rome. I ask you to accompany me always with your most fervent prayers and with those acts of virtue and generosity that so move the Heart of Jesus and cause Him to favor us with His gifts.

So many of you ardently desire to come to Rome, but believe me, this is not a propitious time; it is cold, the weather is bad, and the streets are slushy, so it would be impossible to tour the city to see the various churches. The time will come, my daughters; it will come. Stay united with me in the Heart of Jesus, and try to console me with your virtue—a truly generous, solid virtue that has nothing of the human in it but is entirely spiritual. The quickest way to arrive at this degree of virtue is self-abnegation: seek occasions to deny yourselves and desire to be denied by others and to have your defects seen and corrected so that the pure gaze of Jesus may rest with pleasure upon each one of you.

After more than a month of penance, walking a mile and a half daily to receive Holy Communion, we finally have the Blessed Sacrament in the house; having longed for it so much, now we would like to stay with Him always. You go to church perhaps a little lethargically because you don't have the hunger and thirst. Love, love Jesus, and frequently bring Him your spiritual bouquets, but make sure that the flowers are fresh and fragrant. Always insert purity and humility into each bouquet; without these virtues they are unacceptable.

I urge Sister Carmelina to look after everything while Sister Salesia is ill; consider that you must give an account to God, so do your duty well. See that everything is clean and orderly. Tell Sister Felicita that she will come to Milan later.

I remember you all. In chapel I cannot pray for myself, but only for you; so you pray for my intentions. I am not saying anything about the graces that God is bestowing upon our Institute because Monsignor will tell you; only I beg you not to render yourselves unworthy.

May the Heart of Jesus bless you and make you understand the obligation you have of living up to your vocation, which you have received through the pure bounty of Christ.

Dearly I greet you.

Affectionately in the Sacred Heart of Jesus,

M. FRANC. SAVERIO CABRINI

P.S. Remember me to the girls and tell them that I pray for them every time I visit the tomb of Saint Agnes so that they will become as angelic as she was. Sister Carmelina, see that they don't dance under the excuse that they are taking lessons.

April 24, 1888, Rome

Written during the springtime, this letter speaks of the soul as a garden.

J.M.J.F.
My Dearest Daughters,

The precious month of May, the month of flowers, is drawing near. Let everyone cultivate the garden of her soul and gather flowers from it to place on Mary's altar every day. May these flowers be fresh and fragrant and of the best quality.

You are intelligent enough to know what virtue goes with each flower, so enter into the interior sanctuary of your soul, see what virtues are lacking, and promise to study assiduously how to practice them in very difficult moments; then you will have a beautiful bouquet to present to Our Lady each day. She, however, will not be outdone in generosity, and you will see what graces she will bestow upon you for our dear Institute.

In the cultivation of your garden—that is, in the practice of virtue—let your guardian angel assist you as well as the angel of the Institute and Our Lady herself who, like a tender mother, will help you every time you invoke her intercession in your endeavor to conquer self.

Decorate the altar nicely in the usual way. I wish to observe the month of May with you so as to be moved by your devotion and your example and by the fragrance of your virtues.

I intend to speak with each one of you individually. I think we understand each other, don't we? It is now time to make the monthly day of recollection; prepare yourselves well.

Let Theresa wait for me if Monsignor agrees. Her entrance into the convent will be the first fruit that you offer me.

Fr. Savaré says that if we are to have many boarding students, we must pray to Saint Anthony to find them. I believe that the Blessed Mother can help us too. Tell Sister Carmelina both the one and the other.

May the Sacred Heart of Jesus bless all my good, generous daughters, and may He make you the real religious I desire you to be.

Affectionately in the Sacred Heart of Jesus,
M. FRANC. SAVERIO CABRINI

December 21, 1888, Rome

Mother encourages her Sisters to prepare their souls to receive the Christ Child at Christmas.

J.M.J.F.
My Dearest Daughters,

I really do not have the time, but I wish to communicate with you, especially since I cannot have a spiritual meal with you. Prepare yourselves well, I beg you, for the reception of the Christ Child into your hearts and prepare yourselves in such a way that it will procure the choicest graces of holiness for the motherhouse and the Institute.

Unite yourselves with Mary, if you wish to prepare well, meditating frequently and profoundly on her virtues, through which she was able to draw the Eternal Word from Heaven to earth. Admire her humility when she declares herself His handmaid and the angel tells her she is to become the Mother of God. Ponder on her resignation to the will of the Most High when she says her *fiat*, thereby submitting to that series of bitter pains that she will encounter for the rest of her life in carrying out this great mandate. Think about her charity in submitting to all of them out of the great love she has for God and sinners, especially for her poor daughters who will one day answer the call to become Missionary Sisters of the Sacred Heart of Jesus. Oh my daughters, see how Mary teaches us to dispose our hearts for Christmas!

Do we have these three sublime virtues that Jesus wants each one of us to have in the measure He requires of us? . . . Do not be discouraged if you find yourselves short on these virtues, for that would be a sign of pride. Run to Mary and be generous when the occasion demands it.

I will not say anything about the purity of soul you should have so that the Christ Child will not turn away from you. You all know how to deport yourselves in this respect, and you know how I want you to practice this angelic virtue, you who should be angels on earth.

In the examination of conscience you make before Vespers, examine yourselves rigorously, and if you discover that some bird has been pecking at your heart, heal it quickly by making a perfect act of contrition coupled with the firm resolution to flee from the occasion of sin. Guard your eyes and your feelings, and do not fall into a certain kind of falsity that is unworthy of a spouse of Christ and displeases the Christ Child to the point of tears.

Pray much for my intentions, especially on Christmas Night. I hope you have advised the Sisters of the other houses that I have obtained permission to have Midnight

Mass. I have not been able to notify them since I have had so much writing to do.

I hope to have an audience soon with the Holy Father; at his feet I shall implore that blessing that will be of the greatest assistance to all. The other day I went to the Vatican to have some religious articles blessed, and I happened to see the Holy Father coming down into the garden. How serene, how joyous his countenance was! He seemed like an apparition from Heaven and left me greatly comforted.

What will it be like, oh daughters, when we see Jesus Himself, when we greet Him joyously with a pure conscience?... May the Sacred Heart of Jesus bless you.

Affectionately yours in the Sacred Heart of Jesus,

M. FRANC. SAVERIO CABRINI

February 2, 1890, Rome

Mother Cabrini summarizes the spiritual retreat she has just made with the Sisters in Rome.

J.M.J.F.
My Dearest Daughters,

Having organized the house in Rome, we finally organized ourselves with a one-day retreat that we made in the company of Our Lady. Like her, we sought to ransom Jesus, searching here and there for the few coins that were necessary. And this is how we found them:

1. By imploring the Heart of Jesus with a lively faith to grant us light. Surely if we had sufficient light, we would have great faith.
2. With the holy fear of God that is the product of love and that fears to offend the good Lord and therefore

is most careful not to commit even the smallest fault. This, I believe, is that true, holy fear that the saints call "the beginning of wisdom" [Ps 111:10, Prov 9:10].

3. Sorrow for sin, or profound displeasure and real humiliation at our falls. True humility always obtains pardon and an increase of grace. God resists the proud and gives grace to the humble.
4. Great confidence in the mercy of God. We are nothing and can do nothing; by ourselves, we can do only evil, but with God we can do all things; therefore, let us always have humility and confidence; let the proud, who rely upon themselves, distrust themselves.
5. We made serious resolutions to serve our good Jesus faithfully. We often make resolutions that are not efficacious because we do not do all we should to conquer and sacrifice ourselves. Yes, we would like to do everything—but without effort, without injuring our pride, and without disrupting our passions. This is the reason why we fail to keep our resolutions.

Procure these five coins immediately and ransom Jesus so that upon my arrival I shall find Him feasting among you. Do not let a month go by without making a day's retreat, and if you want to gain a special grace in that way, cultivate humility—humility always and in all circumstances. It is still the same precious stone that I trust you have already found, but beware of losing it because it is so tiny. It is a gem that can be easily mistaken for costume jewelry. Ask Jesus for light with confidence and perseverance; empty yourselves of all earthly affections for creatures, and the light will come.

Pray for a Protestant young lady who will come to us tomorrow to be instructed in the Catholic faith. Pray for various intentions of mine; I pray for each one of you and for your needs every day. Have you attracted any more candidates to the novitiate by your prayers and virtues? Why haven't you told me? Ah, my daughters, why don't you obtain so many necessary graces for me? Are you perhaps lukewarm, cold, distracted, or proud? I exhort you to become saints. Jesus and Mary help you. Dearly I greet you.

Yours aff. in the Most Sacred Heart of Jesus,
M. FRANC. SAVERIO CABRINI

May 23, 1890, New York

With Pentecost approaching, Mother Cabrini reminds the Sisters of the power of the Holy Spirit.

J.M.J.F.
My Dearest Daughters,

Distance may separate material things, but it cannot separate spiritual ones, for in spirit I am always in your midst, close to each one of you, my daughters. I watch how you deport yourselves and I notice the efforts you make to render yourselves perfect religious and true Missionaries of the Sacred Heart. I shall have no fears after you receive the Holy Spirit, for He will remove all difficulties and will give you the strength and ability necessary for your spiritual progress.

Oh my daughters, have great confidence in the Holy Spirit! He can soften the hardest hearts, pacify the rebellious, sweeten embittered souls, inflame lukewarm souls, fortify the weak, steady the wavering, and convert the proud to humility, the disobedient to obedience, and the avaricious to poverty of spirit.

Therefore, my daughters, by examining yourselves for these powers of the Holy Spirit, you can understand well whether He has descended upon you; if not, I beg you to recollect yourselves and not to cease inviting Him to come to you until you are truly transformed.

In this manner you will prepare for our most solemn feast—that of the Sacred Heart of Jesus. Thus prepared, you will renew your vows on that day with great sweetness and joy, and from then on, your humble and fervent prayers will obtain for me all the graces I need to expand the Kingdom of God on earth by means of my daughters. Truly we must be holy, my beloved daughters, for Jesus has said that if he who has been called to perfection falls away from it, he will be counted as one of those who works iniquity.[1]

Therefore, oh daughters, let us be faithful in all things; let us beware of little faults as much as we would of big ones, and let our pure affections rise unsullied to the Heart of Christ, our only love, our beloved Spouse. Let us endeavor to be very humble, for if even a little pride nestles in our hearts, we shall never be able to understand spiritual things; we shall delude ourselves by thinking that we are nearing a safe harbor when in reality we are miles and miles away.

Recently I accepted a good and humble postulant; I hope she succeeds in becoming a good missionary. Other candidates presented themselves to me, but they were only capable, not humble. One candidate went so far as to say that she was doing us a favor by entering our Institute because we needed someone who spoke English. I dismissed her, saying that the Sacred Heart does not need anyone but that the one who wishes to enter the Institute has

[1] See Hebrews 6:4–6: "For it is impossible to restore again to repentance those who have once been enlightened, who have tasted the heavenly gift, and have become partakers of the Holy Spirit, and have tasted the goodness of the word of God and the powers of the age to come, if they then commit apostasy, since they crucify the Son of God on their own account and hold him up to contempt."

need of the Sacred Heart; it is He who grants us the grace of admitting us among His missionaries. Do you think I did well in saying this? I would like to have your opinion. I need many subjects, but I wish to have only those who are humble, detached from themselves and from their talents, for I am positive that one humble subject can do the work of fifty or more. Without humility, peace is lacking and grace departs.

Goodbye, my good daughters; be always happy and serene, but serious in all your undertakings; in a word, be holy, as you know I want you to be. Pray for me as I do for you. Say the prayer to the Providence of God for me daily until you hear from me again; also make a special triduum.

May Jesus bless you all and enclose you in His Sacred Heart.

Yours affectionately in the Sacred Heart of Jesus,
M. FRANC. SAVERIO CABRINI

February 7, 1891, Rome

Mother Cabrini makes spiritual recommendations to her Sisters as they enter into Lent.

J.M.J.F.
My Dearest Daughters,

In these days of carnival, the world reaches the heights of folly by going wild and thinking that everything is lawful, unmindful of the thorns it is placing in the adorable Heart of Christ. Yes, my daughters, Jesus is tortured, manhandled, agonizing in excruciating pain. He looks around to see if there is someone to say a kind word to relieve His oppression; He turns to you in a special manner, the

Missionaries of His Sacred Heart, who once offered yourselves as victims of expiation.

Now is the time to do your duty, oh Missionaries! Fulfill it scrupulously by making reparation to the Heart to Whom you have consecrated yourselves. It is not necessary that I show you the way; He Himself will show you if you humbly and magnanimously place yourselves at His feet. Humbly, I say. Let each one enter into herself, recognize her own wretchedness, and acknowledge her faults; then she will receive God's grace and approach the suffering Christ to console Him. Who shall comfort Him most? She who best understands my treatise and puts it into practice.

Study it, then, word by word, and seriously meditate on it. From true humility will spring great fervor of spirit, that fervor that will allow not fits of temper but an equanimity that will develop tremendously in God's sight almost without your knowledge.

I cannot like proud people; neither do I like those who allow themselves to be carried away by some wild fantasy, and I believe I have a reason for this: they are not true to themselves but very volatile, subject to change, sometimes happy and sometimes sad according to circumstances. Such subjects will never be real Missionaries of the Sacred Heart, because they have created a piety according to their own ideas and get along very well with great attachment to self, to their own inclinations and fancies. Death to such an idea! We wish to fly like doves or walk always leaning on our beloved Jesus, Who knows how to repay love with love.

Prepare yourselves well for Lent, and humbly ask for the singular grace to learn how to meditate effectively on the Passion of Christ. Oh, blessed will you be if you obtain this grace! Ask for it for me as well. Pray much for my intentions and for important affairs I have at hand for the welfare of the Institute.

Do you love the Institute? Do you really love it? Show it by your actions, especially when the occasion demands it. Meditate on humility; with this virtue you will obtain the graces that I wish would really fall into my hands during these days. I expect much from you, my good daughters. Make a pilgrimage for my intention to Saint Joseph's Chapel for nine days.

May Jesus bless you and keep you as diligent students in the school of His Sacred Heart. I appreciated your letters and the victories in self-conquest that some of you have won. I seem to see Jesus caressing those souls in a special way. Courage, my daughters: Suffering is brief; the reward will be everlasting. I have need of your prayers, so in charity pray for

Yours affectionately in the Sacred Heart of Jesus,
M. FRANC. SAVERIO CABRINI

November 14, 1891, Granada, Nicaragua

Mother Cabrini reminds the Sisters of the value of making sacrifices for the Lord.

J.M.J.F.
My Dearest Daughters,

You want me to give you a present, and since I know your taste, I am sending you an examination of conscience that I made for the nuns during retreat and that Sister Virginia recorded. I hope it will be useful for the retreat you will make in preparation for Christmas. The Holy Child will then give you a spiritual warmth comparable to the one we endure physically. Yes, I cannot believe that December 25 is Christmas Day—the perspiration is running down our faces and the temperature on Christmas Day will be the same as today's.

The Sisters want me to tell you that they are being very good, that not one of them will complain this winter about the cold and frostbite; nor will they bother anyone for additional heat, not even the wardrobe Sister for extra woolen blankets. All joking aside, I really don't know which to choose when it comes to this equatorial heat and the northern cold. All I can say is that I am greatly consoled by our good Sisters who endure the heat without complaint. They are animated by the promise they made before leaving for the missions; they have one thought only: forgetfulness of self and the offering of themselves as victims for the salvation of these people in whom we find a great deal of ignorance but a lively faith by means of which we hope to unite them to the Heart of Jesus.

You must help this mission by your fervent prayers and little sacrifices. I say "sacrifices" because I presume that not all have conquered themselves entirely; some may still possess a great deal of self-love and pride, and these souls may think they still have high mountains to climb. Well, these are the sacrifices:

Destroy your pride and self-love, and these victories shall be blessed by the good God Who offers you all the great mercy of His divine Heart.

Nothing will afflict you, my beloved daughters, if you are possessed by this pure love of God. Remember the saying of Saint Francis de Sales: that present crosses carry with them their own particular grace, and in them we see the hand of God, but disturbing future crosses are outside the limits of God's decrees and are not accompanied by grace; therefore, they are more difficult to tolerate. In them, everything is sad and unendurable, everything appears to be without remedy. This is a fitting chastisement for a soul who wants to taste the forbidden fruit—setting her mind on that which pertains solely to God. Walking in this path, the poor soul will meet with death and the rebellion of all her passions without finding any comfort in herself.

Let us abandon ourselves lovingly to the adorable Heart of Jesus with profound humility and detachment from all creatures, no matter how holy or necessary they appear to us. I wish you detachment from yourselves, and I will implore this grace for you from God; you also beg this grace for me. This will be a nice act of charity that will be rewarded by the beloved of your soul Who, loving me tenderly, through His bounty will reward all who will in some manner help me to sanctify my soul while working for the welfare of the Institute.

As I don't have the time to write to all the houses as I desire, you will do me a great favor if you send a copy of this letter to them so that we may all follow the same road. Who would want to fail at the end? May God keep us from such a misfortune!

Spread the fragrance of your virtue around you so that as true missionaries you may save all and know how to draw countless young souls to the Institute; after becoming your Sisters, they can work with you where the harvest is great and the laborers are few—at least let the spouses of Christ come here to save so many souls gifted with faith but deprived of doctrine.

Yes, my daughters, your good example, your life of abnegation and virtue, can attract a large number of candidates. Let this be the best present that you give me on my return: a large number of vocations drawn by your example; but make sure that they are detached from all things and from self, disposed to be used everywhere and in all things by obedience. So we have an agreement: don't forget!

May Jesus bless you and grant you all the graces I mentioned. They are the ones I think are the most suitable and best for your real happiness. If you have need of me, go to the Sacred Heart of Jesus and to the feet of Mary Immaculate; there you will find me disposed to grant your needs. Pray much for

Your affectionate Mother in the Most Sacred Heart of Jesus,
M. FRANCESCA SAVERIO CABRINI

October 15, 1910, London

In this letter, Mother Cabrini encourages a group of Sisters who are about to espouse themselves to Christ. She also reminds them to be careful of becoming too attached to other Sisters at the expense of their love for Christ.

A.M.G.SS.C.J.
My Dearest Daughter,

The day of your espousals draws near, and the heavenly Spouse comes to you with innumerable benefits; so open your hearts, my beloved daughters, and lift your thoughts to Heaven. Yes, depart from Babylon to attend more diligently to the sanctification of your souls. "Go from this people", Jesus seems to say; "separate yourselves from it and come to Me. I will be your Spouse and loving Father. Let the dead bury their dead, renounce yourselves in all things, carry your cross, and follow Me faithfully all the days of your life."

Give, oh dearest daughters, your heart to your dearly beloved Jesus; let none of your affections rest disorderedly on any creature. Don't be too quick to excuse certain blind inclinations of the human heart that tend to substitute earthly sympathies for the pure and sublime motives that religion proposes.

There is nothing more common among tenderhearted people than that natural inclination to strike up a particular friendship with certain people whose exterior or personality attract them. Well, according to the masters of the spiritual life, nothing is more opposed to true charity or more harmful to souls who follow this inclination and to the congregation of which they are members.

It is commonly believed, especially by young Sisters, that nothing is more innocent than to form such friendships with people who appeal to them. It is a necessity of life, they say, to have someone to confide in and open one's heart to; only hard hearts can do without virtuous friendship. Oh my daughters, don't talk so foolishly. These ideas, which are full of danger in all states of life, are especially to be feared in a religious community. When one is consecrated to God, she must regulate her friendships differently from one leading a free, private life.

By becoming a religious, you have sacrificed yourself to obedience, and you no longer belong to yourself. If you are no longer in charge of your time and work, neither can you be in charge of your attachments, which, if they persisted, would take away your time and attention from spiritual matters. When you form ties not approved by your superiors, you disobey and enter unconsciously into a particular spirit that is contrary to the general spirit of the community. You run the risk of falling into jealousy, anxiety, and passion for the interests of the beloved.

Particular attachments often make you resistant to changes of assignment that would take you away from the person you love; maybe you will even become bitter toward the superior or obedience and seek a thousand pretexts to evade it. You often break silence, have secrets to confide, absent yourself from the community, and lose your serenity.

Oh, it is so true that a quarter of an hour spent in opening our hearts intemperately to a beloved person does more harm than all the conversations that could take place where the community is assembled. You become irritable and suspicious, all the charitable remedies that the superior uses are judged as cruel, and you complain that no one cares about you, that the superior is inflexible in an innocent matter, etc., etc.

The poor superiors see the evil and can hardly explain it. They discern that a secret friendship is insensibly poisoning the heart and don't know how to prevent this poisoning. The Sister first gets angry, then gets bitter, and finally rebels. See, my daughters, how good beginnings have evil consequences. But this is enough; I don't have any more time to continue. I leave it to you to ponder how a particular friendship is capable of destroying unity and peace and creating disruptive factions.

Resolve never to have particular friendships, to keep your heart free, to guard it with great jealousy so that it will never break open into vain affections but love all whom your Spouse commands you to love: your community.

Direct the affections of your heart toward the greatest good, from which you will never suffer. Open your heart to the love of order and obedience, love the work of God in your Institute, taste the sweetness of charity that embraces all, love unity and peace in the house where you live, and let your conversation be serious, simple, and edifying.

I regret that I am unable to be with you on this grand day of your investiture and profession, but I will be near you in spirit, and I shall invoke the spirit of God upon each one of you.

Pray for me and my intentions so that God will bless this mission I am preparing in London. It is situated on a hill from which I seem to see the universe and the immense work of God.

May Jesus bless you and make you taste the joys of Heaven on such a great day.

Affectionately in the Most Sacred Heart of Jesus,

M. FRANCESCA S. CABRINI

3. The World Traveler

Mother Cabrini never slowed down—except when she was on a steamship. All the demands on her time as superior general were placed on hold when she stepped onto a steamer and spent several days on the ocean. Of course, she still had to care for the Sisters who traveled with her and who were often seasick. But the sea air seemed to help her weak constitution, and she spent hours composing long, beautifully written letters to her Sisters, describing the ups and downs of her journey.

* * *

April 1890, Voyage from Le Havre, France, to New York

When Christopher Columbus crossed the Atlantic Ocean in a sailing ship, it took him about two months. Four centuries later, steamships could make the crossing in less than a week. But, as Mother Cabrini describes, her second voyage from Europe to America, accompanied by several Sisters, took ten days due to engine failure, fog, and icebergs.

A.M.G.SS.C.J.
My Dear Daughters,

When I left you last Wednesday, I thought of myself as traveling only to Milan, not too far from you, for if I had let myself dwell on the thought of going so very far away, I would have quickly begun to feel overwhelmed. In Milan, when I was truly leaving you, I felt as if I was being crushed beneath a huge weight. The only relief came from the thought of the promises each of you made to study to become true brides of Christ, worthy Missionaries of His Sacred Heart.

How much this thought, my daughters, eases every pain! It makes me find sweetness in any labor or crosses I have and gives me great joy. If we reflect well, for us there are no distances: the Missionaries of the Sacred Heart of Jesus are a worldwide order and must participate in the immensity of this Divine Heart, Who embraces all, comprehends all, animates all, unites all in Himself. It is He Who sustains us in these temporary separations, Who makes us share in His strength, Who communicates to us every grace. He is our true Treasure; love Him with all your hearts, serve Him faithfully, encourage all souls to be detached from creatures, from all things, even from themselves, so that they may succeed in possessing His perfect love, which is an anticipation of Heaven. Let all your affections, my daughters, be centered on this beautiful Heart, and you will always be happy; but if, instead, you foster private affections that tie you to self, or to creatures, you will always have annoyances, times of tedium and melancholy. Free yourselves, and put on wings, I beg you, in order that you may rise above the earth.

Arrival at Paris. The journey has been very happy. While we were passing through those high chains of mountains, and admiring so many beauties of nature created by God just to give pleasure to His creatures, our souls felt raised to sublime meditation. It was beautiful to notice the sweet impression the many and various sights they saw made on the minds and in the hearts of the Sisters, for this was the first time they had made this journey. When Sister Eletta noticed the change in the color of the water between Italy and France, she thought she was seeing the equator. Then as we crossed over certain bridges, she wondered if the train might be frightened.

About two A.M., when everyone was sleeping, someone opened the door of the compartment and asked us to get off quickly, but we did not want to obey, responding that we were not getting off until Paris. Three minutes later they returned and begged us again to leave the compartment, but they received no satisfaction, because I did not understand what they were saying. Sister Ignatius, half-asleep, contented herself with answering, "Close the door." To bring us to our senses, the stationmaster, accompanied by several porters, told us that the carriage we were in had broken down. At last we understood and left the compartment in haste, some with our shoes in our hands, some with no veil, some holding a white handkerchief, some with our hair down, some still putting on our collars. Quicker than I can say, our luggage was transferred to another compartment, where we remained very comfortable until we arrived in Paris. We then thanked our dear Spouse for the great love He had shown us in protecting us. We made a very fervent Spiritual Communion and went to sleep again!

We arrived in Paris an hour and a half late on account of the incident. Nevertheless, we found Mrs. Gabin awaiting us. At once she took us to the church of Our Lady of Victories, where we all received Holy Communion, to the great joy of our souls. This being our first visit to this sanctuary, it left a great impression on me. The most Holy Virgin, our loving Mother, invited me—maybe because I have placed our Institute and each one of you in a special manner under her protection, and through her, in the

Heart of the Child Jesus. What beautiful graces will shower down upon us, for our sanctification, for the good of the Institute, and for the salvation of souls! We spent a few hours touring Paris in the company of our guide, seated on the upper deck of the tram so as to see better. A little after midday we took the train for Le Havre; we arrived there about five o'clock in the afternoon and spent Friday evening relaxing on the ship.

Saturday, April 19. This morning we went to visit and pay our respects to the captain and commissioner. They received us with great courtesy and offered their help in all our needs. These persons did not know us, but they were so kind to us. From this we can learn to appreciate the great love the Heart of Jesus has for His spouses. He heaps upon us benefits and favors we do not merit. Let us be ever grateful, so that gratitude may obtain for us greater graces. This morning we went on deck and saluted the sea, the image of the immensity of God. Then we recited our prayers, which arose fervently without effort from our souls. We then recited the "Ave Maris Stella". We did not sing, because we were afraid of disturbing the other passengers on board, but the Most Holy Virgin, who had blessed our departure, listened to the melody of the affections of her devout daughters, if not the melody of their voices.

At nine A.M. we left the port, and in a short time we were on the open sea and had lost sight of land. It was raining a little, but the passengers said we would have a good voyage. We did not feel anxious about this, because we knew we were in the hands of God, enclosed in the Most Sacred Heart of Jesus, and this thought kept us safe and peaceful in every situation. As soon as Sister Battistina saw the boat move, she said she felt a dizziness in her head. Half an hour later she was very sick, and one after the other followed her example. I was the only one who remained unaffected. I wished the boat would stay steady, so that I could go on with my work, but I found I had to abandon that idea. However, I continued to feel much better, and by degrees I felt I could breathe more freely.

This, too, helped me raise my soul to God, and I could almost say in all seriousness what I said jokingly a few days ago, that if the Sacred Heart would give me the means, I would build a ship called the *House of Christopher* ("Bearer of Christ") to sail the seas with a community, small or large, so as to carry the Name of Christ to all people, to those who do not know Him yet, and also to those who have forgotten Him. But these are useless thoughts, and I do not permit them to occupy my mind, although they serve for a little recreation.

At ten-thirty the bell rang for breakfast; everyone found the courage to come to the table with me. But a minute later, they all ran, one after another, to the side of the ship to begin that unpleasant task. Sister Ignatius tried to force herself to eat to keep herself strong, but halfway through the meal she also had to follow the others. They left me alone at the table, and I kept up to the end like a sailor. In fact, I've never had such an appetite.

Sunday, April 20. Yesterday, at dinner, all the Sisters came to the table and took a little refreshment. Then we all went on deck to breathe in the air and revive and refresh our lungs. At seven-thirty we returned to our cabins. We stayed for a short time and said our prayers. Toward nine o'clock we went to bed and slept all night. The sea was very calm. Sister Assunta thought she heard a hurricane, but it was only a little rain beating against the windows. You should see poor Sister Assunta! She looks so woebegone. How would she be if the sea were at all rough? However, she laughs heartily when asked what is worrying her and making her look so miserable.

This morning the sea is still very calm. I have never seen it so calm. It is literally like a lake. The boat is moving so quickly, and we don't feel the motion at all. The sun is shining beautifully, and the air is good. There is no odor in the cabin whatsoever. The boat is so well-built and well ventilated, it's as if we were traveling on land. Even so, all the Sisters were not able to be present at breakfast, and the few that came were not able to stay. I soon found myself alone like yesterday. The steward, who sits near us at the table, gave orders to the waiters to bring something special for the Sisters who were sick. Poor Sisters! At every movement of the boat they think we are in a great storm. Sister Eletta would like to have the boat stopped, at least during meals. I told the steward this just to make him laugh; he is so kind, he looks like a Saint Francis de Sales.

How many beautiful thoughts the calmness of the sea suggests. We see in it the happiness of a soul that lives in the tranquility of the grace of God. In such a fortunate soul, all is calm; there is undisturbed peace; it has the capacity to raise itself to the sublimity of the divine mysteries. It also gives us a vision of the immensity of the power of God, Who commands this endless sea, which could rise in whirling billows but instead remains calm and tranquil. God commands, the sea obeys. If every religious Sister would obey her superior with perfect submission, without relying on her own judgment, what calmness, what tranquility, what a sweetness of Paradise she would have! My daughters! Act in this way, be obedient, be most humble, not using your own judgment, submitting with great peace and simplicity to your superiors, and your houses will have a true Paradise in them that anticipates the eternal one awaiting you. It seems as if the Risen Jesus Himself has said to the sea, "Peace be with you." This is an image of a pure soul without anger, who is detached from everything and united exclusively with her beloved and divine Spouse. She rests on His left arm while He caresses her with His right hand.

My dear daughters, be purely selfless; be detached from all things and all persons, including yourselves, from your desires and inclinations, and thus be like a peaceful sea. You will become like a great ocean, because the pure soul is capable of great things, and the mind is thus able to wander in the infinity of God. The earthly soul, full of attachments, is always small and narrow with limited capacity, lacking in courage, and easily discouraged, and it is never able to throw itself fully into divine service. I don't want any such souls among my daughters, or among my friends. I want you all to have wings and fly swiftly and rest in that blessed peace possessed by a soul that is all for God. I want to be like that too, so pray, my daughters—pray for me; I have many desires, but all of them are barren. If these desires were talents, oh, I would be in trouble, because I would be obliged to multiply them, whereas now I keep them buried and they bear no fruit. The thought that we can always humble ourselves and obtain pardon from God is a consolation for me. Yes, my daughters, let us humble ourselves before God in every moment of our lives, and he will lift us out of our troubles, and we will be allowed a taste of the peace and tranquility that I see pictured in this sea I am now crossing.

Monday, April 21. Here we go: the see-saw has been put in motion by the almighty hand of God, and we must play along whether we want to or not. Yesterday about five o'clock in the afternoon the sea began to be a real sea. It was not possible to stand on your feet without leaning on something for support. Five hours have already gone by since Sister Eletta began to pray to God to calm the sea. But now, at such a scary (for her) sight, she is at a loss for words and thinks the best thing to do is to go to bed, as the other

Sisters have done. I stand firm and remain on deck. I made them laugh so much that Sister Eletta said she almost felt better. After supper, about six o'clock, I wanted to see the other good Sisters, and following their example, I began to feel seasick myself. Patience! Twice I had to resign myself to keeping them company. Sister Assunta looks like a troubled soul. Sister Giovannina is always laughing, even when she is very sick. Sister Augustine also smiles. Sister Bernardina is like a dead person, and so is Sister Battistina! Sister Ignatius is trying to follow my example, but after a while she has to run for her life, or else stay in the cabin so as not to fall.

Of all the passengers on board, men and women, only six or seven come to the table. Woe to those who succumb. The best strategy is to stay on deck. Even if it rains, it is better to stay out in the open. Last night, I stayed out until after midnight, half-dressed (because I believed a storm was threatening) so as to be ready to save myself and everyone; but the good God is continually watching over His spouses, and all the back-and-forth subsided, although the gale still beat round us. I rose early this morning to go on deck to view the wonderful spectacle. Oh! How beautiful is the sea in all its great motion! How the waves swell and foam! Enchanting! The wind is favorable, though, and the boat is moving so quickly, it seems to fly. If you could only see the waves! None of us could stay at the stern because the waves were sweeping over the vessel at every moment. At the bows it is not so bad, and, stretched out in an armchair, I can write fairly well. A single wave could submerge everything, but He Who created the sea and commanded it to rise like mountains would not permit His beloved creatures to be drowned, much less His loving spouses. God loved us before He created the sea; in fact, He created the sea itself for our use and pleasure. He has chosen us for His spouses, and we have answered His call, attracted by His infinite lovableness. Let us remain, my daughters, entirely subject to Him, conquered by His love; and let us run swiftly in His footsteps. The good God has perpetually loved us and chosen us, so let us love Him and serve Him with joy during the few days of our life. If you were all here with me, dear daughters, to cross the immense ocean, you would exclaim, "Oh, how great and loving is God in all His works!" But the ocean of graces, oh my daughters, that the good Jesus pours down upon us at every moment of our lives is immensely superior to anything in nature. All natural splendors are eclipsed by the abundance of riches that God showers upon His beloved spouses. Let us venerate and love, then, our excellent state, and let us examine ourselves frequently and remove all defects that are unbecoming to the virgins of Christ, so that our Beloved may soon lead us into his wine cellar, inebriate us, and instill charity in our souls.

Tuesday, April 22. Today I am only writing a few lines, because I am worn out from what we have gone through. Yesterday evening the movement of the boat increased. It dipped at the stern to such an extent that we thought it would capsize at any moment. Then they increased the speed of the engines so much that about midnight we felt a terrible shock, and the boat stopped suddenly. The engine had broken down. A horn, a bell, and a bugle called all the sailors up. There was a great noise, but no one knew what it was, except we realized the ship was at a standstill. We got dressed in a hurry, even those of us who were sick, in order to be ready to be rescued, if that were necessary. As soon as I was dressed, I went to see all the Sisters. Sister Eletta ran to me first—she was terrified and asked if I had heard anything. I laughed heartily to make her laugh so as to chase away her fears. In her cabin everyone was alarmed, while in the next they were all sleeping as if nothing had happened. I thought it best to leave them there because they were all sleeping soundly. Meanwhile, we went to see what was wrong. They told me we would have to stay here until the engine was repaired; however, the sea had become tranquil, and the boat was just rocking gently from time to time.

We didn't move forward from about midnight until eleven the next morning, when, while we were eating breakfast, the boat resumed its course. Now we are swiftly sailing toward New York on a calm sea, as if nothing had happened. In the meantime, when the boat was stopped, all the Sisters got up, and now I am pleased to see them all with me on deck. If Sister Giuseppina had been paying attention, this morning she would have seen the ship at a standstill in the midst of the clouds, but perhaps she only wanted to watch the sky. Sister Augustine, Sister Battistina, and Sister Assunta are still half-dead. They don't feel able to eat anything, although it is nice to see them smiling, always resigned to the dear and holy will of God. Having lost sleep last night, I am very tired. Nevertheless, I am walking around and eating; I am with you in spirit. Tonight I will sleep, if the good God does not wish otherwise. We are often delighted at seeing the beautiful seagulls, at one moment flying in the air and at another frolicking on the water. They seem to be the image of our guardian angels, or of the many dear young virgins who come to our Institute to become missionaries. This is the first time I have ever seen seagulls.

Wednesday, April 23. We are near the shore of Newfoundland, and, as usual for this spot, the boat is moving in an extraordinary way, which is making everyone uncomfortable. All the Sisters are ill again. They are half-dead, except Sister Eletta and Sister Giovannina, who are now quite used to the sea and are keeping me company. Sister Eletta is our entertainment with her geographical difficulties. She does not understand how the pilot of our ship can be so ignorant as to keep us in mid-ocean, while other boats we see from time to time in the distance are always sailing on the horizon, so she thinks they are nearer the land and thus safer than we are. And she marvels at how the great circle is always the same distance away. Today they have prepared the list of passengers to be given to the officer of New York as soon as we enter the bay. Our names, along with the others, were stamped on a most beautiful card that was given to each first-class passenger. Sister Giovannina was called Sister Giovannona from the beginning. We always end our meditation by gazing at the sea, which evokes such beautiful thoughts and feelings. The sky is blue and the horizon is vast. It is an image of the love of God when it takes possession of a soul and makes it capable of an immense amount of holy deeds. Yes! Grace is an infinite treasure of God, and those who receive it and make good use of it truly participate in the friendship of God. Is it not precious for the immense increase that it brings to our souls every hour? It is true, then, that the ocean is a beautiful image of grace. Let us try, oh my daughters, to attract the grace of God to our souls, by perfect detachment of all and from all, even from our most ardent desires that can disturb the peace and quietness of the soul, which are the fruits of grace.

Thursday, April 24. I am writing to you after having witnessed a spectacle quite new to me and also to some of the sailors. About eleven o'clock we found ourselves surrounded by enormous masses of ice. At first they appeared to be objects of no importance, like white doves resting on the water, but afterward, little by little, they grew much larger. They took on enormous proportions, and when we got nearer to them, we saw that they were about twelve times larger than our ship. The captain reduced the speed of the engines and took a different route to avoid them, but even so, at one point we were only about sixty yards away from them. Now we can see some of them in the distance. We feel afraid of the coming night. Perhaps there will be danger then, but we leave ourselves in the hands of the good Jesus.

A gentleman who had already made twenty-one ocean voyages had never seen a spectacle like this before; this has been reserved just for us. These icebergs look like great crenellated fortresses. The sea is very tranquil today. All the Sisters are well except Sister Augustine, who still looks nearly half-dead. One thing after another is delaying our arrival. According to our calculations, we shall not arrive before Tuesday. Imagine! We thought we would arrive in time for the feast of the Patronage of Saint Joseph; instead we shall have to spend it at sea without Mass, without Holy Communion. We are beginning to feel the gravity of such an onerous fast. Oh yes! When we land, we shall look for a priest at once in order to receive Communion, as we did a year ago. The marvelous spectacle that is continually before our eyes offers us a good preparation for Holy Communion, as we all see this is the work of Him Whom we so ardently desire to welcome in the small sanctuary of our souls.

Friday, April 25. Today it is very hot, just like July. The sea is very beautiful, but the motion of the boat is very marked. The chairs would not stay in place, and stewards had to come fasten them so that we could comfortably enjoy the open air. However, all the Sisters are well. They ate breakfast with me, to my great delight.

The ladies got up late this morning, and we were able to say the prayers of the Office of the Sacred Heart on deck. We also made a little meditation on the beautiful lesson of

Saint Bernard, in which he speaks of the strength and power of the love of God in a soul, and how the possession of this love enables a soul not to feel the weight of any cross anymore, so that the cross becomes instead a great pleasure and delight. Oh, happy the soul that lives in the true love of Christ! My daughters, detach yourselves from all persons and all things, and you will have a foretaste of the Paradise of true, solid, and heavenly love.

Before we went to bed last night, we were thinking of you making the Holy Hour, perhaps for us. We united ourselves with you in spirit and tasted with you the Paradise of holy union with God. Every day we invoke the Star of the Sea with the "Ave Maris Stella", in honor of our loving Mother who truly protects us. Only yesterday we escaped a collision with those enormous masses of ice that were threatening our ruin. We owe this to our dear and powerful Mother. We are reasonably cheerful. The passengers seem to share our cheerfulness, for one after another of them come by to spend a little time with us and favor us with their company.

Saturday, April 26. Yesterday, about three o'clock, a heavy fog set in. It was so dense that we could only see a few yards ahead. Fog is always a source of great danger, more so on sea than on land. Our fear increased when we saw blocks of ice floating all around the boat. The engine was shut down for fear of crashing into some of these masses of ice, but before evening the fog cleared, and we could see the horizon clearly. So the night will be calm. For fear of the ice, the boat changed its route—at other times the route is more northern, toward the Banks of Newfoundland; this time it is more toward the south. Meanwhile, the heat is like summer. For three days, I have been looking like Bacchus. My forehead is very red, even purple, and this redness is spreading all over my face. At first I thought it was an infection. I did not like the prospect, because I would have had to retire from the open, and fresh air is life to me. Happily, however, the doctor said the redness was the effect of the air and of the water spraying my face. I did not want to run away as soon as it began to rain and deprive myself of the fresh air.

Today the skin has begun to peel off my forehead and nose. I am molting like a snake. God wants me to change my life and be converted; to confirm this, my dearest daughters, pray. The Sacred Heart of Jesus will always be favorable to the prayers of children for their mother. Pray! Pray! I am in need of your intercession. When I am converted and begin to lead a good life, it is certain that this will obtain many beautiful graces for the Institute. But I rejoice in the belief that you have been so good as to do that, because in the midst of many dangers, especially those enormous masses of ice, we did not plunge to the bottom of the ocean. Continue to be so good, generous and sacrificing, humble and meek on all occasions, especially in moments when you feel self-love.

A Protestant gentleman came to me last night and asked me to go to a concert along with all the Sisters. I told him we could not accept the invitation, as religious do not attend secular entertainments or amusements. He wanted to stay with us. He presented us with six tickets for a lottery worth fifty cents each, and he promised to be on the alert when the numbers were drawn. I am sorry I do not know English, as this gentleman is a very good man. I like his frankness and the way he speaks of our holy religion. Patience! Pray to the Sacred Heart and Our Lady for his salvation. He is an Englishman who has lived in New York for five years. He promised to come and bring his wife with him to see our orphanage; his wife is a Catholic. This gentleman thinks we have undertaken a very difficult mission with little likelihood of success—a mission to the Italians; but hearing that it was just for this reason that we undertook it, and that we will do this work no matter what the cost, he held us in higher esteem than ever, and he is willing to help us.

There is also a great Milanese adventurer traveling with us. At first he did not reveal that he was Italian, but when he saw everybody coming to us and making friends, he came too and offered his friendship, saying how happy he was to know us. Now he delights in speaking Milanese with all his strength. He also admires the success we have had in a few months, while he, for fifteen years, he says, has found nothing but sorrow and disappointments enough to fill a book. The poor man does not know Jesus and the goodness of His Heart. He puts all his trust in his talents. Thus his days cannot be happy.

Sunday, April 27. Today is the beautiful feast of the Patronage of Saint Joseph. If we could find a priest on board, we would at least be able to hear Holy Mass; instead, this is the second Sunday that 1,300 people are without Mass. On board are 900 poor emigrants in third class, 700 Italians, and 200 Swiss. Poor things! I hope they will at least come to a town or village where there will be someone who will break the bread of the Word of God for them. But God alone knows what will happen to most of them! Perhaps they will become associated with those other poor brothers of ours of the New World who are called barbarians because they have forgotten the noble principles of the religion they were brought up in. For unfortunately, they have a rabid anarchist among them, who often gathers them around him and, like Belial, incites them to revolt against authority and order in such a manner that the officers of the boat have to interfere. In short, there is a small country floating on the waves here that threatens revolution in every sense. This is an image of our own poor Italy, whose sons have lost the true sense of patriotism and are at the mercy of their disorderly passions and civil wars. They rush to their own ruin, with the just punishment of God upon those who have forgotten that the Catholic religion of their country constitutes their principal nobility and security.

Oh, let us pray, my daughters, let us pray for so many of our brethren, and let their blindness be a good lesson for us and teach us to be more faithful in the observance of our Holy Rule, in order to console the afflicted Heart of Jesus and obtain from Him blessings in great abundance for ourselves and for our neighbors. Their mistakes will help us remain very humble in order that we may be enlightened and never allow our intellect to be darkened. God resists and confounds the proud, but He reveals Himself to the humble, draws them nearer to Himself, and caresses them. Let there be no one among the Missionaries of the Sacred Heart who is attached to her own judgment, who wants to defend her own opinions, who takes corrections poorly, wherever they come from, or who submit reluctantly to this or that superior. Each one must consider it a duty—rather, feel it a necessity—to submit to all. The religious who acts in this way will be a true jewel of our Institute who conforms herself to the Most Sacred Heart of Jesus. She will move Him to pour many great treasures upon us. Are you humble, then, my daughters? Do you like to take the last place? Are you pleased to be despised, forgotten, and ignored? Anyone who feels this way, oh, let her pray for me! She is a real gem presented to me by my dearest Jesus; through her I will obtain everything.

Last night the commissioner of the boat presented me with six tickets for the lottery and another gentleman six more—now we have fifteen. The drawing will take place today; we shall see who wins.

Monday, April 28. Today we shall sight land at about three in the afternoon, but we may not arrive in port until late in the evening, and we shall have to sleep at sea again. Our poor Sisters will be as impatient to see us as we are to embrace them. We have been greatly delayed, but here we are now, and it is our duty to thank the Most Sacred Heart of Jesus. We were alarmed on the day the engine broke down, but now we know that the delay was a great grace, because without this delay, our encounter with the icebergs would have happened during the night and been fraught with great danger.

Yesterday we were presented with more tickets for the lottery, in all nearly a hundred lire's worth. They invited me to view the exhibit, but I found nothing of any use to us. Even if we win, it will matter very little, because they are all useless things. I hope to win a greater prize of a more important kind—the conversion, with the help of the Most Sacred Heart of Jesus, of the Protestant gentleman who gave me tickets first. Yesterday we had a discussion, and he ended by saying I was right. He loves the pope very much and feels a profound veneration for him. He also has great esteem for our holy religion, but he does not wish to embrace it because he has seen so many priests without the true spirit; but even on this point, he understood well the reasons I gave him. You should see the patience with which he listens to me when I speak, and then to the Sister who tells him in English whatever he didn't understand. He is very intelligent, and understands what I intend to say from the expression on my face. He asks me to speak English as well as I can, and he helps me with some French words, saying he can understand. Sister Bernardina is going to make a novena for me to obtain the grace "to speak English" [these words are written in English], and assures me she will obtain it. What do you think of that? I am afraid Judgment Day will arrive before I learn English. In any case, I trust in my good Jesus, and if He wants me to bring any souls to His Heart, He will also give me the grace to speak the language of the country I shall visit.

A young lady from New York never leaves our side. She is very frank and lively. She speaks to everyone around us of the work of the "Sisters", and convinces everyone of the advantages and benefits of our little mission.

Now I leave you, my daughters, with this little bit of disconnected news that I have been able to write between one wave and the next. You must always accompany me in the practice of the most beautiful virtues, especially those you know I desire from each of you.

May Jesus bless you and enclose you in His beautiful Heart, where we shall find a true Paradise on earth, and may He make you always most fervent in spirit, in the perfect abnegation of yourselves, and in detachment from all creatures and pleasures.

The Sisters salute you dearly.

Your affectionate Mother in the Most Sacred Heart of Jesus,

M. FRANCESCA SAVERIO CABRINI

October 1891, Voyage from New York to Granada, Nicaragua

Mother Cabrini was invited to Nicaragua to establish her first community of Sisters in that country. As she and her Sisters traveled by steamship, they stopped at other cities in Central America. Mother describes the people she met, the natural wonders she saw, and the storm that she thought would capsize the boat.

A.M.G.SS.C.J.
My Very Dear Daughters,

As you are well aware from the account of my last voyage from Europe to America, we reached New York on September 13, where our Sisters, with many good, benevolent, and affectionate persons, were waiting for us with indescribable anxiety. The day following my arrival was the anniversary of my religious profession, a dear and memorable day for me, and for all my good daughters, who look upon whatever concerns me as theirs. We made a great feast of it. We had two Masses and a sermon by Fr. Bandini, appropriate to the work of our mission, about the solemnity of the Exaltation of the Holy Cross. In the evening, Benediction of the Blessed Sacrament was to have been given by His Grace the Archbishop, as he so kindly promised, but because of his many duties, he was obliged to delegate it to the rector of the parish where our house of 43rd Street is situated, Msgr. Brann, who was assisted by several priests who came to celebrate our arrival. His Grace came to see us the next day, and with paternal kindness, consoled us greatly.

The following days I visited the various houses of the mission. I went to Manresa first, with the twenty-nine Sisters who came here with me from Europe. All the Sisters were charmed by the beauty of the villa, which is located on one of the best sites of the Hudson River. The order and tranquility of the house pleased them even more. The chapel annexed to it inspires one with great devotion and recollection and invites us to the kind of contemplation that makes us feel the divine goodness of our celestial Spouse vividly and makes us understand His will deeply, infusing us with the courage necessary to fulfill it faithfully. Every time I find myself in Manresa, I think that when I have worked sufficiently for the Institute, perhaps this will be where I make the retreat to prepare myself for my journey to eternity. But this is an illusive dream, a childish feeling. Let us leave all thought of our future to Providence. Let us work, day by day, in the Lord's vineyard, seeking the greater glory of God, in perfect detachment from everything that is of very great importance to ourselves, for often without our knowing it, we are the enemies of our own souls, troubling ourselves about many things, while "Porro unum est necessarium" ["One thing is needful", Luke 10:42]. Most of the Sisters remained at Manresa for some days to rest after their long journey and the hardships of the sea, but I could only stay there for twenty-two hours; then I rushed to the city to make arrangements and get everything ready by October 10, the day appointed for the continuation of the journey to Nicaragua.

The 21st of September arrived with a precious and moving celebration. Seven of our American postulants, who had given excellent proof of their good spirit for a year, were preparing to exchange the white veil of a postulant for the habit of the Institute. His Grace came to see us again, and vested in his ceremonial robes to give them the veil (or the holy habit). He performed the ceremony according to our ritual with impressive decorum and devotion. He gave a moving talk, and his sweet paternal words sank deeply into the heart of each religious. I do not need to describe to you, who have often assisted at these beautiful and ever-new ceremonies with me, the emotions we shared, or what a happy and heavenly day we spent in community. Even His Grace, in congratulating us afterward, said that the ceremony was always as touching as if it were being performed for the first time. In spite of all I had to do before my departure, the time flew by without my realizing it, and without a day's rest.

The 10th of October arrived quickly, and everything was ready for the continuation of the voyage. I had already visited the cabins and prepared the places assigned to the Sisters. On the eve of our departure, the archbishop, who is most kind and shows so much affection for our Institute, came again to console us with his presence and to comfort and encourage us on the new journey that awaits us. He gave us one of those heartfelt sermons that sink deeply into the soul, and then gave Benediction of the Blessed Sacrament, which was preceded by the "Ave Maris Stella" and "Tantum Ergo", sung with great fervor by the Sisters who were leaving. This was followed by a prayer to Our Lady. Afterward, His Grace very kindly kept us company, and his holy words were a source of great comfort, as he assured us that he would pray for us every day during the voyage so that Our Lady and the angels might accompany us. His secretary, Msgr. McDonnell, also assured us of his most fervent prayers and wishes for a prosperous voyage and hoped it would be perfectly happy. During the same day, till late in the evening, many good and pious people came to say goodbye and to wish us a successful voyage. Even the next day some came on board the steamer to pay their compliments and express kind wishes for our journey.

But while we were talking about so many beautiful things, the hour of departure arrived. At ten A.M. we were on board the steamer, which is called the *New York*, of the Pacific Mail Line. The agent was very good and assigned a cabin for every two Sisters and a separate one for me. The berths are not as small as those of the transatlantic steamers, but large and comfortable. The cabins open onto the lounge, so that the Sisters can go from their berths to the lounge room without danger of falling, even when it is rough and stormy, for we do not expect this voyage to be as smooth and beautiful as the last one, since we are dealing with a new mission that needs great graces and therefore new sacrifices to render us more worthy of it. The Sisters were accompanied by many kind people. A distinguished and excellent Irishman presented us, and warmly recommended us, to the captain and the purser.

At one P.M. the anchor was raised and we glided slowly out of the port, while the Sisters and friends waved their handkerchiefs. We did the same for about a quarter of an hour, until the distance reduced the Sisters and everything else to an imperceptible dot. As the steamer steered farther down the bay, we lost sight of everyone and found ourselves abandoned to the relentless waves. We coasted along the shore until evening and would have done so all night, I believe, if a terrific storm had not arisen around eleven o'clock and threatened to dash the boat and everything it contained to pieces. At one point, the boat rolled from side to side with such force that it threatened to capsize. The Sisters could hardly keep in their berths. I arose and dressed in haste to save them all, or at least so that we could die all together. Our luggage rolled about in all directions, like so many animated objects. There was nothing to stop it. No one could keep still, not even sitting on the floor. The sea swelled in an extraordinary way. The waves formed mountains as if by magic—one could see, as it were, deep valleys between them. The steamer seemed lost amid these mountainous precipices of water. The wind wreaked havoc on deck and threatened to smash the cabins; but not permitted by God to do so, it limited itself to destroying the doctor's cabin. The following day the poor doctor had to wear somebody else's clothes, his own having been drenched and ruined.

The captain had all the sailors and crew at work to save us from complete destruction, and he only succeeded by steering the vessel toward the middle of the ocean and sailing across it for more than a day. In the meantime the sea became calm, and then we were able to resume the ship's proper route, from which we had only deviated forty miles. But God be praised! During the terrible storm, as the captain told us, no one was lost or hurt. During this tempest not one of the Sisters was frightened; all remained quietly in bed, ready to perish quietly, although they stayed under the blankets. I stayed up all night in the lounge, from which I could see the Sisters resting, and thus we encouraged one another. I was attentive, however, to every movement, for if we had needed to escape in some way, they would have been obliged to dress and try to save themselves when called upon. In the meantime I was praying to Our Lady of the Holy Rosary, in whose month we were voyaging. Then I lighted the candle of Our Lady of Loretto, so efficacious against sea storms, and our Most Holy Mother really did come to our aid, delivering us from the extreme danger that surrounded us!

Oh, how good Mary is! How sweet and amiable. The earth is full of her goodness. From generation to generation, every age has witnessed the wonderful and merciful works of her blessed hands. But this time, we ourselves experienced how much we are protected, how much we are loved. Like a mother full of compassion for each one of us, she pitied us who, in our danger, invoked her with faith. Oh, what joy to be children of such a Mother! We shall always recall the wonders of her love! We then prayed to Saint Aloysius to send angels from Heaven to save us from the dangers we thought to be imminent, and he, having compassion on us, who undertake all our works in honor of his centenary, sent us immediate aid, and now we are enjoying a very quiet, calm, and smooth sea. Yesterday the sea was like a soul who is agitated by remorse and pride, who never finds peace with God.

Today is October 15, the feast of Saint Teresa [of Ávila], and this dear saint, who endured every kind of trial and suffered long and painfully, has obtained for us a most beautiful day: a clear sky, a vast horizon, and a pure, gentle breeze. One could imagine that we were at Heaven's gates, from which there emanates a sweet comfort that allows us somehow to partake of the grand and beautiful feast that Jesus is holding for His beloved spouse today. There is no priest on board, so no Mass, but we have been able to communicate spiritually with great faith. That adventurous prisoner had reason to rejoice at the thought that if she had held Jesus in her heart even once, she could enter the mystical tabernacle of her soul, rejoicing as if it really held her Beloved. We, happier still, have received Him many times, and it is only five days ago that our hearts beat together with His, and that He strengthened our souls and was given to us as Holy Viaticum. Today, then, it was not difficult to draw ourselves around Jesus, for He has wounded us with holy love, as He once pierced the heart of the Seraph of Carmel.

Today they say we shall meet a steamer that will take our letters, so I shall write a few lines to New York and Italy, and in this way quell the rumors that have led you to believe we all perished in the storm. The danger was indeed real, but we were all calm, tranquil, and safe, trusting in our Jesus and the mission on which He Himself was leading us in the company of the Most Blessed Virgin and Saint Aloysius, patron of the new foundation. It is evident that we are making great strides toward the tropics, though we have not yet reached them. We could use our Sister Eletta here with us to teach us about the equator, the meridians, and all the different marks that divide the zones, states, and seas, since we don't know much about it ourselves. Though we were obliged to put on lighter clothes, we are still perspiring. The breeze, however, is refreshing and comforting.

Yesterday, October 15, we expected to meet a steamer that would take on our letters, but the whole day passed without one coming into sight. This morning at seven o'clock we sighted a little island, called the Isle of Fortune, and a tug-boat called *Columbus* came out from it to take the mail.

After some days on the high seas and after experiencing so many dangers, it was a great joy to see land, and we saluted the island with great pleasure. The captain, always so good and kind to us, placed us in the best position so that we might see everything well. I strained my eyes and searched the island for a steeple, so as to salute with double fervor Jesus in the Blessed Sacrament, for it was Friday, and at this hour all our Sisters were making their Hour of Adoration. Oh, you dear daughters, so fortunate to be so near the living center of life. Blessed are you who feel His Heart beat, who hear His ardent words that fill you with great strength and instill in you a powerful realization of the necessity to return the Love of our Beloved. Therefore, put into practice the holy resolutions you have made, generously sacrificing yourselves for the glory of God; always humbling yourselves with all your might and loving humiliations with true and sincere affection; being obedient till death and seeking the perfection of obedience, being careful to avoid even the slightest transgression of the orders of your superior, who speaks to you in the name of God; being charitable, willingly abandoning all your own inclinations in order to make others feel better, especially your Sisters; seeking to give consolation to your superiors by perfect renunciation of your will, which you left at the door of the convent when, with the cross, you entered saying, "[I come] peaceably; I have come to sacrifice to the LORD" [1 Sam 16:5]. Oh, yes, my daughters, foster peace by sacrificing yourselves always, and never be the cause of sorrow to your superiors, thrusting thorns into their hearts by your conduct, by your own ideas, which, however lovely they may appear to you, are but offshoots of a poisonous self-love. The more you are attached to them, the more poisonous they are to you. Renounce yourselves entirely if you wish to enjoy peace, and let those who are around you partake of your joy, and thus also gain the desire, when the occasion arises, to co-operate for the salvation of souls.

Since I started writing, we have sailed a very great distance and have reached another island called Castel, where we, just as fortunate as you, were able to salute Jesus in the Most Blessed Sacrament of the Altar, attracting Him to us with the most fervent Spiritual Communion. This morning, October 17, at five A.M., we entered the Caribbean Sea, after having passed the island of Santo Domingo, which we were not able to see because of the darkness. We were told that this sea is always very rough and stormy, but the good God deigned to show us that He is the master of land and sea and that all the elements are subject to His omnipotent hand, and so He gave us the storm where all expected calm, and gave us calm when we expected the storm.

Today is the feast of one of our most powerful patrons, Blessed Margaret Mary Alacoque,[1] and she, in her ineffable enjoyment of the Divine Heart, has surely obtained for us a drop of that celestial and sublime dew to dilute the sea through which we are now passing and make it into another sky, clear and blue, smooth and beautiful. Over it gracefully fly a number of very white birds called birds of paradise, which look like angels descending to tell us, in their silent but eloquent language, of the feast being celebrated in honor of that spotless dove Margaret, bathed in

[1] Margaret Mary Alacoque (1647-1690) was declared a saint in 1920.

the deep red of the flaming rays of charity that burn in the Heart of Jesus. What a marvel of grace God has wrought in the heart of His beloved! Let us also be faithful to the work of the Holy Spirit in our souls! Let our minds be pure, disinterested, humble, and pliant, and then we shall see what beautiful and wonderful things the Holy Spirit will work in our souls. Even the angelic spirits would fall into an ecstasy of wonder at the marvelous workings of the Holy Spirit. It is a work worthy of the infinite wisdom and goodness of God. This Spirit works within us, inspires us, instructs us, encourages us, and comforts us with His abundant and eternal light, with His promptings and impulses toward every holy work. Finally, He surrounds us with loving solicitude in keeping us within the enclosure of His eternal and infinite love.

Let us seek the right and sure path of perfection, encouraging ourselves in true charity toward God and toward our neighbor. The one should never be separated from the other. We should endeavor to attract all those who approach us to the Sacred Heart; that is the object of the life of the missionary, the spouse of Jesus Christ. Blessed Margaret Mary Alacoque saw beautifully engraved in the Most Sacred Heart of Jesus the names of those who sought to make It known, and the Divine Heart made it known to her that these would never be blotted out. The fire of His love is great and wants to spread, and those souls who endeavor to extend it are loved in a very special manner and filled with heavenly graces. Who among us, oh daughters, would not wish to be such a soul? Otherwise, we should be like the foolish virgins, who, for want of reflection, became unworthy of seeing their Spouse and entering with Him into the marriage feast. Let us always have our lamps burning, never weary, and, as soon as we see our oil is diminishing, let us go to the Fountain of Life with profound humility to renew ourselves and to gain new courage. There is little time left, oh daughters, so let us work quickly, for the reward is already prepared, and will be given in the measure in which we are prepared for it. Jesus is with us. In Him we can do all things. By ourselves we fall, but with God all things are possible. Take heart, daughters. Let none of you ever stray from the center of the path, lost in the shadow of a little pride—or of pride's child, dejection. Pray hard for me, too, that I may not, after trying to encourage you, forget these lessons and thus make myself unworthy of the tender kindness and friendship of my Beloved, who is our treasure without parallel. Compared to him, the whole world and all its delights are nothing—or rather, muck and affliction of spirit.

All the Sisters are feeling well and are on deck, admiring the work of the Omnipotent and the immensity of God and imploring graces and blessings for the land that they see. Last evening we passed Cuba on the east side, with all its beautiful elevations. To the west lay Haiti, where we saw what we thought was a beautiful and enormous palm plant. A few gentlemen who were traveling with us saw it too, and they passed around a telescope to get a better look at the lovely palm. Our Sister Pauline was overjoyed to describe to us the big leaves that hung and swayed, but when we approached, we noticed that this plant, about which we had made so many predictions, was really just a piece of a sail spread over the tall mast of a merchant ship. The gentlemen still did not believe it, but finally, once they got closer, in the brilliant moonlight, they saw their error, and everyone cracked up laughing. Even those who still felt seasick were in a good mood.

I have not told you of our sweet and simple strategy for maintaining a good sea, and even making it more attractive and tranquil. At night I beg the Sisters to make great acts of humility, acknowledging our misery. This is very easy when we live in the truth and do not delude ourselves, and with this kind of humble supplication we obtain the grace of seeing the sea spread out like a beautiful blue cloth, slightly wrinkled, but brilliant with beautiful colors, creating a charm with which diamonds, gems, and precious stones cannot compare. To tell the truth, during the days of the storm we had quite forgotten about this most powerful form of petition: deep, sincere acts of humility.

Oh humility, how powerful and beautiful you are! My daughters, be humble in your intellect and thinking, as true religious placed in the school of perfection should be. Have the lowest opinion of yourselves. Let each one consider herself the least of all the Sisters and the only one unworthy to live with the spouses of Christ, the beloved of His Most Sacred Heart. Be grateful for God's mercies, for gratitude is the noble sentiment of humble souls. Be humble, therefore, and always sincerely so, loving to be held of no account, unnoticed, forgotten, ill-treated, despised, and calumniated; even in such cases one should remain calm, resigned, and content, as in a garden of flowers. Prefer to obey rather than to command. When you are corrected, do not justify yourselves; never say, "I speak because I have reason to do so." Keep silent and practice virtue whether you are right or wrong; otherwise we may dream of perfection, but we shall never reach it.

With humility, you will increase in grace and virtue, the serenity of the angels will shine upon your faces, and you will not be discouraged in adversity or elated in prosperity. Your only thought will be to please Jesus in everything, and then you will be like those pure white doves, beautiful and lovely in the sight of God. Your voice will be sweet to the Sacred Heart of Jesus, your prayer will be as perfume in the sight of the Most High, your life will be as a burning lamp in the community; and finally, your death will be that of the just, with an immense trust in Him Whom you have imitated, and Who is your All and the center of all your aspirations.

Now, I must tell you how the feast of Blessed Margaret Mary Alacoque, our greatest patroness, ended. At four P.M. a bell rang long and loud, and the crew appeared, in a great commotion. The sailors were running here and there, calling out, but softly, "fire!" In less time than it takes to tell, everyone was ready with a life preserver to jump into the sea in case of danger, but carefully, for, as the captain says, this sea is full of sharks, which are seen very frequently. Men were employed in lowering the lifeboats. It was a fine sight to behold, for a dear old lady, who takes such good care of us, told us it was only a fire drill carried out occasionally to keep the crew skilled in the event of a real fire. May God spare us such a catastrophe!

At six P.M. we went to dinner as usual, and several people, accompanied by a colonel from Guatemala, addressed us, saying they were going to give a concert in honor of the captain, and hoped that we would participate. We hesitated to give our consent, not being accustomed to this sort of thing, but, remembering that we were in very refined company, and that, after Our Lady of the Holy Rosary, we owed the safety of our lives to the brave and valiant captain, we yielded, begging the colonel to put our names at the beginning of the program, so that as soon as we did our part, we could retire. This was graciously accepted, and half an hour later, we found ourselves in the first-class lounge, where we read an address that was graciously applauded, and then we went back on deck, leaving the other passengers to finish their entertainment, which was really very nice and sensibly arranged. But after all that, they were not satisfied. The colonel came on deck, accompanied by the doctor and other persons, and begged us to sing some of the little hymns they had heard us sing a few days before. So we sang, in chorus, "Gesù mio ver conforto" ["Jesus, My True Comfort"] and then "Maria, che dolci affetti" ["Mary, What Sweet Affection"], and our voices, blending with the sound of the waves, were raised to Heaven, while the listeners' faces brightened with a new pleasure, which some may have never enjoyed before. It was Jesus and Mary who were passing their celestial rays over these souls, whom we were secretly praying might be given the precious gift of faith. The captain, not knowing how to show his gratitude, invited us to the bridge. He showed us his tricolored lantern—white, green, and red—that is used to avoid collisions, his compass and other nautical instruments, and the plumb line for measuring. The captain told us that the Caribbean Sea is a mile deep, and that the depth of the sea near Nicaragua is unknown, for no one has been able to fathom it: and I hope I shall return to you without having to measure such a profound depth myself. We also saw the captain's bed, which is a sort of hammock with a small mattress, suspended from the ceiling of his cabin. But the poor man must get very little rest if the weather is not good, as he is responsible for all the lives on deck, about which he is most anxious and careful indeed.

Yesterday, the 19th, at seven A.M. we arrived at Colón, a port that has the reputation of being very unhealthy and a place of yellow fever. For us, however, it turned out to be very pleasant; the air, which for the last few days had become cool, contrary to every law of nature, became still cooler as we arrived in the harbor, which amazed everyone. We were able to enjoy for the first time a view that was wonderful to us: a forest of palms surrounding the bay, a charming sight. The railway was quite near the steamer, but the captain would not allow us to disembark until everything was ready for our departure, which was at one-thirty P.M.

So, we were spared the trouble of finding food and shelter on land. When the signal was given, our luggage, which occupied six seats, was put on the train free of charge, thanks to the thoughtfulness of the purser, who assisted us greatly on this first sea voyage. When we were all on the train, the captain, accompanied by all the officers, came to bid us goodbye and told us to keep well and assured us we would have a pleasant voyage up the Pacific. Even the servants came to say goodbye. One would think we were leaving our own families. But while we were pleased at such an exhibition of kindness, nevertheless, it made us feel sad to leave such kind people, among whom it seemed we could do so much good. God, however, wants us elsewhere, and so, after the signal was given for departure, we find ourselves flying across the Isthmus of Panama, through a forest of palms, and then through a country where nature puts forth an immense amount of vegetation. There are immense stretches of coconuts, royal palms, bananas, breadfruit trees, tamarinds noted for their beautiful tiny leaves, and another tree called in Spanish *asquiera*, from the roots of which a particular kind of flour can be extracted. There are thousands of other trees displaying fruits and leaves that are a source of great wonder. I must say I really saw something new this time that interested me greatly, for up to now I had only heard them described in the annals of the propagation of the faith. You would almost think we were in India or in China, especially as the train passed through villages of wooden or thatched huts, inhabited principally by Chinese emigrants and Negroes.... The further we go, the happier I feel in being out here: this is real missionary territory. It is true we have been sent to an uncivilized country, but I hope it will be the cornerstone of a large foundation, from which we may go forth from time to time to bring the knowledge of Christ and His most holy laws to those lands that the missionary has not yet reached. In fact, we see no churches, or if we see anything of the kind, they are only pagodas or Protestant churches. The sight of this spiritual poverty filled our hearts with zeal, though for the moment we can do nothing but pray for these, our unfortunate brethren, dwelling in the darkness. As we can do nothing else, we say our Rosary and recommend these souls to our great heavenly Mother, who, by the mouth of the Church, says to herself, "Quasi palma exaltata sum in Cades et quasi plantatio rosae in Jericho." ["I was exalted like a palm tree in Cades, and as a rose plant in Jericho" (Sir 24:18, DOUAY-RHEIMS)]. Let the Blessed Virgin be honored in these countries of palms and flowers, which are an image of her, and may there be a perfect and complete conversion of all these souls. To obtain this, we trust in your prayers, dear daughters. Pray, pray much without ceasing, and make your prayers efficacious by sacrifice, which you can practice hourly by a perfect observance of the rule that imposes certain acts of self-denial, to which I invite all, for Jesus wishes this of you.

We have been crossing the isthmus for two and a half hours, and we have not arrived at Panama City, situated on the Pacific—which extends in front of us with a calmness worthy of its name. Here the boat awaits us, and we are the first to board it, while the person to whom we were recommended by the captain carried our luggage. Very soon it was filled with passengers who were going our way, and we were then transferred to the steamer, *St. Blas*, which awaited us in the bay, and which could not come close to the shore because of the great rocks there. We went on board two hours before dark, expecting to continue our voyage at once, but when we got there, we had to make a day's stay, which eventually turned into one of two very long days. But even then Our Divine Lord remembered His own, because in Panama there is danger of yellow fever, and

He thus placed us on the sea to enjoy the sea breeze for two days. We would love to run to our mission immediately, but Our Lord wants us to have two days' delay. We must take this rest in peace.

After a ten days' fast from Holy Communion, we had an ardent desire to approach the Center of Life. Our desire was about to be realized, for now we see a little rowing boat coming toward us that we hired and that rowed us to shore. It was my first experience in a rowboat, and I assure you I was frightened indeed to find myself so close to the waters of the great ocean, especially as the little craft seemed about to capsize every time a passenger stepped into it; but the purpose of our trip enlivened my faith, and I encouraged the others to follow. In a few minutes we were rapidly making our trip of two miles to Panama City, singing hymns in preparation for Holy Communion. At the sound of our voices, a flock of birds approached and accompanied us to the shore. In the cathedral we were able to satisfy our desire: Jesus came to live in us, to co-operate with us, to unite Himself with us. We went to the bishop's house, but the bishop was absent and we were received by his secretary. It was about ten o'clock when we got back to our boat, and as at this time the sea was at low tide, we had to walk half a mile over the long beach in order to get to our boat. We could therefore admire the beautiful stones, many of very fine marble, that are usually covered by the salty sea. We amused ourselves by gathering shells of all colors and sizes.

Then we rowed out once more amid the waves, singing hymns of thanksgiving. Here again the birds hovered over us, drawn either by the hoarseness or sweetness of our voices, to adore and praise their Creator, Whom we carry in our hearts as in living tabernacles. The Sisters, still a little superstitious or perhaps just playful, wanted to know what this procession meant, and I replied that they represented the religious of those countries who might enter our Institute someday, but some of the Sisters were not convinced by my interpretation, since there were about a thousand birds, and responded, "Aren't they rather the souls that shall be saved by us?" I was still arguing when another flight of other aquatic birds appeared, a thousand or more, and eventually we decided that they represented the souls that were to be saved by us in the course of time. Nevertheless, it was a sight I had never beheld before in the five voyages I had already made. Up until then, we would be awestruck when a flock of just fifty birds came into view. Nevertheless, this is the marvel that awaited us in the Pacific.

We arrived on board to the joyful exclamations of all the passengers, who love us like family. Some of them tried to frighten us for fun, saying we would never reach the shore, especially as we were hidden from view by a shower that fell near the steamer while we were crossing. The shower only threatened us, for we intoned the "Ave Maris Stella", during which the spirits of the air vanished, and we only experienced the rocking of the boat, encouraged at the same time by the realization that Our Lord was master of that piece of wood that separated us from the ocean's abyss. Sitting at the stern of the boat, I put my hands into the water, bathing them in the sea, but I withdrew them quickly when I felt one of them being pulled down vigorously. It could not have been one of those seven-foot sharks, but was surely something of the crab species that kept a tight hold once it grasped.

We spent the day in devotional readings, interrupted now and then by the arrival of new passengers or fishing boats carrying a quantity of corals for those who wished to buy them. We amused ourselves by watching the little islands, which according to the ebb and flow of the tide appeared correspondingly very small or very large. These islands are joined by narrow stretches of land. At low-tide we spotted the remnants of a shipwreck. Who knows from how many years ago? The old vessel is so lodged in the sand that no tide can set it afloat. How many poor creatures may have been victims in the disaster! What feelings of compassion the thought awakens in us and how we are moved to pray for the repose of their souls!

Yesterday, the 21st, we wanted to return to Panama to receive Holy Communion, but the passage cost too much, and in order not to spend another twenty lire or more, we contented ourselves with the thought of having received Our Lord the day before and by drawing Him into the Mystic Tabernacle of our hearts through Spiritual Communion. During the course of the morning the Sisters were anxious to visit the islands nearby. This could be done easily, as the tide was low. They could be reached by boat and then on foot, thus passing from one isle to the other. The trip only took ten minutes and cost very little, so I was able to satisfy their desire. I did not go myself, however, for, to admit my weakness, I am afraid of the sea, and if there is no very holy motive in view, I have no courage to go where I fear danger, unless I am sent by obedience, when, of course, one's actions are blessed by God.

Oh blessed voice of obedience! When it speaks, the missionary crosses the ocean and gives no thought to the roaring waters, the rising and sinking of the billows, but the ocean becomes a sublime and magnificent sight that fills her with admiration and induces her to praise the Creator for the beauty and wonder of His works.

The Sisters enjoyed themselves immensely under the shady trees. They found other shells, but none as pretty as those on the beach at Panama.

Finally the two days of rest were over, and at seven P.M. the steamer set sail to the salutations of the passengers on the other steamers in the harbor, standing around as though they were in a piazza, and of hundreds of little boats manned by boatmen who stand there like carriage drivers and greet the people as though they had known each other for years. This is more of a pleasure trip, for we are coasting all the time. The steamer does not seem to move, no sound of the engines is heard, and still the boat is going rapidly. The waters of the Pacific Ocean are really quiet—it does not appear to be what it is in reality.

Yesterday, at five P.M., the Vigil of Saint Raphael, we reached Punta Arenas, Gulf of Costa Rica. Here the steamer stopped for the mail of the first republic of Central America. Because of the low tide, the steamer was obliged to remain two hundred yards from the shore. Some rowboats conveyed passengers to and from the steamer. Among these was a gentleman who approached us, and hearing that we wanted to send a telegram to Lady Elena Arellano, he offered to do it for us. He further told us that the bishop had come to Punta Arenas for the feast of Saint Raphael, that he would inform him of our arrival, and that he would surely be glad to see us.

In about ten minutes he returned to the port, and in half an hour's time we perceived a boat coming toward us with two persons in it, and presently we recognized the prelate's dress. In no time the bishop was ascending the gangway, and he met us as a father awaiting the arrival of his children. We all approached the most excellent prelate, who, sitting in our midst, listened with interest to the account of our voyage and the work we were about to undertake. Now and then he whispered to his secretary, "We must get them here, too," and his secretary said, "Why don't you at once?" He encouraged us greatly, but told us we would encounter great difficulties, but we would overcome them and do great good if we maintained the true spirit. Finally, he told us that if we encountered serious difficulties in Nicaragua, to write to him and he would do everything to support us in his diocese. He blessed us and then went, leaving behind him an excellent impression of his zeal and holiness. He is German, with an intelligent mind and good spirit, a strong physique and energetic character. He is just the type of person for these countries.

Today, which is the feast of Saint Raphael, is the last day of our voyage. Just as this angel conducted Tobias to the land of fortune, so he conducts us to these countries where we can accumulate treasures for Heaven by working hard for these abandoned souls. Even here on board, ladies and gentlemen approach us and tell us how necessary it is to have missionaries in these parts who will work with true zeal for the good of the people. Oh my God, bless our intentions, and give us zeal for the salvation of our neighbors' souls, and communicate to us that energy that knows no measure and overcomes all difficulties by confiding in the Sacred Heart of Jesus.

Yesterday afternoon we saw what seemed like a small canal, with waters of different colors, flowing like so many streams in the midst of the salty sea. We asked the captain the cause of this phenomenon, and he told us it was due to a phosphorous element, and that at night we would be able to see the phosphorescence, which is quite common in the Pacific Ocean....

Here we are, at the equinox—twelve hours full night. It is interesting to see the succession of day and night. At six P.M. we are in full daylight, and at six-thirty, not only does the sun disappear, but we have complete night. It is the same in the morning. At five-thirty A.M. we are still in darkness, and at six A.M. the sun is high in the heavens. There is a difference of six hours between here and the time in Italy and Granada, so while we are hearing Mass, you are making the Particular Examination of Conscience, and when we are going to bed, you are about to get up, and thus we are always praising God, which I always greatly desire.

While I am writing, we have arrived at the end of our voyage. This morning, the 25th, the steamer entered one of the most beautiful gulfs I have ever seen, the Gulf of Nicaragua, off the coast of Corinto. It anchored at seven A.M., about two hundred fifty feet from the shore, and soon, amid the strains of a very fine band, we saw two boats adorned with flags and steered by soldiers rowing toward the steamer. Everyone was asking what it meant, and we were among the inquirers. When the boat reached the steamer, a priest and an old gentleman came on board; then other priests and gentlemen who had accompanied them followed. They are the representatives of the president and of the bishop, sent to meet us. Everyone made way for them to approach us, as we were standing at a distance and were far from believing that such distinguished personages could be approaching us. They presented us with greetings from the great men of the republic and asked us to go with them, saying our luggage would be seen to. Having saluted the captain and passengers, some of whom were crying because we were leaving them, we boarded the boats that brought us ashore. At Corinto a good breakfast had been prepared for us, which we ate with pleasure; it was already ten o'clock, and our appetites had been somewhat sharpened by the pure air. In the meantime, a dispatch arrived from the president, welcoming us and giving us and our luggage free passage. Thus, after receiving several visitors, we boarded the train at three P.M., accompanied by the same people who had met us on board the vessel.

At six P.M. we arrived at León, where a crowd was waiting for us, to see what we were like, I believe, but the place was so full that we could not get off the train, so we were compelled to go further back and take another exit. All precautions seemed useless, for the people were determined to see us. While all this was going on, the vicar general, sent by the bishop, came on board the train and read an address to us in the bishop's name, which was certainly an honor we did not deserve.

At last we were able to get off the train, surrounded by soldiers so as not to be crushed to death. Then we got into carriages that took us to a hotel, where, by order of the bishop, apartments had been prepared for the night. The owner of the hotel is a Florentine who had great pleasure in serving us and treated us as well as he could.

In the evening some ladies and gentlemen from León came to visit us and ask us to send seven Sisters to León to open an academy there. It was very hard to convince them that such things were quite impossible for the moment, but in the end they resigned themselves when I promised to let them have some Sisters in a few years.

In the morning the bishop sent carriages to take us to his palace, as he wished to see us, and though seriously ill because of a stroke that had paralyzed his tongue, he got up to see us, making efforts to speak and assuring us that as soon as he was better he would come to Granada to see us.

At eight-thirty P.M. we were on board the train, and at ten A.M. we reached Momotambo, where we took another trip up the lake after a second breakfast that had been ordered by a telegram from the bishop the day before. At eleven A.M. we crossed this beautiful lake. Opposite us were several volcanoes; only one of them was active, but only smoke was coming out of it. At four P.M. we arrived at Managua, where a train for Granada was waiting for us. One of the senators and a deputy of the government, with other people eager to see the Sisters, came to greet us.

At six P.M. we arrived at Granada, where the entire population was waiting for us. I really think no one could have stayed home—everybody seemed to be at the station. The people prevented the carriages from coming up to us, as they wanted us to pass through the crowd so that they could see us, but the number of people was so great that order could not be maintained, and we were afraid we would be crushed. I was particularly anxious, as some of the Sisters were not feeling well. I feared they would make martyrs of us through their great devotion toward us. I therefore asked the soldiers, who were there to maintain order but who didn't dare come closer, to draw near. As soon as they understood our wish, they established order, forming a great procession to the parish church, where the parish priest, accompanied by other priests, awaited us to sing the "Te Deum", after which we were taken to the house that was assigned to us and where we are very pleased to prepare to open an academy.

All the children of the town want to attend our school, and boarders from the neighboring districts are applying, but for the present we can only take fifty boarders, for although the house is big, it is not big enough for this tropical climate, where the heat is intense. Now, since it's winter, it's about 95 degrees in the day and 60 to 70 at night, but a providential breeze blows by from time to time, like the flutter of an angel's wings, and refreshes us greatly with its purity and coolness. We have three courtyards, one of which is very large, surrounded by wide cloisters, in the middle of which are many tall plants bearing a large quantity of oranges, and other shorter plants loaded with flowers of every shape and color. It looks like the very beginning of spring, and so it will be on Christmas Day.

The good Lady Elena Arellano had all the dormitories in order for the Sisters, and a very nice airy chapel, so that the director of the seminary, who by the order of the bishop had accompanied us, could celebrate Mass and give us Holy Communion. In the afternoon he gave a beautiful sermon inviting people to thank the Sacred Heart for having bestowed on them the favor of having religious amongst them. At present, Lady Elena is preparing the desks and everything for the school, and we are designing the curriculum, which will be examined by the heads of the families, and so far has been approved by them, for they say we have brought them true progress. We hope this will be of benefit for their souls; for this reason alone have we undertaken such a long journey. May the Sacred Heart and Saint Aloysius, who is patron of this house, help obtain these graces.

Help us, oh daughters, with your prayers, for we would like to combat a great vice of these parts; namely, that the poorer women go around dressed quite immodestly (while the ladies cover themselves much more than in Italy). We have been making efforts, and at first the serving-women made a great many excuses, but some, to make us happy, have covered themselves—and then approached the Sacraments with great joy, saying that only now did they feel they could approach the Lord worthily.

All the Sisters are well and working hard to open the academy very soon. Perhaps they will begin around the middle of December. Those Sisters who had been afraid of earthquakes are not afraid of anything now, although we do experience some tremors. We have a volcano quite nearby. Some ladies have already come to take us to see everything in the country that is new to us, and I agreed to do this a bit later, so that upon my return, I can give you some news about this country, and not be like those who go to Rome without going to see the pope.

I beg you to become true missionaries, capable of those sacrifices that your Sisters have made with the aid of the Sacred Heart. Seek to perfect your spirit and the observance of the Holy Rule, for you must be holy to be able to go to the missions: that is, be perfectly observant.

[Saint Francis Xavier said:] "He who goes to the Missions holy will find many occasions to sanctify himself more, but he who goes poorly provided with holiness runs the risk of losing what he has and of falling away." I become more convinced of this truth every day, and as experience is a great master, let us take advantage of the lessons it teaches and never let a day pass without examining our conscience and making serious resolutions to acquire the virtues we need.

May the Sacred Heart bless and enclose you in His sweet Heart, imprinting His love on yours, and giving you perfect detachment from yourselves.

Your affectionate Mother in the Sacred Heart of Jesus,
M. FRANCESCA SAVERIO CABRINI
Granada, November 3, 1891

October 3, 1892, Voyage from New Orleans to Paris

This brief letter establishes that not every sea voyage was dangerous. Note the kindness and respect that others show toward Mother Cabrini and her Sisters.

J.M.J.F.
My Dearest Daughters,

We are nearing the harbor. The voyage could not have been better or happier. The weather was as cool as springtime, the sea was as tranquil as a lake, the sky was a heavenly blue, and the sea was the same color. We could not have wished for anything more.

On board, as soon as you left us, I became acquainted with the minister plenipotentiary of Colombia, who had been assigned by Fr. Cardella to take care of our needs during the voyage. He was certainly faithful to his assignment. He came every day to check on our needs, and in the evening he kept us company with his secretary until ten o'clock in order that we might enjoy the fresh air on a sea illumined by a splendid silvery moon.

The captain, remembering that he had had me on board with twenty-nine nuns on a previous trip, came to congratulate me on my return and asked if I would come back next year. The commissioner to whom Mr. Lech recommended us was always most courteous. He placed us at the captain's table and ordered the waiters to give us whatever we wanted, so I was able to eat some meat.

With such favorable weather it was easy to pray daily and unite ourselves with your prayers at all times. I was able to read the small book of psalms. I greatly appreciate your lovely gift. How beautiful the psalms are, and what comfort they bring in times of pain and tribulation! David, a man after God's own heart, certainly knew how to sing His praises. Oh, let us belong wholly to God, do everything for Him, and renounce the world and all creatures for Him; then our words and works will also be after God's own heart.

I hope you are doing your best to put the school in perfect order. Go from house to house among the Italians and collect a good-sized group. Now you are not limited to a parish; you are missionaries in general. So take good care of the Italians, seek them out wherever they may be, and help them, as the archbishop desires.

Now that we are in Paris, I'll bring this to a close. Our old people are full of concern for us. We shall be in Milan on Wednesday. The voyage was really miraculous, for I have learned that there were storms everywhere except where we were. Goodbye, and may Jesus bless you all. My regards to everyone, especially the archbishop.

M. FRANCESCA S. CABRINI

September 1894, Voyage from Genoa to New York

How could Mother Cabrini serve as a spiritual guide to hundreds of women when she could not see them in person for years? Here, she describes her voyage to New York (including her rare, though brief, experience of seasickness) and also injects her spirituality into her depiction of every event.

My Dear Daughters,

The peace of God be with you and accompany you everywhere in the love of the Most Adorable Heart of the Divine Jesus.

Two years have passed since I left the missions of Central America and the United States and returned to you, and having to leave you again now is very hard; for I had become like one who is accustomed to the pleasure of gathering different fragrant bouquets of the most beautiful flowers of your virtues every day, but who is now going forth to wander in an endless desert, where nothing but weeds can be found. But I consoled myself with the reflection that if when I was near you, I could gather bunches of edifying flowers, now that I am far away, the memory of your steadfast and virtuous practices, which make you exemplary religious, true spouses of Christ, will give me comfort. Meanwhile, a voice seems to repeat in my ear and engrave upon my heart, "Go, Mother, and do as the vicar of Christ has told you. Do not worry about your daughters far away. They will relieve your mind by the beautiful and consoling news they send you. They will do their duty faithfully and keep their promises."

Should I believe that voice, my daughters, that whispers within me? Certainly you are very good-hearted, and you would never wound the heart of a mother with bad news; you are sensible and you never break your word. You will try to grow in virtue, try to make sacrifices yourselves—real, true sacrifices—in order to ensure that my time and labor is not spent in vain, and that I may find good ground, good seed, a good harvest. "Euntes ibant et flebant mittentes semina sua: venientes autem venient cum exultatione portantes manipulos suos" ["He that goes forth weeping, bearing the seed for sowing, shall come home with shouts of joy, bringing his sheaves with him" (Psalm 126:6)]. So wrote the most eminent Cardinal Parocchi in the commendation he sent. But the first part is no longer applicable to me, since my daughters follow me with their virtues, sacrifices, and beautiful and admirable fidelity. Shall I fear weather, privations, bad treatment, and injustice? No, for the missionary should fear nothing, outside of sin—an offense, however small, against God. What, then, can disturb me? One thing only: to receive news that one of my daughters has lost the spirit of the Institute, become weak and unfaithful: this would be a sea of bitterness that would disturb me greatly.

But enough with sad thoughts; I have confidence in you, and I ask you to assume the usual cheerfulness of the missionary and to join the company of the good Sisters who surround me. We are fifteen in number, and so represent the fifteen mysteries of the Holy Rosary. Our Lady of the Holy Rosary is our guide, our star, and our comfort. We each drew a mystery, and the one I love most—the

Descent of the Holy Spirit—fell to me, so I shall remain in the upper room during the whole voyage, and from this dear solitude I will send a thought, a word, to you each day, providing you always say the "Veni Creator" for me.

September 14. Today we commemorate the Exaltation of the Holy Cross, and the Sisters, unable to honor the day in any other way, have thought it fitting to feel somewhat unwell. The sea is calm and beautiful, the air is mild and soothing, the service on board is very much like what we have been used to, but, for whatever reason, one after another began to feel seasick and retired to their "boxes", as they call the small berths in the cabin. At dinner I wanted everyone to come to the table, but they had to leave at once, not wishing to disturb the others. It is three P.M., and all of them, feeling well again, have come on deck to see the Balearic Islands, near which the *Fulda* is coasting.

We also saw Majorca, the homeland of Saint Alphonsus Rodríguez, and there we sent up our sighs, begging for some of those sublime and great virtues possessed by this saint, which I would love to see imprinted on the hearts of my daughters.

This morning (as we had arranged to do yesterday evening), everyone wanted to make the regular meditation, but they changed their minds very quickly as they were feeling too ill. Some of the Sisters tried to resist but had to give in at last. At present all are in contemplation, admiring the landscape, sea, and sky, which present us with an enchanting scene. Of course it is not like the scenery of Liguria when coasting along the Riviera. There we see a real amphitheater from the sloping top of the Apennines to the sea—the mountains, hills, beach, sharp peaks, lofty pines, soft green undulating slopes, peaceful olive trees, and thousands of fruits and flowers, while the palms and woods and fruit gardens that reach to the sea are beautiful to behold from the deck of the steamer.

From Genoa to Nice, the cities seem to vie with one another in presenting a continual change of view. To tell the truth, until I became acquainted with the beauties of the Eastern Riviera [La Riviera Levante], and still more with those of the Western Riviera [La Riviera de Ponente], I never realized how beautiful Italy is. I am happy, now, however, to be able to describe our peninsula to the people of other countries through which I pass.

The Sisters remembered it was the anniversary of my profession and were sorry that I was not able to receive Holy Communion, for which kind thought I was most grateful. It is only one day since I received Jesus in my heart, and I imagine He is still there. One remembers Jacob's mystical dream in which he saw a mysterious ladder with angels descending and ascending who revealed many mysteries and secrets to Jacob and assured him and his descendants of God's protection. Though we are far from the Holy Tabernacle, even here on the sea there is a mysterious ladder that touches Heaven, and the angels ascend and descend upon it for us as well. From its summit, the good Jesus looks down upon us and makes generous promises. We can, therefore, repeat with Jacob, "Surely the Lord is in this place; and I did not know it" [Gen 28:16]. We are in the bosom of the Catholic Church. We always lay our heads on the dear and mystic stone that is Jesus; we agree with Him in everything, and abandon ourselves to Him, tranquil and secure, and by doing so, we merit in Jesus and by Jesus to share in the good and the graces He brings us. And so I am quite happy to celebrate on the sea the most beautiful day of my life, the anniversary of my profession. Jesus is looking at me from the top of the ladder; I invite Him to come to me spiritually, and He descends at once into my heart. He deigns to come down to this steamer, the *Fulda*, to bless those who are traveling with us. What a gift, and we did not know it!

September 15. We are even more fortunate than yesterday, for we do not feel as if we are at sea, but rather as if we are wrapped up in a cloud like that of the Transfiguration. There is a charming blue sky above, and below us one can hardly distinguish the sea from the sky. Some of the passengers say we are in the third heaven, others, the seventh; the glorious splendor renders everything so bright and brilliant that the passengers exclaim, "How lovely, how beautiful." We seem to see the portals of Heaven that do not close at the end of the day, because there, daytime never ends: the day up there is eternal, and the light that emanates from the Divine Face never fails. In that abode, there exists no night, no ignorance, no blindness, for everything is seen in God; there, no hardships exist, no tears, no sorrows, no sighs. No, daughters, in Heaven there are no clouds to obscure the Divine Sun, the Eternal Sun of Justice. There is no fear of losing God; no wiles of the enemy, for he has been routed; the world is far away, and the body is spiritualized and lives in harmony with the soul. No, there is no night in Heaven, and the door is always open. Friends arrive at every moment, every instant; they arrive in a way that does not cause any disturbance, but rather that renders the repose serene and sweet. Oh, sublime city, send down your beams of light into these regions of darkness, this shadow of death under which we are still miserably living. Come, oh supernatural light, to reveal to us the beauties of that blessed country, and detach us from the miseries of this earth; make our eyes so pure that through the shining crystal of faith, they may behold the eternal good that awaits us after a short time of sacrifice and self-conquering. He who fights will be victorious, and to the victor, the prize is Heaven.

September 16. Between one thing and another, two days ago we reached Gibraltar. The steamer steered into the harbor, remaining, however, a third of a mile from the shore. The small tenders came for passengers who were bound for Spain and for those who wanted to visit Gibraltar. Two of us went ashore to make a visit to the Blessed Sacrament, but the churches were closed, and the cabman told us that they would not reopen at that hour, as the priests had gone to dinner. We then went to buy some Spanish books for our new mission, but all they had to offer were English novels. None of the booksellers had what we wanted. The cabman tried to console us by telling us there was very little devotion in Gibraltar. Then he took us to the Borgo S. Rocco to show us what was interesting. In the Public Gardens we found all sorts of plants. The cabman, acting as our guide, picked bunches of pretty berries for us, and we brought them back to the Sisters as a souvenir of this Spanish land.

Gibraltar is grand with its rocks and mountains, which render it one of the strongest fortresses that England has acquired in the Mediterranean. There is stationed here a garrison of six thousand soldiers, with an enormous amount of artillery and cannons of incredible size. The city is small and contains three Catholic and three Protestant churches. Though I was told there was very little religion in Gibraltar, all the Spaniards I met appeared to be good; they told me they were apostolic Catholics, an expression that greatly consoled me. Moreover, they wanted to introduce us to the Sisters they love so much, but we were pressed for time, the captain having allowed us but two hours, so we hurried on board, where we were received with great joy, just as if we were members of one family. We are very fortunate indeed. Our company is composed of very kind ladies and gentlemen, who are most thoughtful and respectful toward us.

Among the passengers is a good Conventual Franciscan father, whom I met four years ago at Hoboken. We were rather importunate in begging him to say Holy Mass, at least on Sundays, but he could not comply with our request, for he had no vestments or other requisites with him. So, here again on this voyage we are deprived of Holy Mass and Holy Communion. But, after all, God wishes it thus, so let us cherish the memory of the last reception of Him, as Holy Viaticum, in Genoa. As I have said before, He helps, consoles, and comforts us. We are representing the fifteen mysteries, and God, in His immense goodness, leaves us to enjoy Him. He is our Paradise—the Heaven of our desires.

We left Gibraltar yesterday, and steering through the Straits, passed Spain, or had a glimpse of it; but we turned our gaze to the other side, where Morocco presented itself. We sent sighs and groans toward Morocco, that poor land to which we would willingly fly to give succor to those poor souls that the Word of God has not yet reached. It is true that great crusades of Christ's missionaries are already on this soil, but the land is vast, the ignorance extreme, and the help insufficient. May missionary priests and Sisters multiply! The harvest is great, the laborers are few! To you, Christian virgins, I speak especially: love God, and make yourselves active with the zeal that burns in you; help your poor abandoned brethren, whose price is the Blood of Christ, join our band, and try to give a large number of souls to the Heart of Jesus.

Your love must not remain hidden, but become active, alive, and sincere. "*Sitio!*" repeats Jesus, as from Golgotha: "I thirst for souls!" If you love God, come forth, have courage; the devil laughs at the weak, at the timid, whereas he fears and flies from energetic souls. Are you fearful? She who trusts in God and mistrusts herself has nothing to fear, because stripped of herself and strong with the strength of

God, and with faith and humility, she can face anything. Besides, dangers only exist for those who put themselves in the way of them, who mix up the things of the world with the things of God. On the other hand, those who are unencumbered by the things of the world and seek God alone and His service and glory encounter no danger.

Worldly people look upon religious who despise the pleasures of the world with esteem; they revere them and turn to them when they need help. What an honor, Christian virgins, if God calls you to extend His Kingdom! Arise and go forth! Do not refuse and incur the rebuke given to the Foolish Virgins by neglecting to take advantage of the opportunity that the Institute affords us of co-operating in saving souls, and thus gaining merits, which in Heaven will yield an immeasurable weight of glory.

Virgins are chosen spouses of the King and therefore queens. If they are queens, they must have a people over whom to exercise their power—their celestial mission of peace. Just as the virgin, working as a missionary, gains souls for Christ, so she extends her dominion, and her scepter becomes more powerful and more glorious. Come, wise virgins, and enlarge the missionary army; come, and make all nations offer each other the kiss of peace. Come, for the borders of our kingdom extend to the ends of the world. Come, and let your glory be the glory of your celestial Spouse, the exercising of that celestial talent—the sublime vocation of co-operating with Christ for the salvation of souls. Come, for in the fields of the great Father of the family we are to gather rich and abundant sheaves by the armful. There are some who may think they are too poor, ignorant, and weak to undertake such work. Do not be afraid of anything; as I have already told you, mistrust yourselves and put your trust in Jesus, for "Omnia possum in Eo qui me confortat" ["I can do all things in him who strengthens me" (Phil 4:13)]. He who calls us is that same Jesus who said, "You, therefore, must be perfect as your heavenly Father is perfect." But how are we to attain such perfection? By the grace of Him Who deigns to command it of us. With God, all things are possible, and when the virgin of Christ distrusts herself and puts her trust completely in Jesus Christ, she becomes powerful, and can repeat at every moment, "With God I shall do great things."

But now I must continue my letter. You will certainly forgive the digression, which was inspired by my great desire to see your numbers increase. I long to help those nations who elicit my compassion. Today I am alone on deck. All the Sisters have remained in their berths. As we passed through the Strait of Gibraltar and entered the great Atlantic, we felt the roughness of the ocean at once, and that, coupled with the swaying of the steamer and the roar of thunder, unnerved the Sisters, and they began to fear a storm. Sister Alphonsus tried to be brave and came on deck to keep me company, but she was hardly seated when she was forced to go back down. Then Sister Xavier gathered her courage, and to be honest, she did well enough, by resting her head in bed and then coming back on deck. In this way, she will eventually become a good sailor. Sister Alacoque is quite a success; she lays her head on a chair or a table from time to time, but then runs off generously to be everyone's nurse. Sister Giovannina made several attempts also, but was eventually forced to retire to her berth. Sister Constance is always up and comes to her meals regularly, for she thinks that by eating, she will be able to resist the seasickness longer. I believe she is quite right, but today even she is laid up and can eat only what is brought to her. Sister Benedict sighs and believes she is ill, but one can see she is looking brighter than ever. All the Sisters seem very happy and are making the best of their little discomforts.

Today the captain and the commissioner begged me to tell them what the Sisters needed, as they were sorry to see them suffering so much. The kindness with which we are treated is incredible. Thank heavens we were always well taken care of as passengers on the Transatlantic Company's steamers, but the North German Line merits just as much praise. Captain Thalenhorst is a typical sea captain, and his good-heartedness and sagacity make him as the right man for this position.

September 17. Today I made up my mind to stay in my berth and rest a while after the incessant fatigue of the preceding days. I had hoped the Sisters would remain there also, as they had done during the past days, but to my surprise they were on deck, bright and happy and as serene as the lovely sea we are enjoying today. The sea is a charming deep blue and reminds one of the Heaven of a soul in the possession of God, with a very peaceful heart, a celestial look. Such a soul is always made more beautiful by Jesus. It listens to His conversation, and loves it because it is purer and more precious than gold or silver; it listens to the precepts of its Beloved and feels they give it life and salvation, for such souls are fragrant with the sweet balm of grace and wisdom. Such a soul should exclaim, "Enlighten my mind, give light to my intellect, help me with Thy grace that I may happily run the paths of Thy sweet commandments. Do not permit me to stumble on the way, but make me strong with Thy virtue, that I may faithfully do Thy holy will. Work in my weak and unstable heart, that I may fervently desire all what Thou willest, my Jesus, and reject that which Thou willest not. Guard Thou Thyself this Tabernacle consecrated to Thee." To this beautiful soul consecrated to God, every sign from Jesus is invaluable. Such a religious not only performs what is prescribed for her hour by hour, but joyfully anticipates His every desire. She lives no longer for herself but for her Beloved; she has, as it were, wings to fly wherever the Divine will calls her, to do and suffer anything for Jesus. Again, this soul imitates the life of Jesus. He was obedient unto death, and the obedient religious imitates Him in her perfect obedience to her superiors; to her, every command is easy, for in obedience, her path is safe, her work sure, her spirit strong. She is joyful, happy, and smiling; she feasts on heavenly fruits; she acquires eternal merit at every moment, and follows in the footsteps of the saints.

It is obedience that distinguishes true piety from false piety. The obedient religious is victorious over her enemies, for by subjecting herself to her superior, she acquires perfect mastery over the devil, who was cast out of Heaven for disobedience. She has promised to give up her life rather than be unfaithful to her loving Lord. In the exercise of obedience, she has the same merit of martyrdom. In martyrdom we sacrifice the body; in obedience we sacrifice the will, our liberty, the supreme power of the soul. Obedience is a penance of the mind, a sacrifice immensely more pleasing to God than any other sacrifice you could make of your own choice. One act of obedience is more pleasing to God than a thousand other acts of your own will. The saints teach us that it is better to eat by virtue of obedience than to fast to gratify one's own will. Saint Mary Magdalen dei Pazzi used to say that the simplest act of obedience is greater than the highest act of contemplation. In fact, we read in her life that when she was in ecstasy, the voice of obedience was sufficient to recall her to herself. Learn to love this virtue, which forms the character of a true religious. The readiness of your obedience indicates the readiness of your heart, for the hand moves and the feet run when the spirit is fervent. In serving Jesus

Christ, you see Him in your superior. You must consider the orders of your superior not only as rightly given, but as being the best for you. If thoughts against obedience come to you, chase them away as you would drive away thoughts against our holy faith. See in your superior not only the authority of God but the will of God. Remember that holy obedience is ordered by God in the Holy Scriptures; therefore, it is orthodox, and in faith there can be neither deceit nor illusion. Conform your will and judgment to that of your superior, and you will reach a great height of perfection. Do not consider the natural gifts and good qualities of your superior, for by so doing you will change divine obedience into mere human obedience. See Jesus Christ in her, and all will be well. Make all your actions, however small, precious by obedience, not by doing your own will. Beg Jesus often to give you the spirit of obedience, and on your part, do everything you can to merit such a beautiful grace, and blessed will you be if you receive such a remarkable gift. Let us trust in the Heart of Jesus, which has always beat with precious obedience!...

It is almost evening now, and we have sailed 389 miles in twenty-four hours. The Sisters seem fairly well, sewing and praying, and meditating either with the aid of a book or by gazing upon their sublime surroundings, which excite sublimer thoughts. Sister Alexandrine, afraid she will lose track of the days of the week, is keeping a record of them, and she reminds the Sisters scrupulously every morning what day it is. Yesterday, Sister Constance, staying in bed, asked for a bit of chicken, but they brought her soup. She asked again, and they brought her salad. Once they realized that they had no idea what she was saying, they asked her to speak English, but she answered that she could not, since her language is European. Sister Claver thought she was very sick yesterday and kept saying that she would never make it to

New York if they did not stop the steamer. Today, however, she is fine, though she has another annoyance: she has gotten a tear in her habit and she does not know how she will tell Sister Augustine....

Our fellow passengers are taking better care of us than they are of themselves; they give us everything they can to avoid seeing us suffer. They treat us with great respect, and have reverence for the religious habit. Some of the merchants ask for our advice about their business affairs, and we try to reassure them with the inspirations we receive from the Sacred Heart. Yesterday a waiter told me how sorry he was that he could not speak Italian, so that he might be of better service to the Sisters. He wants me to act as interpreter, but my knowledge of English is limited, barely sufficient to prevent me from losing my way or dying of hunger. When we are on deck, there is a very nice gentleman who always acts as interpreter. In short, the adorable Sacred Heart of Jesus, who sent us through his vicar, seems to be blessing us in a very special way on this voyage.

Well, my dear daughters, help us praise and bless Him Who guides and comforts us with so much care and ineffable love.

Tomorrow, at ten A.M., we shall see the Azores, and we shall be able to tell you something about them, though we may not be able to visit them as we did Gibraltar.

September 18. At five A.M. we heard a whistle that notified us that the Azores were in sight. We stayed at rest because we did not know the meaning of the whistle or understand the cause of the commotion on deck, but it was not long before our friends came knocking at our doors to inquire why we were not on deck.

It really was a lovely sight! Some call the Azores the Azures, and they really do look like a bit of heaven dropped into the Atlantic. What beautiful mountains and hills! The grand slopes are covered with a cheerful green that changes its color every fifty feet. The grassy plains, the heavy-laden vineyards, the leafy woods, and the enchanting villas make one long to visit these charming islands. More than one passenger wanted to ask the captain to stop the steamer, at least for an hour, to go ashore and see these most fertile Portuguese possessions, divided into fields, cities, and summer resorts, with everything so pretty. Surely wealth and comfort reign there. The good captain steered the vessel in such a way that the cities of these islands could be seen quite easily. The city of Ponta Delgada could be seen sloping down to the sea. Its towers, steeples, and monuments were reflected in the waters. Just as we were passing, a most beautifully colored rainbow appeared in the sky, which seemed to unite the inhabitants of the city with the passengers of the steamer. The rainbow seemed to announce the peace of the Divine Heart that draws the hearts of all people together in ardent charity. Behind this arc there was a still larger and more extended rainbow with fainter colors; it was a sight that took our breath away. It looked like a heavenly light spread out to purify the mind and make it capable of raising itself to praise the Maker of creation, so immense and enchanting and inimitable by man. And while the arched rays of this beautiful rainbow increased in splendor and this unparalleled view fascinated us, big bright drops of rain advanced at lightning speed and sprinkled us, and we were obliged to take shelter. The Azores are beautiful and healthful; they are a resort for invalids, especially for those who suffer from chest trouble. How good God is!

This morning the rainbow reminded me of our celestial Mother, the real ark who guides our little company across the sea. Mary is heavenly, and in her loveliness and serenity, she reflects the rays of the Divinity. She is a shining and burning wave of love for us, because the splendors in her descend from God, Who is not only an ineffable light but a burning fire of love. How many wonders we meet with in the love of Mary; how many graces, how many gifts, how many good things come from her benevolent hands, and all are sealed with great love. One look from her, one thought from her, fills us with her burning charity. Mary, our sweet Mother, is an ocean of goodness, a fire of charity that burns, inflames, and transforms. She is a sun of perennial light, grace, and beneficence. No one is excluded from her beneficial warmth, for her charity is universal and continual. To all she opens the bosom of her ineffable goodness; she is ready to help all, and even anticipates their desires.

Mary is like a beautiful olive tree in a field where all can see her and have access to her. From her fields flow perennial streams of water wherein the thirsty may quench their thirst. Do not wonder if you see yourselves overloaded with graces and tenderness from Mary, for she dispenses gifts and graces that flow like a stream from that immeasurable ocean of love she bears for us.

September 19. At two o'clock yesterday, after lunch, we saw the last of the Azores. The great Saint George [São Jorge] did not seem half as beautiful as Saint Michael [São Miguel], though it also had cheerful green mountains and valleys and enchanting slopes. In one of the great cities, we saw a very beautiful and artistically built cathedral, but no one could tell me the name of the city. There were several boats full of people, but none of them could approach us because of the formidable waves created by the movement of the *Fulda.* They waved their hands and handkerchiefs to us. How I longed to tell some of them to go and visit Jesus in the Most Holy Sacrament of the Altar. They certainly would do so, I'm sure. All on board seem quite disposed to believe what we say about God. They are very reserved in manner and speech. We joined the Portuguese and Flemish people in sending our greetings to the churches. We could also see volcanoes; some were extinct, while the sharply pointed cones of others seemed about to burst at any moment and send out fire, smoke, and lava.

The scenery of the Azores disappeared among rainbows that came two at a time, one after another. The passengers were surprised, but we saw the eye of Mary looking down upon us, as though to console us. Then another thing happened that astonished those Sisters who were strangers to sea voyages. A huge number of water birds appeared. The sea, disturbed by a north wind, tossed the vessel, and the passengers began to whisper to one another and then to exclaim aloud, "A storm, a storm!" Like the Apostles, they gathered around me, and begged me to tell the sea to be calm. I had to tell them they had little faith and little courage, and it takes more than that to qualify as a storm. If a storm does come, we need not fear, for we are traveling in the name of Jesus and under the mantle of Mary. Neither sea, nor wind, nor waves will frighten us. Our faith obliges us to trust in God, and that trust will make us strong even unto death.

The sea continues to be rough, but today the barometer reads "fair weather", so we hope to recover the calm that marked our passage from the Mediterranean to the Azores. Sister Constance asked me if I would allow her to complain aloud, but I told her to repeat the words, "How wonderful!" This she does, though she can hardly bear it at all. Sister Pia cannot get up, so she remains in her berth. She is able to eat whatever is brought to her. Sister Xavier is not feeling well, but she keeps me company on deck, as she does not like her berth. Sister Alacoque is quite the sailor, healthy and active. She is still infirmarian, and knows how to make the Sisters eat. This is the best thing she can do, for it is very bad not to be able to eat while traveling, for fasting increases the nauseous feeling and one suffers more. Sister Frances is suffering silently and serenely, and forces herself to eat for the sake of obedience. Sister Claver is suffering more than anyone else. Our Sisters have made a Heaven of their cabins. One Sister will dream she is at Holy Mass but cannot receive Holy Communion, and then another will see a saint who comes to console them. They are always praying. The goodness of God is so great that He consoles us in a thousand ways. To raise us up, to provide for us, to console us and to enrich us—He has thousands of ways. Have faith, my dear daughters; whatever you ask you shall receive, for by prayer born of faith you can obtain everything. If, sometimes, we do not get what we want, let us examine ourselves and see whether the cause does not lie in our lack of the proper disposition—perhaps a lack of proper spirit, of fervor, of supernatural motives; perhaps our prayers are said with the tongue only, with weariness, in a hurry or without recollection and perseverance. My good daughters, what cannot prayer animated by living faith accomplish! Prayer and faith united are powerful beyond belief. If the saints have worked wonders and miracles, they did it through prayer with faith. Have faith! He who prays with faith has fervor, and fervor is the fire of prayer. This mysterious fire has the power to consume all our faults and imperfections, and to give merit to our actions—vitality, beauty, and merit. The fervor produced by a lively faith is like a shower of limpid crystal waters that revive and animate. It lightens all our sufferings and troubles, and purifies all that is faulty and earthly, and gives everything its proper virtue, value, and splendor. But, note, I am not speaking of merely emotional fervor, but of that substantial fervor that is the product of a lively faith. I refer to that fervor and ardor of spirit that consists of the union of the soul with God, in the perfect conformity of our will with the will of God. You will obtain this fervor by keeping a mastery over the powers of the soul, and by watchfulness over your senses—rejecting, as far as it lies in your power, all useless, vain, and troublesome thoughts. A soul that is recollected in God receives the fervor of God in its prayers; therefore, it can obtain from Him all it desires.

Accustom yourselves to uniting your prayers with those of Jesus Christ, so that yours are purified and sanctified by coming in contact with His. Be assured that after Jesus Himself has purified them, He will present them to His Eternal Father. Pray always with Jesus, always remembering that a soul united with Jesus can do anything. Bear in mind the maxim, "Omnia possum in Eo qui me confortat" ["I can do all things in him who strengthens me" (Phil 4:13)]. Have faith; pray with faith, and "good measure, pressed down, shaken together" shall be given to you [Luke 6:38]. Oh faith, beautiful daughter of Heaven, come to our souls and let us honor thee; thou who hast enveloped us with the beautiful mantle of Baptism, and hast always enriched us by means of the other sacraments!

September 20. Another gorgeous day! The sea is so calm and serene that one hardly perceives the movement of the vessel! Everyone is up and well. Weary from the rolling and the pitching of the steamer, we said our prayers last evening. We began by humbling ourselves, knowing that humility is the secret that penetrates the walls of the Holy City and the rock of the Omnipotent. Humility is the foundation of every meritorious and virtuous work and of prayer. It is impossible to please God without the heavenly virtue of humility; it is a "measuring rod of gold" [see Rev 21:15] that measures the strength of our prayers, and thus their weight in the Lord's own scales. The humblest obtain the most graces, the least humble obtain the least grace, for it is written: "Deus superbis resistit; humilibus autem dat gratiam" ["God opposes the proud, but gives grace to the humble" (1 Pet 5:5, Prov 3:34)]. Chase away all sentiments of pride and self-love if you want God to be with you. God will be our strength, and if we are humble, our prayers will ascend, like a sweet perfume, to the throne of Heaven, where they will be fully granted. The humble religious is like a bunch of spikenard, which, though the smallest and humblest of flowers, is one of the most fragrant. Spread the perfume of humility around, study this celestial virtue profoundly until you possess it completely and perfectly, and then you will be able to say someday, when this life is over, with the Spouse of the Canticles, "Nardus mea dedit odorem suavitatis" [from Vespers; see Song 1:12], while the loving Savior, delighting in such sweet perfume, will give you the embrace of eternal beatitude.

The Franciscan father inquires daily how we are faring, and tells us the feast of the day, and thus helps Sister Alexandrine, who, having been ill these past two days, has given up keeping her diary, and so we run the risk of losing our bearings. I have met kind friends on my journeys, but never anyone kinder than our good captain. He is just like a father, always anxious about everyone being well cared for. He watches over the Sisters especially and sees we have the best service. The Sisters, now that they are well, are thinking about invoking the Holy Souls in Purgatory before the weather changes. These Blessed Souls cannot help themselves, but they can do so much for us. Let us have pity on them; let them be the main subject of our prayers, for the mitigation of their sufferings depends upon our charity and our prayers. One might almost say the keys of their prison have been entrusted to us. The Holy Souls love their Divine Spouse—they desire Him and yearn for Him—but they rely on the hand of benefactors to settle their debts. These doves would love to fly to the bosom of their God, but woe to them if there is no pitying hand to break their chains of fire! Come, beloved daughters, draw down upon them a celestial dew that will cool and allay their inconceivable heat. Your prayers will be the dew that quenches the flames of Divine Justice. Comply with the just desires of these souls. It will be to your own advantage too, if you relieve them by offering your Holy Communions, indulgences, Masses, and all satisfactory works for them. This, you see, will be a work of perfect charity, of immense glory to God, of great joy to the Church Militant, Suffering, and Triumphant, because with your prayers you will send many saintly souls to the Kingdom of the Blessed. Have no fear that you will lose anything by giving your prayers, indulgences, and satisfactory works to the Holy Souls, but rather, rest assured that by so doing you will become rich in grace and merits in this life and in sublime glory in Paradise. And rest assured that the intrinsic merit of this work of suffrage will always be yours, since it is inalienable by nature; only the portion that gives atonement goes to the Holy Souls. If we offer, then, this portion of our works to the Holy Souls, which some do by means of the Heroic Act,[2] we do nothing less than convert every act of satisfaction into merit, and be assured that in the scales of God, one degree of grace and merit is of more value than all the works of atonement we may apply to the Holy Souls. Be generous to the Holy Souls, for he who gives shall receive, and he who is merciful shall obtain mercy. The souls whom we set free will become so many advocates, so many protectors who will pray for us and intercede for us, and, what is more, interest themselves in our eternal salvation.

[2] The Heroic Act of Charity is an indulgence decreed by Pope Leo XIII in 1885, wherein Christians offer all their works and merits for the souls in Purgatory.

September 21. The sea is now as smooth as a tabletop. Our sailing is delightful. The passengers are very happy and come to thank us, for they say they owe everything to our prayers. The captain says that each of us must bring a lovely day, and, as we are fifteen in number, if we have fifteen fine days, there will be a surplus of four days' fine weather, for the *Fulda* only takes eleven days to go from Genoa to New York. At present all the Sisters are feeling well. I always feel better at sea than on land, so the passengers call me a sea lion. But, for a change, I woke up with a sickness in my stomach that very quickly obliged me to hand over my tribute to the sea, perhaps because the fish demanded it. Truth be told, they have kept asking me for it since yesterday. All the passengers were quite surprised that I should have to pay the toll at the very end of the voyage. It is usually leveraged at the beginning. But Jesus, the Master, does as He wills. Our only duty is to praise and thank Him, for everything that He permits is good.

We have entered the Gulf Stream, where everyone says the sea is very rough, but up to now we have enjoyed wonderfully fine weather. Everyone is astonished. So we have reason to praise and thank God for His goodness in commanding the elements to adapt themselves to our comfort and convenience. Love the good God, for the sky, earth, and sea tell us to love Him! The immense ocean which surrounds us on all sides, set with wonderful gems, reveals clearly the ineffable care of our loving Creator who surrounds us with His graces and blessings. We behold the sea, oh daughters, and it speaks to us; you behold the earth with its inexhaustible fecundity, the firmament with its stars, and the whole universe that reflects God's attributes, His power, wisdom, and goodness; and together we exclaim with admiration, "How wonderful is God in His works!"

The Sisters are quite well again today, so we found a nice cozy corner on deck where we enjoyed our lecture on humility. We then read a chapter on charity, that sublime virtue that offers a foretaste of Heaven. Those souls united in charity peacefully repose in God and await with security great graces from God's goodness. Magnanimous and generous souls are those united in charity; they are blessed by God; they soar on high; they ascend to Heaven, where they repose at God's feet, and He, rejoicing in them, crowns them with glory. Be charitable, my dear daughters; love one another in holy love in the adorable Heart of Jesus. Sacrifice yourselves willingly for your Sisters; be meek toward each other; never be sharp or resentful with each other. Try to be the one who always soothes with the balm of peace. Learn how to use that precious stone of the charity of the adorable Heart of Jesus to alleviate pain, to dress wounds, and to console in tribulation. Admire what is good in your Sisters, pity their faults, and do not envy anyone. What a wonderful sight to see so many souls of different nationalities and different languages united in one religious family, joined by the ties of the sweet charity of the adorable Heart of Jesus.

Though the distance between us is widening more and more each day, I am nearer to you in spirit than ever. Not a moment passes without my thinking of you and working with you. You must do the same and accompany me in the spirit of holy charity. Help me with your prayers and sacrifices. When you wish to console me, withdraw into the mystic sanctuary of your soul to see if you have acquired the sweet virtue of charity. I could desire nothing more. Love all in the adorable Heart of Jesus, as the saints love each other in Heaven; love, and God will take care of the rest. Study charity, love one another in charity, let charity rule your souls, and then you can repeat triumphantly, "Dotavit me Deus dote bona" ["God has endowed me with a good dowry" (Gen 30:20)].

September 22. Yesterday the crew was making great preparations to protect us from the breakers, as we had to pass over the Grand Banks of Newfoundland tonight, but the precautions were unnecessary, for the Blessed Virgin covered us with her mantle and the Holy Souls interceded for us, and the result was that we had rain the whole night, which proved very advantageous, for the sea became quite calm. Fresh water and saltwater mixed together to make a calm sea, and this lesson teaches us how to behave with those who are against us. Let us raise our hearts on high and accept God's will without murmuring against or criticizing those people who afflict us. Pity them and excuse them, as David did his enemy, for on hearing himself reviled, he did not defend himself, but said, "Let them talk, because it is God who permits them to speak against me; it is little, indeed, they are saying. I deserve more [See 2 Sam 16:11–12]." Thus behaves a soul according to the Heart of God. If we obtained such virtues, we would become saints very easily. Never complain, never criticize; if you are inclined to use your tongue, use it against yourself. Or, better still, as Saint Francis de Sales impresses upon us, say neither good nor bad of yourself.

Today on deck (I spoke of this yesterday) we were able to enjoy the sun and say our prayers and make our meditations together. As we were rapt in contemplation, the sun, covered with graceful clouds, seemed to form the border of Our Lady's mantle with its rays of gold. It seemed to us that Mary, the perfect image of Jesus, was gazing down upon us. As a cloud brightened by the rays of the sun becomes beautifully bright, so does Mary, the perfect image of Jesus, appear brilliant in her divine beauty. We imagined we saw Jesus and Mary, beautiful and refulgent, looking down upon us and offering us their patronage so that we might become converted.

But how shall we obtain Mary's patronage and protection? By imitating her. Engrave upon your minds the life of Mary, her sentiments, her habits, her immaculate purity, her words, her actions. Beg Our Divine Lord to imprint, with the fire of His Divine Heart, Mary's image on you, and to make you loving models of His Immaculate Mother.

Mary, oh my daughters, is the mysterious book of your predestination to glory; she is lovable, so love her. She is sublime and glorious, so praise her. She is benign and merciful, so appeal to her. Mary is your Mother, mistress, and foundress, so obey and fulfill her desires. Mary speaks to you plainly, so listen to her, trust her with all your affections, so that they never turn toward mere creatures, and you, as angelic spirits, will take refuge in the Heart of Jesus. Offer yourselves often to Mary; pray, work, suffer, take your recreation and your rest with her; walk with Mary and beneath the gaze of Mary, and never sadden her in the least.

September 23. Yesterday, to our great surprise, the captain invited us on a tour of the steamer. I wish I knew how to describe the complicated machinery of this great vessel, which transports thousands of people from the Old World to the New. The steam power used by the propeller to drive this ship forward is the power of fifteen thousand horses. The noise the propeller makes when it is out of the water is great. I commend you to Sister Frances, whose knowledge of ships and their appurtenances is more extensive than mine. She will give you more satisfactory details than I am able to. She will explain either out of the store of her own knowledge or by reference to ancient and modern works on the subject. I can see quite a library of such books spread out in her berth. I was advised to ask Sister Xavier for information, as she knows something of these things, but she replied, "Whoever wants to know about the sea, let him come and see, and we have to pity the poor thing!" Sister Ignatius set out to give you a very full and learned account of everything, but so far she has written no more than four lines.

The captain asked Fr. Mazzetti to celebrate Mass, but he did not have the necessary vestments, and we had no Hosts. Taking advantage, however, of the captain's exquisite kindness, we all—passengers and Sisters—assembled in a large space and recited the Rosary, priest and passengers alternately, just as we do in the convent for our benefactors. This was followed by a sung litany. We formed quite a fine choir, and our voices, which filled the air, seemed to arouse in the souls of those who stood around (no less than a thousand in number) a host of pious sentiments. A beautiful sermon was given on the day's Gospel by the reverend father, who spoke with great zeal and emotion, touching the hearts of all and bringing tears to the eyes of many. Then we sang hymns to the Sacred Heart and Our Lady and said other prayers. Partly because of the father's religious habit, which made him seem like Saint Anthony come back to life, and partly because of the solemnity of the devotions, our poor countrymen almost thought they were in church, though there was not even a cross to be seen. After the father's simple blessing, they accosted us and asked us why we did not sing the "Tantum Ergo".

Now that the voyage is at an end, we are sorry to part from these people, who have been such good friends to us on the voyage, who were as close to us as if we were their mothers, and for whom we could have done a bit of good. Oh, if only we could impress upon them again the happiness that awaits them if they are faithful to prayer and to the sacraments! If we could make them understand that Heaven is the great prize or reward granted to good Christians, to those who are faithful to the laws of Jesus

Christ! Oh Heaven! Who can conceive of or express the inconceivable delights that God has prepared for those who serve Him with that internal and external worship He requires of us? The holy prophet spoke well when he said, "Rejoice and be glad, ye who love the Lord." "Drink large draughts of that river of peace." "Fill yourselves with joy, glory, and happiness, because the Lord has said: I shall pour upon Jerusalem celestial torrents of glory that will inundate it with the purest consolations and delights" [see Is 66:10, Is 55:1–2, Is 66:12–14]. On that most blessed eternal day, we shall be rapt in ecstasies of love and gratitude, and there will be an immense jubilee as we contemplate God face to face. We shall be rapt in His infinite beauty, illuminated by His light, inebriated by His peace, and fortified by His divine consolations, because to see God and to contemplate His divine beauty means to love Him with the most pure and perfect love, and that love will increase exceedingly the joy and contentment of our souls. Speak often of Heaven to those who approach you, my daughters; seek to make them love the virtues that are required before we can be admitted to that blessed country. For if you know how to draw souls by your zeal, your good example, and your exemplary religious conduct, you may be assured the gates will be opened for you also.

September 24. I wanted to go to Heaven, but what with one thing and another, we have entered the New York Bay. The superintendent of the customs house officers and the doctor are already on board. We are asked to give our names to a New York representative while the *Fulda* is being towed down the bay by three tugs. We disembarked at Hoboken Docks, where we were met by our dear American Sisters, who received us with great joy. An excellent customs officer came up to inspect our luggage and asked us to say a prayer for him.

I found everything in perfect order here, with much to console me. I cannot, for the present, give you further details, for I have a great number of friends to greet. But I will send you further news as soon as I embark on my next voyage.

In the meantime I commend myself, as well as my intentions and new enterprises for the good of souls and the glory of God, to your good prayers. I'll work hard and you'll pray—adding some extra sacrifices, I'm sure, especially that of self-abasement. Offer everything as a perfect holocaust to the adorable Heart of Jesus, Who loves us so much and has done so much to merit for us our beautiful and sublime vocation.

May Jesus bless you and enclose you in His Sacred Heart.

Your affectionate Mother in the Most Sacred Heart of Jesus,

M. FRANCESCA SAVERIO CABRINI

October 1895, Voyage from Panama to Buenos Aires

After establishing a new community of Sisters in Panama, Mother Cabrini was invited to establish her Sisters in Argentina. In this letter, she describes how she crossed oceans and mountains by boat, train, and mule, as well as Soldier's Jump, a narrow bridge that spanned a dangerous precipice.

My Dear Daughters in the Sacred Heart of Jesus,

Peace be with you, and may you repeat often, "Omnia possum in Eo qui me confortat!" ["I can do all things in him who strengthens me" (Phil 4:13)].

How wide is the opening
Of the wound in His side!
There, the port is ready.
Cast away every fear, O daughters;
I am holding close to the Virgin.
Soon, I will come into harbor.[3]

"What a long voyage, what a hard voyage Mother is undertaking at present!" This is what I hear you say, and I detect sadness and fear on your faces. I believe I am the calmest among you all—I really am, as far as my voyage is concerned. Jesus still lives. Mary, the Mother of Grace, is always my most tender Mother, because she is the mother and foundress of our Institute. It is Jesus and Mary who have always seen me through thousands of difficulties; will they abandon me now? No, I shall never wrong them by failing to trust in their power and protection. During the sixteen years the Institute has existed, they have done everything for me. They have accomplished everything wonderfully. If there have been failures, it was because I acted too much on my own initiative; when I left the work to them, I had nothing to regret. I move forward, then, as tranquil as a child resting in its mother's arms; in that safe ship of the Sacred Heart of Jesus I go to fulfill my mission. Holy obedience and the blessing of the Holy Father accompany me and remove all fears. I fear nothing, repeating continually my motto, "Omnia possum in Eo qui me confortat!"

The wind roars, the heavens darken, the treacherous waves arise and beat against the steamer, everything is topsy-turvy. We are threatened with a terrible tempest. None of this matters; I have committed myself to trusting;

[3] This appears to be a poem Mother Cabrini composed.

I must keep my word of honor, and do so with faith and confidence. I hope, with God's grace, to go on repeating, "Omnia possum in Eo qui me confortat!" We are missionaries, oh daughters, and a missionary should never shrink from difficulties and dangers, but rather, confiding in Jesus and relying on Mary, she will overcome all difficulties and escape all dangers.

Difficulties! What are they, daughters? They are the mere playthings of children amplified by our imagination, which is not yet accustomed to focusing itself on the Omnipotent. Dangers! What are dangers? Specters that surprise the soul, which although it has given itself to God, or thinks it has, still retains the spirit of the world, or at least many sparks of it, which fly up from the ashes and flare at every gust of contrary wind.

It is necessary, dear daughters, to clothe ourselves with the true spirit, to live a life of true faith, lively faith, and not to deceive ourselves or the grace that is always in us.

In Holy Baptism we solemnly renounced the world, the devil, and the flesh; but we must prove that renunciation by our daily actions. When we entered religion, we said, "I am crucified to the world and the world is crucified to me [Gal 6:14]." But such a promise should not be a mere empty saying; in reality, we should live as if we were people of a holy nation that belongs no longer to the world. When we took the crucifix of the missionary and became more generous in the service of God, we said, with the impulse of the ardent soul, "I shall be happy to shed my blood for Jesus Christ, and will welcome the blessed day on which it shall be given to me to suffer something for the holy cause, for the salvation of souls and the glory of God." Sublime words! And who would be false to such an oath made by so courageous a soul? Oh daughters! Let us meditate profoundly on the sublimity of the state to which

God has called us—that of working for the salvation of souls! With such reflection, may we never shrink from our promises or lose courage just because of the judgment and reasoning of the world!

"But I am weak!" With God's help we can do everything; He never fails a humble and faithful soul.

"But I am so fragile!" If you are humble and constant, God will be your strength, and having been made strong with the strength of God, what shall we fear?

"The devil is terrible." The devil is a chained dog—he cannot disturb you or hurt you without God's permission. Therefore, a humble and faithful soul need have no fear of the devil.

"I have failed in generosity. I have fallen at the first temptation. Now I shall not be able to do anything well." Have you fallen? Then humble yourself, and with a lively act of contrition from the depths of your heart, ask pardon with great humility and renew your promises to God and those who represent Him; then onward, with more courage than ever to repair your defects.

October 12. Yesterday was a day I will never forget.

The thought of leaving, after four months, our dear Sisters, who so edified me and whose virtues made the convent of Panama a sweet habitation, was painful. And to leave those young ladies, our pupils, who endeared themselves to me by their nobleness of heart and the way they responded to the care and sacrifices of the Sisters on their behalf; who gathered around me daily to hear a few words of advice in their own language, which I still speak so poorly; who made efforts to overcome themselves and make me happier each day by anticipating my wishes ... all this combined to make my departure more painful. The steamer was lying at a distance of three miles from the shore, and they all came on board to see me off. The noble and generous Don Ernesto

Icasa, the father of one of our dear pupils, had placed his comfortable tugboat at their disposal. The representatives of the heads of families in Panama and the patrons of the new school also came on board and introduced me to the captain and the head steward. They are very distinguished persons, not only on account of their social position, but for the virtues and generosity that set them apart.

From the very first moment I arrived in Panama, they did everything in their power to further the development of the school and to ensure its preservation and progress. Many were the sacrifices and acts of self-denial they made to this end. The evening before my departure, the committee came together to assure me that during my absence they would do everything in their power for the Sisters, and even attested to their commitment in writing, adding a letter of recommendation for me to present to their friends when I reached Ecuador, Peru, Chile, and Argentina. Many ladies, our good friends, came to the port to see me off. There was also the bishop's secretary and the parish priest of the cathedral, who came with good wishes, which, because they are accompanied by God's blessing, are always valuable. This good priest had been invited by our chaplain to give us Benediction of the Blessed Sacrament so that my voyage might be blessed. So many demonstrations of kindness touched my soul indeed, and made it all the more deeply painful to leave Panama, which has so many noble and generous people.

On board the steamer, Messrs. Icasa, Espinosa, Della Ossa, and Lewis introduced me to the captain with many expressions of recommendation. Mr. Icasa put the finishing touch on the leave-taking by paying for the voyage and handing the tickets to the bursar himself, making sure that I should enjoy all the advantages procured for me. There was also a comic element that served to mitigate the sadness of the last moments, for the consul, Mr. Della Ossa, took the captain by the arm, saying, "You know, Mother has not had supper yet." "Of course," he said, "she shall have it soon." But Mr. Della Ossa persisted so much that the captain thought he wanted him to go to the kitchen himself to get me my supper. The captain was very amused, and called the steward to conduct us to the dining room, but I begged him to wait a few moments, as I wished to see the Sisters and children return, since it was six P.M. and the tugboat was leaving at once. Night comes on remarkably quickly in these equatorial regions. The waving handkerchiefs could not be distinguished after they had gone about 150 feet, so we went to our cabins, Mother Chiara and I. These were just like a little convent. The two cabins communicated with each other and opened out onto the deck, which is fifteen feet wide and three hundred feet long and where we can walk around freely and enjoy the air. The dining room is very close and very comfortable; we might have wished for all these conveniences, but we could hardly have expected to find them. After having supper and saying some prayers, Mother Chiara went to bed, while I sat alone facing the lighthouse of Panama. Looking to the left of it, I thought I could see the Sisters at recreation gazing in the direction of the steamer *Mapocho*, and afterward absorbed in prayers in the chapel. I also thought I could see all five lamps burning, three before the Blessed Sacrament and one each before Our Lady and Saint Joseph, which, by the up and down of their flickering lights, seemed to wish to join the Sisters in praying for a good voyage for me. I then united with you in spirit and prayed in return that you might always receive the most precious graces that you need to accomplish your mission: to lead all the souls brought into contact with you to God.

Between nine-thirty and ten P.M., very quietly, the steamer began to move, and having turned round, it passed in front of Flamenco hill and made straight for the south. I continued as long as I could to look on the left-hand side of the lighthouse, but little by little the darkness that surrounded us became so dense that even this became indistinguishable. Then, having lost all hope of seeing any more of you and hearing your voices raised in the hymn of the "Ave Maris Stella" as an invocation and prayer for me to Our Lady, I also retired.

October 14. On the morning of the 12th, as soon as I had arisen and said my prayers, I turned toward Panama to see if I could catch a glimpse if not of the town, at least of the coast, but the water that surrounded me was like a sheet of lead. The sky was so cloudy that I could not determine the points of the compass, which might have helped me look in the proper direction. I then fixed my gaze on the Sacred Heart, where I could see you in deep contemplation like so many seraphim inflamed in preparation for Holy Communion. It was a most consoling vision for me, and I hastened to unite myself with you in Spiritual Communion, offering it to the Eternal Father in union with your sacramental Communion....

The atmosphere seems to have changed, for as we move toward the equator and even when we are on the equatorial line itself, instead of feeling the great heat that we were told to expect, we felt cold—so much so that we were obliged to put on heavier clothes. One would think the steamer had gone off course and had steered toward the North Pole instead of going to the equator. Two blankets were not sufficient, and we had to wear shawls on deck, but even so, I feel the cold to my very bones. I would have loved to have used those two cushions you so thoughtfully provided for me, but no matter how much I stretched my arms, I could not reach Panama to take them; I also imagined how disappointed you must be that we forgot them, but there is no need to be upset, for everyone is so attentive to us on the steamer that we lack nothing.

While crossing the equator, it is not fitting to wish for too many conveniences, because we are close to and directly aligned with Quito, where Blessed Mariana[4] lived in such austere penance, though this is to be admired rather than imitated. What a pity that Mother Gabriella is not here, now that we are passing the equator, since she wished to see the line so much. It is like a shining dark blue band stretched just above the globe, and it is really beautiful to behold. The sea seems to end there, or if there is more, one would have to leap over the band to get to it. To one of the lady passengers who desired to see the line, the merry company placed a thread across a pair of eyeglasses, so that she thought she really saw a great beam dividing the two hemispheres. However, all joking aside, the combination of sky and water makes such a beautiful spectacle that one would think it was the actual line of division where the South begins and where a real division appears to exist, for while the thermometer registers 80 degrees, the air is so cold that it made us shiver.

You must not think it is always like this; in fact, everyone is surprised at this phenomenon. I am not so surprised, accustomed as I am now to see so many beautiful and unexpected things from the hand of God, Who, in the economy of His Most Holy Providence, always has new wonders for those who completely abandon themselves to Him. But I rejoice to be able to give you a new description of these equatorial regions, of which I have heard hardly anything except that the heat is excessive and unbearable. It might be that the Lily of Quito, the Blessed Mariana, from her sepulchre in the Andes, or rather from Heaven,

[4] Mariana de Jesús de Paredes (1618-1645), a mystic known as the "Lily of Quito". She was canonized in 1950.

where she sits happily at the side of her loving Jesus, sent us this fresh breeze to mitigate the heat of the voyage, which we undertook from Panama in honor of Saint Rose of Lima, the patroness of America. We shall visit her tomb and receive Holy Communion at her altar.

October 16. Yesterday we arrived at Guayaquil, where we intended to go ashore to receive Holy Communion, but two hours went by before the custom officers and doctors came on board. Then there arrived a Peruvian priest, who had left Ecuador and settled in Peru during the revolutions. He had hardly reached Guayaquil, when he was banished to Peru again and embarked on our steamer. I made up my mind after hearing this not to go ashore and have the police follow us, as everybody is held in suspicion, since Mr. Alfaro[5] has not yet fully settled his government.

Guayaquil is a beautiful port. Its entrance resembles that of the Mississippi at New Orleans. One has to sail up this river for more than six hours to reach the port. They say the vegetation is charming, but I cannot describe it, as we arrived at night, and after twenty-four hours we will sail at night again. The town resembles Genoa in its scenery, only it is at a lower elevation and less healthy, because they do not keep it clean. Seen from the steamer, the city, with its beautiful houses built with architectural regularity and well painted and set in a natural semicircle reflected in the water, is very fine and not inferior to a European city. When illuminated at night, it is a wonderfully pleasant sight, and judging from the tall steeples towering over the houses, the churches should be beautiful.

But at present these churches are deserted, for the first thing the revolutionary Alfaro's followers did upon taking power was to banish as many priests as they could, along

[5] José Eloy Alfaro Delgado was the liberal President of Ecuador during this period.

with a great many Sisters. The latter took refuge in Panama and then returned to their motherhouses. I hear that some of these Sisters were not officially banished, but were treated so badly that the poor frightened women had to flee the country—a troop of soldiers entered their convents, looting anything valuable and destroying everything else. Some of these poor women suffered so much that they were still ill when I visited them. But you are not to be frightened. If you are banished from one place, you should shake the dust from your shoes like the Apostles and enter another country. If you are chased away from the second, you can return to the first, and so you will not abandon a large number of souls who desire to take advantage of the good you can do them. At the present moment, having no business in Ecuador, I simply pray to the Blessed Mariana to look down upon her country so that the dominion of darkness may soon end and it may be enlightened with the light and faith of former days.

October 17. Yesterday we left Ecuador and entered the waters of Peru, and at seven A.M. we arrived at the port of Paita. It looks like a desolate city, and at first sight it saddens one's heart. No trees, no grass, no fountain is visible. Surrounded by low and dry mountains, it is a real desert. Yet it is one of the healthiest ports, and large numbers come here even from Ecuador to treat many maladies, especially of the blood. In fact, the air one breathes here is pure, light, and balsamic, and really restores one. The sea is tranquil, and they tell us it never gets rough at this spot. It has such a beautiful soft blue color that one would think it was a fallen piece of the sky. But to us it appeared especially beautiful and most unique, for as we looked around to see if we could find a steeple, so as to turn our thoughts and hearts to Jesus in the Blessed Sacrament of the Altar, a flock of white birds suddenly whirled around us, making a strange noise, upon which Mother Chiara broke the silence, saying, "What can this mean?" "Oh," I replied, playfully, "they are inviting us to their country as they did three years ago in Panama, and we will go there when we can." While we were talking and amusing ourselves with these peculiar birds, a priest came on board and approached me. After we exchanged greetings, he asked me what the object of our voyage was. Without further ceremony, he said, "Your place is here. I will take you to a nearby city where you can open a beautiful mission. I will see to your disembarkation." I had a difficult time persuading him that it was impossible for me to stop here, telling him that, if the Most Sacred Heart of Jesus should will it, I would come back later. He seemed very disappointed. However, determined not to be outdone, he appeared shortly afterward with the governor and mayor, who promised me all sorts of things, including a stipend. At first I thought that as there was a great deal of business being carried on on board, these people wanted to trade with us, but I soon discovered that their intentions were very good, and that they only desired to obtain a religious education for the youth of their country. Of course, I could not fulfill their wishes, and they finally took my address, and I theirs, with the hope of satisfying their wishes at a later date. Meanwhile, two beautiful days have passed without our being able to receive Our Divine Lord or hear Holy Mass: the feasts of Saint Teresa [of Ávila] and of Blessed Margaret Mary. Had we been without the consolation of prayer, this long voyage would have been intolerable. What a gift prayer is! It is the real treasure of our soul, to be able to give to God the worship of perfect adoration. Prayer is the channel through which the most precious waters of grace continually and copiously flow from the Heart of God. These are precious waters, daughters, for while they sanctify us, they also bring joy to our holy Church, of which we should try to become more worthy every day. Prayer is always useful, because it can penetrate everywhere, and where there is misery and poverty, there it enters to enrich, to give life, grace, comfort, and salvation; its zeal is like that of God's angel, its activity is greater than the most ardent fire, its velocity is like the thought of the cherubim. Oh, the spirit of prayer knows no obstacles, allows no delay, despises dangers; its aim is the glory of God, the prosperity of Christ's interests, the extension of His Kingdom, our own sanctification, and that of our neighbor! Oh, what happiness, daughters! I am accompanied by the powerful and wonderful means of prayer. I am, then, most happy in the midst of the foaming waves of the sea. And you, dear daughters, pray—pray always, and incessantly practice the spirit of prayer, which must form your happiness.

October 20. On the 18th we had two landings—one at Puerto Etén and the other at Pacasmayo—and yesterday morning we had another at Salaverry, where we still are, though judging from the scenery and commerce, it does not appear to be a place of much importance. There is an extensive trade here in sugar, cocoa, rice, and cotton, which form the principal wealth of these countries, apart from the mines of gold and other metals that still abound in Peru, though not as much as they did at one time. Now it possesses another source of wealth: the natural guano composed chiefly of bird droppings. From the equator to Chile, the whole coast, whether plains or mountains, is one big desert. There is not a blade of grass, not a tree, nothing that gives the slightest indication of vegetation. Nothing can be cultivated, for there is no rain except at intervals of five to seven years. In the years in between, millions of birds, provided by Providence, deposit quantities of droppings in certain places, from which is extracted the guano that is so greatly valued all over the world for the fertilization of fields.

In these parts we have seen many practical innovations. The sea is almost always so rough that boats coming to a ship with passengers cannot always get near the ship ladder, and then how can they get the passengers on board? Well, something very curious and funny takes place. They take a barrel cut open on one side and place the person in it. They then attach it to the chain that they use for hauling cargo. The person is then pulled up and let down into the ship. The poor creature, who is suspended between the sky and the water, seems very much afraid, and this applies not only to the women but also to the men, for even when they reach the deck, they appear stupefied, as if they are not quite sure they have escaped some sort of danger. Yesterday one of the usual stowaways at these ports, taking advantage of the conveyance of merchandise, managed to get on board, but the officers, who are quite practical, accosted him as soon as they saw him and told him to leave the steamer at once. It was a most difficult task for him to climb up to the ship, but it was more difficult to go down, so they took him, put him into a sack, and then attached the sack to the chain and let him down. He must have been accustomed to this sort of thing, for he remained indifferent and as fresh as a rose.

We were detained in this port of Salaverry, which is as important as it is inconvenient, for two days because of the large quantity of cargo we had to take on board. Some years ago, a large dock was built here to facilitate the work of embarkation. It was hardly finished when there arose a tremendous gale that destroyed it completely, leaving no trace of the work, and the expense of construction was so great that the promoters did not feel disposed to rebuild it. The ocean is very rough here, and the waves break so violently that they actually frighten us. The cargo is brought across in large and strongly built boats, but even though they are so big, they often seem to be on the point of foundering as the great waves sweep over them and hide them from sight, while we remain in terrible suspense until we see them rise again above the tremendous waves. Amid the force of the waves, these unfortunate boats roll from one side to another, though they are manned by ten strong rowers with long, broad oars. The one at the stern, who acts as steersman, has a bigger oar than the others and works with all his might and main. Others come with *balzas,* a boat of somewhat primitive construction made out of tall, thick balsa trees. They are as light and spongy as cork and offer great resistance to the water. With these boats they transport bags of charcoal, which is used in these parts. It is said to be a safer form of transport than any other kind of boat. However, I would not care to entrust myself to one of them except under obedience, in which case fear ceases and is replaced by a trust that brings security.

Obedience! Oh dear word, obedience! The revealed word, ray of true light, that descends upon us from the Father of Light, as a manifestation of the divine will by means of His representatives on earth. He who does the will of God feels great peace and gets a taste of Heaven in advance; and what great joy is ours, oh daughters, we who live under obedience—or rather in the state of obedience—really, actually, and continually doing the will of God. "Ego quae placita sunt ei facio semper" ["I always do what is pleasing to him" (John 8:29)]. Those who live under obedience are sure of their way, because in the practice of obedience there are no errors, no deceits, no illusions, no darkness. Obedience! Obedient souls are the delight of the Heart of Jesus, Who has said His treasures are always open to His beloved and faithful spouses. It is they whom He makes the dispensers of His possessions, on earth and in Heaven. Do you love Jesus, daughters? Do you want to be His faithful spouses? If so, love obedience. Obey always, for God's sake. Let every command be easy to you, on account of the faith you have in holy obedience. Only in obedience will your steps be sure, your actions firm, and your spirit strong. In the way of obedience you will not only walk, but fly like royal eagles and spend a quiet and happy life, being able to repeat to yourselves, "I am sure I am doing God's will." Remember, no one ever became a saint without obedience, for it is obedience that is the favorite virtue of all the saints. Do not do things by halves, but let your obedience be entire and perfect, just like that of Jesus. First, in the performance of it, by following promptly, entirely, and cheerfully all that is ordered by the superior; second, with regard to the will, by not wishing for anything but what the superior wishes; and third, with regard to your judgment, by judging and thinking as the superior judges and thinks. Which of you, daughters, has not contracted debts with God in the course of your life? Well, a sure way of paying your debts to God is by submitting yourself to a true and perfect obedience, since obedience is of far greater value than any penance you can imagine. "Melior est obedientia quam victimae" ["To obey is better than sacrifice" (1 Sam 15:22)]. Most sweet will be the death of obedient souls.

Late as always, we did not arrive at Callao until the 22nd. I rose at four o'clock, and at five-fifteen I called to Mother Chiara to get up in the hopes of going ashore at six A.M. and then taking the train for Lima, where I wanted to satisfy my desire to receive Holy Communion at the sepulchre of Saint Rose. But very soon our hopes vanished, for at seven-thirty, none of the customs officers had arrived, and no boats were allowed to come near the steamer under penalty of a heavy fine. They came at last, but imagine our surprise when we learned that there was no train to Lima until nine A.M. I didn't know what to do. Mother Chiara had been fighting the sea long enough, and it was impossible for her to keep fasting much longer. As for myself, I did not want to miss my promised Communion in honor of Saint Rose, having made many promises to her and having entrusted to her care the rest of our journey and the interests I am engaged in furthering. I could manage the fast all right, having had no trouble with the sea, only playing with the waves, as it were, delighting in their impotence and their breaking and rising like foam and mist, which at times resembled Niagara Falls, which I saw near Buffalo, U.S.A., about three years ago.

We took the train and arrived in Lima at ten A.M. We hired a cab to the Dominican church, where we were able to make our devotion. Above the altar where I received Holy Communion there was a statue of the Infant Jesus with His arms extended and a celestial smile of extraordinary beauty on His face. He seemed to gaze on me and to say, "It is here I have waited to favor thee, through the merits of my beloved Rose, whom you have come to honor." The look of this Infant, so lifelike, penetrated the very depths of my soul, and I felt such comfort that I forgot all about my fast, as well as all other human wants, and I realized I hadn't taken so much as a sip of coffee, and it was one P.M. If Jesus rewards a small sacrifice this way, what will He not do for souls who are really faithful to Him?

But let us return to the Dominican basilica, where, after Holy Communion, the reverend fathers showed us the different altars, especially the one where Saint Rose's head is venerated. The saint's head is enclosed in a silver urn placed above another urn that contains the remains of

Blessed Martin de Porres.[6] The altars are all adorned with big statues, some of which are truly beautiful and represent the saints so realistically in life-size that one would almost think they could speak.

On leaving the church, we saw many women placing their finger on a leaden seal at the mouth of a leaden pipe, which was embedded in a column where the holy water font was placed. With a finger in that position, they prayed with great fervor. I asked them why they did so, and a woman, surprised at our astonishment, answered, "Do you not know that this is an authentic seal from Rome, and that by placing your finger on it and saying an Our Father, you free a soul from Purgatory?" To avoid further surprising these good people, I touched the seal with my finger too, and then said a Pater Noster for the Holy Souls. To tell the truth, I never heard of such a devotion in Rome.

We were not satisfied with venerating only the head of Saint Rose. So the guide told us to go to Santa Rosa de los Padres, where we would find the rest of the relics. Following the directions given to us, we soon found ourselves in the indicated place, where there was a beautiful new church, very devotional and well-kept. The good sacristan showed us the relics of the saint, which are distributed among the different altars. In one of the chapels there was a large crucifix and a glass case where we found the remains of the saint. The crucifix is the one she used herself. At the two sides of the altar there are two glass cases, each containing an arm of the saint. On another altar we saw the cross of wood on which she used to pray prostrate on the floor, and to which she used to tie herself in order to imitate her Savior, her Spouse, when she was not undergoing other crucifixions—those of the spirit, which are better—real

[6] Martin de Porres (1579–1639) was declared a saint in 1962.

crucifixions in the strictest sense, which serve so well to purify souls and unite them intimately with their Beloved. From such crucifixions, this beloved of the Crucified, of whom I speak, had much to suffer. On another altar we saw the discipline and the instruments of her penance, with a framed letter written by the saint herself.

On this same altar was a picture of rare beauty of Our Lady with the Divine Infant in her arms. This picture captivates the soul simply by looking at it. It is believed that the picture represents the Infant Who gave the mystical wedding ring to Saint Rose, and to Whom the saint always had recourse for advice before beginning any new enterprise. The sacristan then took us to the spot where the saint's house stood, which is beside the sacred shrine we had visited. It is a large plot of land with the foundations of a large church in the shape of a Latin cross. When the large, beautiful, and strong colonnades had been built almost up to the cornice, a terrible rebellion broke out and threw the whole city of Lima into chaos. The religious were ill-treated, many being sent into exile and their convents destroyed. Since that unfortunate episode, there has been no thought of continuing the magnificent work already begun. It is a great pity, for the place would quickly become a celebrated sanctuary, seeing that it holds the well of the saint at the center of the church, and there is the grotto in the garden where she used to withdraw for prayer, which would become one of the aisles of the church—to say nothing of the precious relics mentioned above and others that are deposited in various convents of the Sisters. Having satisfied our devotion to the saint, we went to visit the apostolic nuncio, Msgr. Macchi, who received us very kindly and gave us a very kind letter of recommendation to the superintendent of the South American Company, asking him to let us have tickets at reduced fares, which was the reason I had visited him. We spoke of our voyage, and he gave us instructions to visit certain places in order to transact business matters connected with our missions. He knows the coast as far as Valparaíso very well, having traveled on this very steamer to pay a return visit to Msgr. Casanova, archbishop of Santiago. With the blessing and good wishes of this good prelate, I visited another part of the city so as to have something to write about to you. Lima is beautiful in comparison to the other cities I saw in South America, but I cannot call it really beautiful. It resembles the old portion of New Orleans, U.S.A., where the poor people of that great town reside. We only saw something really beautiful when we entered Saint Peter's. You can compare Saint Peter's with churches found in Genoa. Dressed-up saints are banned from this church. Everything is well ordered, fitting, and richly appointed. It was one P.M. when we entered Saint Peter's, and Mass was being celebrated, at which we assisted with great consolation, after ten days of privation of the Most Holy Sacrament. The architecture is superb, a good style, with rich and varied kinds of marble. From the altar hang beautiful tapestries, elegantly and profusely embroidered in very fine gold. The statues are also numerous here. They seemed life-like and in good order. It was the last day of the Octave of Blessed Margaret Mary Alacoque, and on one side of the high altar there was a temporary altar in her honor, adorned with lilies and roses, with a background of beautiful pink cloth that threw the roses and lilies into high relief. How happy I was to see our patron in the middle of this triumphant altar, truly appropriate for this virgin, whom the good Jesus, in the loving designs of His goodness, preordained from eternity to establish and propagate the devotion of His Divine Heart, manifesting to her Its wonders of piety, clemency, power, and love. This dear virgin, worthy daughter of Saint Francis de Sales, was so true to the designs of her celestial Spouse and worked with such ardent and generous zeal to fulfill her vocation that both Heaven and earth were moved to admiration. Words are inadequate to express how much she suffered and worked to spread such a rare and salutary devotion, for the devil, who knew the incomparable benefit she would bring to the people of every nation, worked against our dear virgin protectress with such satanic violence that to human understanding, it seemed impossible to conquer and overcome his attacks. But truly loving and faithful souls are not discouraged, and so it was with our Blessed Margaret. She knew that the work she was destined to establish came from Heaven. Her courage and confidence did not waver. By entirely abandoning herself, like a strong and true missionary, to the loving mercy of her beloved Jesus, coupled with the industry of an enlightened and generous charity, she knew how to triumph over all obstacles, meriting thus to see this Divine Heart known, loved, and glorified by a large number of devout souls before she died. As a reward for such generosity of action, Blessed Margaret Mary now contemplates the beauty of the Divine Heart in Heaven. She enjoys peace, happiness, and sovereign delights and can speak to Him unveiled at every moment, imploring and obtaining great graces, and she will certainly implore them for you if you honor her—but especially if you imitate her. She will comfort you with her most powerful intercession. She herself carries your ardent prayers to the throne of God, and as a reward for your zeal, she will place you all in the loving Heart of Jesus, and obtain for you the grace to live that same life, which is all humility, all meekness, all obedience, all sacrifice, all love.

At Saint Peter's we met the Jesuit fathers, who told me to visit the Ladies of the Sacred Heart, where we could get some refreshments. They have a government school, a lovely house close to Saint Peter's. Many years ago, before the great rebellion destroyed everything, this house belonged to the Jesuits, a famous college and novitiate. Now the Jesuits have a smaller house opposite the Convent of the Sacred Heart, but it will be enlarged in time, as their schools are always attended by the principal families of the town. The reverend mother of the Ladies of the Sacred Heart received us very cordially, and while they were getting our lunch ready, she gave us a tour of the house. It is a very nice place indeed and suitable for organizing the different classes of children who frequent it. The good Sisters wanted us to stay overnight, but I could not do so, having some business to attend to at Callao concerning our voyage.

I wanted to visit the cathedral, but they dissuaded me from doing so, as it is ugly inside and out, the exterior having been ruined by the cannon fire that was directed against it. This will surprise you, but I can explain the fact at once. One of the first acts of these revolutionaries is always to attack the cathedral of a town, and the first of the two hostile parties who gains possession of the cathedral is considered the victor. Perhaps their intentions are good, for those are declared the victors who have the good fortune to secure the sanctuary for themselves, but we cannot deny that they deface God's temple and destroy the most beautiful statues. They say "adelantados mucho", which means "very enlightened", but to tell the truth, their customs and manners are those of uncivilized people.

I like the custom of having Holy Mass at one P.M. This is done daily in all the churches, and many men and women attend with a truly edifying devotion. There is a society in Lima that defrays the expenses of these late Masses.

In Lima, there is a fairly respectable Italian colony. The Italians are very well loved, and it is only over the last few days that Peruvians have begun to look at them with an evil eye, since a few fanatics decided to celebrate September 20 [the day of Italian independence] with such solemnity that they made a ruckus in the city. Even the president of Peru, who lives in Lima, lost some public respect, because he permitted the Italians to raise their flags and make a very open display of the celebration.

Most Peruvians are sincere Catholics, and they cannot stand anything that directly or indirectly injures the august figure of the Holy Father. What Italians consider a great achievement for national unity [namely, the 1871 unification of Italy] is actually the cause of its disorder, disrupting it and apparently dissolving it. September 20 is a sign of shame for Italians, and may God quickly change its fortunes so that we may once again walk with our heads held high, rather than being ashamed to be daughters of a nation that has always been great and even today could be the greatest of them all, not only because of its intelligence, industry, the arts, and the sciences, but more so because it holds in its bosom the Vicar of Christ, who is a global king for all Catholics. Yes, the pope is the glory of us Italians, and the glory of Italy will find its wellspring in the good treatment of the Venerable One at the Vatican.

We returned to Callao toward evening. Our steamer had already reached the docks, so there was no need to take a small boat to go on board. Both officers and crew were glad to see us again and inquired about how we liked Lima and how our trip was going.

The next day the captain introduced us to the superintendent of Callao, Mr. Mackennie, and obtained a thirty-three percent reduction of the fare for us. We, who could not expect more, were quite satisfied; but not so the good captain, who said that as soon as we reached Valparaíso, he would go to the general agency and get us a fifty percent reduction, as he admired our life of sacrifice, for which he said we deserved every consideration.

Callao is a very important port. It has a very nice, large dock, which is only open when the steamers are arriving or departing.

October 29. We have been sailing along the coast since the 15th, that is, since we left Guayaquil. The coast is so dry and sandy that one would imagine we were sailing along the great desert of Arabia, instead of on the waters of the Pacific. There are no trees, no grass, only a variety of rocks. For two days we have been sailing alongside certain mountains whose peaks are all the same height and look like a long high wall, broken by a few valleys and watered by torrents that descend from the Andes, which, before rushing into the sea, form creeks, but eventually yield to the force of the formidable waves and then mix with the salty waters of the sea. In these valleys are cities and towns that export vegetables and fruit to other places that suffer drought, and where the inhabitants have never been able to grow any trees or plants whatsoever, the soil being too poor for even a garden. This occurs especially at Chala and Antofagasta, where all the mountains contain great quantities of saltpeter, which evaporates and rises up during the day and then falls on the earth at night as a thick fog that burns up every kind of vegetation. These great mountainous walls arise like impregnable fortresses defying the heavens. Sometimes they take the form of heights from which the slope comes down like a mantle and ends in a scarcely perceptible bay. There a town arises with a port that many steamers enter, especially sailing vessels, which lie in the harbor for weeks awaiting a cargo of saltpeter, which they transport to Europe through the Strait of Magellan; if the vessel is a steamer, it goes around Cape Horn; if it is a sailing vessel, it takes about four months to complete the journey. This saltpeter is used in Europe to fertilize the soil. Here the proverb applies that we take the best part of the bread and leave them the crust, which means that they make little, if any, profit. But the proverb does not apply in the commercial or financial world; much money is made from various silver, tin, and iron mines, as well as from saltpeter and guano.

During this part of our journey we stopped at sixteen ports: Guayaquil, Tumbes, Paita, Pimentel, Puerto Etén, Pacasmayo, Salaverry, Callao, Tambo de Mora, Pisco, Chala, Quilca, Mollendo, Ilo, Arica, and Pisagua. It is lovely to watch the train as it travels through these mining countries, playing, as it were, on the edges of the precipices, which lie below the zigzag rails. In some parts there are funiculars because of the steep slopes, and accidents are frequent. But all this does not deter these lovers of buried treasures from their endeavors. These great mountains are called small hills by the people here, and so they are when compared with the great Andes, just as we regard the hills in Piedmont as small in comparison with the Alps and Apennines. To reach the Andes it is necessary to cross this desert for about nine miles or more. The Cordillera is really portentous and imposing. It begins in the island of Diego Ramírez, southwest of Cape Horn, enters South America through Patagonia, and then runs northward, forming a reef first along the Pacific Ocean, whose waters little by little penetrate the Cordillera, creating a deep inlet. But even here, the Andes are not very high, the lowest parts measuring two or three thousand feet and the highest nine thousand feet. Entering Chile, the chain rises until it reaches a considerable height in Bolivia. One can admire what is supposed to be the highest peak of the Andes, the Aconcagua, the height of which is from twenty-three to twenty-four thousand feet above sea level. With a height of from eleven to fourteen thousand feet, this formidable range continues all through Bolivia and Peru, now and then thrusting up other heights or peaks perpetually covered with snow. At intervals one sees traces of paths connecting different regions, and at this point the lowest height is about sixteen thousand feet above sea level. Even at this height there are fields like those on the plains, for the Cordillera is about four hundred miles wide. On one of these is to be found the famous Lake Titicaca, which is the highest in the world. All along the coast of Peru and reaching the line of the equator, this range runs until it unites with the volcanoes, the most famous of which are the Chimborazo and the Cotopaxi. There we see with wondering eyes peaks that seem to touch the very heavens, and often appear cut off by the clouds or reduced to vapor. These peaks then branch off into three ranges. One goes northwest until it reaches the sea of the Antilles, another passes through the center, joining the above and reaching the Antilles, and the third turns to the northeast to the east of the Orinoco, enters Venezuela, and reaches the sea of the Antilles. It is said that the hottest part of the earth's interior is at the equator. Those who live in the isthmus say that the mouth of the interior furnace, that is, of Hell, is on the isthmus. It is also said that one can go straight to Heaven from there, if not too immersed in earthly things—but if one is so immersed, one falls into Hell, where, among other miseries, there is the gnashing of teeth. Along the length of the Andes there are active volcanoes, and the ones in the neighborhood of the equator are so violent that one of them, the Cotopaxi, formed another mountain right beside it when it erupted. The Andes continue into Colombia, presenting to the view many pretty and imposing sights; then they continue on through Central America and Mexico, where we also find extremely active volcanoes. When they enter the United States, they take the name Rocky Mountains along the West Coast. Then, running through Alaska to Asia, they reach the Aleutian Islands, forming a connection between the Arctic and Antarctic, with the Pacific Ocean to the west. In the north of Asia there is another chain that runs along the other side, and to the west there is another volcanic chain that seems to merge into and lose itself in the sea, though it reappears in Australia, where it throws up volcanoes, famous for their uniqueness, which are crowned here and there, as it were, with lakes of fire. The Pacific Ocean seems surrounded, both on the east and the west, by an unbroken chain of volcanic mountains.

I have described the Andes for you because our fellow passengers, who know we are traveling over and will probably cross the Andes at Valparaíso, speak a great deal of the Andes, their beauty, and the facts that make them famous—very often with maps in their hands—and thus every point is described so vividly that I imagine I can touch it with my hand. Since I must cross the Aconcagua, I shall have something to tell you about it later. In the meanwhile, I think the Cordillera makes a good lesson for the missionary, running, as it does, all over the earth, without fear of treacherous sea voyages, weather, unhealthy places, etc. and always preaching to us, both when it rises toward Heaven with its great heights and when it humbles itself, hiding itself in the waves of the sea; it also preaches when it sends out fire, smoke, and lava, adding force to the winds that lash within its gorges. In Boyacá, for instance, especially in Popayán, where we have been invited, it thunders terribly every day, with lightning that seems to reduce one to ashes; in all this, one can very easily find food for pious meditation on death.

October 31. Iquique. Within the space of a few days we stopped at four ports—Iquique, Tocopilla, Cobija, and Antofagasta. We had hoped to reach Iquique early in the morning so as to be able to receive Holy Communion, but the steamer arrived at Pisagua a little late, and the superintendent of the port would not let us land, so we had to spend the night there on board. In the morning the crew was very busy importing and exporting the merchandise, as well as in boarding and disembarking passengers. Having arrived at Iquique at night, the vessel was loaded very hurriedly, for we were a day behind, and the captain did not wish to lose any more time. We had sufficient leisure, however, to go ashore before sunset and pay our respects to the bishop, as Msgr. Macchi wanted us to do, and so we seized the opportunity of meeting that worthy prelate, who is a real missionary to a population of twenty-five thousand inhabitants. The first thing he did on assuming his episcopal duties was to build a beautiful and very devotional church, and he has since laid the foundation of a second, which he hopes to complete in six months—an easy task here, as the churches are built of wood. We visited the Blessed Sacrament rather hurriedly, as night was approaching and we did not relish the prospect of committing ourselves to the waves in the dark, especially in this open port, in a small boat that had to travel for five miles to bring us on board.

Mother Chiara, who finds this voyage very long, thought we had reached the Red Sea to open a mission in Africa; it is very strange indeed that the waters are a bright-red color—the color of blood, in fact—perhaps to remind us of the fierce battles between Chile and Peru in 1880, which caused so many casualties, especially among the Peruvians who were defeated, losing the richest part of their country. At the summit of the mountains, which run along the coast and form a kind of wall, the Peruvian soldiers took up their position, but were surrounded by the Chileans, who are noted for their strength both on land and sea. They were driven over the edge and then thrown, horses and men, into the sea, and to such a depth (in these parts it reaches several miles) that the Peruvians could not even recover their remains.

Iquique is lovely; its roads are broad and straight, and it has pretty houses, though they are not very tall, and well-kept shops, especially those of the Italians, who are quite numerous and who are very well-off and respected. There is, however, not a tree or a blade of grass to be found anywhere. Neither is there a well or a stream. Water for drinking and for domestic purposes has to be procured at the distance of a day's journey from the town, as do grains, flour, fruit, vegetables, wine, olives, sugar, coffee, and animal feed—almost everything has to be imported by sea from other countries, so you can imagine how much it costs to live in this city. Fortunately, it is inhabited by the rich, who pay the poor well, so that everyone lives comfortably. The air is good, but the people here do not live long, and they say that foreigners, unless they are exceptionally strong, deteriorate little by little here. Notwithstanding, the emissaries of the devil have penetrated here and have done grave harm. How is it that the emissaries of the devil have less fear than the followers of Christ? Let us reflect on this to humble ourselves, for often we think of health and dangers before we give ourselves over to our Divine Lord, the glory of God, and the salvation of souls.

Since we left Panama, we have had a Protestant minister on board, one of the worst types—an Irishman from the northeast of Ireland. This minister came from Chicago and is stopping at Iquique. You should have seen how he tried to ensnare first one and then another of the young men. He stayed with one of them until midnight preaching his errors. Fortunately, the young man made light of him and his statements, as did the others. When he saw that they were making fun of him, he began preaching freedom of conscience, but he only made matters worse for himself, and then, with his Bible in his hand, he tried to force his diabolical interpretations on his listeners. He ended up an object of ridicule, along with his wife. So far things were most consoling. He thought he was going to find those who would imbibe the doctrine he offered them, but instead, he met with excellent Spanish-Americans, who were well instructed in their religion. But at Iquique—where there is already wild liberty and libertinism among those who flock there for the great, important mines—I fear he will wreak havoc. The only hope lies in the strength of the bishop, who is studying every means to weaken the efforts of these proselytizers and repair the damage they do. See how dangerous these times are to our faith, to our august religion and to sound morals; for the emissaries of Satan, violent apostles of unrestrained liberty and freedom of speech, make use of all kinds of opportunities and snares and go not only into the towns, but even into remote villages to spread their errors and doctrines, which are, as you know, condemned by the Church. It seems as if all the diabolical powers of Hell have come together to direct their satanic efforts to combat and persecute the Church, her doctrines and her morals, her laws, her worship, her ministers, and all that she possesses of holiness and reverence. In the meantime, the weak, lukewarm, and incautious drink in the venomous errors, the fatal maxims that pervert the mind and corrupt the heart, miserably dragging innumerable souls to eternal perdition. One can do nothing but grieve over this terrible war that the demon never ceases to wage against our holy religion. One trembles at the frightful future that awaits the world if God does not provide a quick and efficacious remedy, which must be something out of the ordinary, as the evils that are now affecting the Church are extraordinary.

Continuing our journey, and passing several ports, we arrived at Antofagasta, an important port for the merchants of Sucre and Potosi. It was a lovely morning, and we were longing to receive Holy Communion in order to be able to overcome the dangers and force of the foaming waves, which at every stroke seemed about to capsize the boat. Antofagasta is a lovely city, which is being enhanced by the construction of beautiful houses and squares and pleasant walks. It has one Catholic church, which is really beautiful and which is an aid to devotion and recollection. On our arrival, one Mass was just ending, but another began immediately, as if providentially arranged for us. So we received Holy Communion and refreshed ourselves spiritually after the long fast we had been forced to make. When we had finished our devotions, we visited the parish priest, who is a very pious and zealous man. He was delighted to see us, hoping we would open a house there, but he was equally disappointed when he heard what our destination was. He learned all he could about our colleges, hoping that someday we might settle there. We made calls at Tocopilla, Cobija, Taltal, Caldera, Calligol, and also at Coquimbo, where we spent the day, and where we rejoiced at seeing a bit of green, after having sailed for so many days along the dry, arid coasts, where at night one could not enjoy the bracing sea air because it is ruined by the fog that rises from a land steeped in saltpeter. This fog falls in the form of very fine rain, and instead of being restorative, dries up every plant it encounters and shortens the lives of the people who live there. At Coquimbo we found that spring was well advanced, and from the neighboring city—La Serena, so famous in Chile—there arrived an abundance of lovely fruit: peaches, pears, figs, melons, and cucumbers, and everything one would expect not merely in spring but also in the summer and autumn. The grape, however, ripens only once a year, in the month of January, when it is full summer, while we in Lombardy are freezing like crows.

The following morning the dear steamer, *Mapocho*, arrived at last at Valparaíso, our destination. After passing through the length of that long desert, it is like entering the Vale of Heaven. It is a beautiful harbor, much like that of Genoa, favored by nature. It is really charming. It seems like a large city, but it appears larger than it is, for it is built on the slope of a hill, or, more precisely, on the foothills of the Cordillera. It is so steep that from the lower part of the town, which consists of a long row of cottages, you ascend by means of a funicular railway, which resembles an elevator, and looking out the windows, you discover you are hanging over a deep precipice. Mother Chiara closed her eyes, for it made her feel faint.

As soon as we got to Valparaíso itself, we went to Mr. E. Escobar, who is a very distinguished person and to whom we had been recommended, but there was great sorrow and grief in his family, for Mrs. E. Escobar was very ill and almost at the point of death. The relatives, who had come to help and console him, were ill also. Mr. Escobar, however, wanted to see us and to show his interest in us. He sent us to the excellent parish priest, Fr. Manero, who, in return, recommended us to the Ladies of the Sacred Heart, who have a very nice school here. These good ladies received us as if we were their Sisters and would not let us leave them. We had our luggage to see to, as well as arrangements for crossing the Cordillera. We then went to visit Mr. Severin, another friend to whom we had been recommended. He was very kind and very energetic. He took all our luggage and stored it in his own business premises, ready for dispatch to Buenos Aires at the proper time. As his family is in Santiago, he asked us to go there and visit them, as well as the city itself, which is really beautiful and deserves a visit. The Ladies of the Sacred Heart extended a similar invitation. They wrote to their house there to prepare a room for us. Four days later we boarded the train and rode along the charming coast, which resembles the western coast of Genoa. We passed through superb villages and entered the mountainous region at the foot of the Cordillera. After passing through the great plains, we reached Santiago. The journey lasted four days. We headed for the convent as if it were our own house, and were received with great cordiality. The next day we visited His Grace, Archbishop Casanova, who is held in great esteem by the whole republic.

He received us very kindly, thinking we had come to open a house, but when he learned that I was on my way to Buenos Aires, he assumed an authoritative tone and said I should rest there a few months after such a long voyage, and in the meantime visit the country and establish a foundation, to which I should return as soon as possible. Though his words were very pleasant to listen to, they were really like so many thorn pricks to my heart, as I saw that I was losing time in traveling when I had so much to do, and time seems to pass so quickly. But it is useless to worry about it, as the company of the Cordillera cannot provide us with passage anyway, as the mountain roads are closed to traffic because of the snow, which is about ten feet high, and the road will not be passable until November. We must have patience, for nothing happens by accident. Everything takes place according to the all-wise timetable of Divine Providence. God has His designs and wishes me, perhaps, to acquire a good knowledge of the Republic of Chile. In fact, both the Sisters and Mr. Severin are so good to us. Mrs. Severin takes us out for carriage drives almost every day, so we have the opportunity to get to know the country well. Santiago is very nice and interesting. It has wonderful churches, beautiful buildings, stupendous squares, and magnificent gardens, with enclosures for animals and fountains for fish, displaying plants representative of every climate and country.

The character of the Chileans is lively, open, strong, and energetic. They love progress to the point of excess. We showed them several of our syllabi to acquaint them with the kind of education we offer in our schools, and they tried their best to make us stay, promising to fill our school with children. One of them, a high-ranking government official, who has a child four years old, said, "You must come back in two years; if not, during the next war we have with the Argentines, we'll take you prisoner, and then make you open a school for us here, as I want to send my little girl to you."

I spent twenty-five long days here, feeling that I was wasting time. Finally, they informed us that the roads were open and that the first caravan was about to start. Both the Ladies and other good friends tried to detain us, saying that the first journey over the Andes is often dangerous, and that if we were to be overtaken by bad weather, we would be in danger of losing our lives in the mountain passes. But nothing could induce me to stay longer and continue that involuntary vacation. I felt I was ready to face any difficulty.

We first visited a chapel of Saint Philomena, the wonder-worker, so venerated here. We received Holy Communion at her altar, begging her to join Saint Rose in protecting us. We made our thanksgiving at the back of the church, near an altar on which a picture of the martyrdom of the saint is venerated. While I was absorbed in prayer to the saint, who inspired me with great confidence, telling her all my needs and necessities, a very gentle voice whispered in my ear, "Esta es una pequeña limosnita"—"This is only a small offering." I was so absorbed in placing my petition before the saint that I thought the words I heard were an illusion of my imagination, and so I made no movement. Again the soft voice repeated the same words. Then I raised my head, and looking round, I saw someone offering me gold pieces. It was the holy man Canon M. Marchian Pereira, guardian of the sanctuary, who kept on saying very humbly, "Es pequeña, es pequeña mas es S. Filomena que la da"—"It's small, it's small, but it's Saint Philomena who gives it"—and then he quickly withdrew. The gift was of the value of about a hundred lire, which the good man felt moved to give us without being asked, and I received it all the more gratefully, as the good saint had obviously begun to help us even before we had finished our petitions to her.

Having finished our thanksgiving, we went to thank the good canon, who said he was only too happy to help us, as we were missionaries. He presented us with books, pictures, and the cords of the saint, which her devotees wear around their waists. Then he gave me an image of the wonder-worker, asking me to keep it in my pocketbook. He himself placed it there, saying, "Keep it there, Mother, and you will never be in need of money for your Institute." I was very much impressed, as he seemed to be inspired. You may imagine that I shall treasure this picture as a precious relic.

On the 23rd of November, supplied with large baskets of pastry, fruit, wine, honey, etc. and accompanied by a number of ladies and Sisters, we took a train for Los Andes, a town at the foot of the Cordillera, where we were to pass the night, in order to be ready on the 24th after having observed the feast of the day, for the journey by caravan, which was to pick us up farther on.

At Los Andes we were received most kindly by Sisters called Hospitallers, to whom we had been recommended by the people of Santiago. They gave us the best room in their poor convent. The next morning, other Sisters of the same order, from another house in the neighborhood, came to bid us farewell and accompany us on the train as far as the Chileans have been able to go, up to the present, with their railways up these great mountains, which seem to want to overwhelm us more and more with their immense height and steepness the farther up we go.

We heard Holy Mass and received Jesus in the Most Holy Sacrament of the Altar, Who, like a mighty giant, was going to conduct us over these great heights. We had a good breakfast, which was more appetizing than usual on account of the pure air. We were favored with the blessing of the good parish priest of the town and accompanied by a larger company of the good Hospitaller Sisters, who came in great numbers. Then, at eleven A.M., we boarded the train along the river, which has its source in the Aconcagua. We passed through a chain of mountains in a pleasant and picturesque country, whose awe-inspiring scenes greatly delighted the passengers. We crossed a small bridge called the Soldier's Jump, which is feared by everyone. It spans a chasm between two rocks of gray stone so narrow and deep that the bottom cannot be seen. One only hears the strange rumbling of the rushing waters in the fearful depths below. Certainly, if anyone had the misfortune to fall into this abyss, he would never again behold the light of day, nor would the manner of his death be known. It did not make much of an impression on me, because I seemed to remember having seen many such horrifying chasms. However, I enjoyed the impression it made on these good Sisters, and how enthusiastically they spoke of it as they drew near to and passed over it, and how they pitied us because of the rest of the journey that awaited us. Shortly after we had passed the Soldier's Jump, the train stopped and we alighted to take our places in the coaches that were drawn up to convey the passengers. The good Sisters returned by train, after making us as comfortable as possible, while we followed the course of the same river with good mules—six to each coach—penetrating those vast gorges where only now and then a few pines of somber dark green appeared.

The river was swollen, and in several places its foaming waters, with their milky spray, made a terrifying noise. Further on it looked as if we were going to be covered by the mountain, as a part of it appeared to fall over the river. At some points the heights were magnificent, while behind the mountain the river descended as a steep waterfall. Then suddenly it narrowed into a small stream, the waters playing around large rocks and amid the enormous rocks deposited in the bed of the river. Then it widened again into thousands of capricious twists and turns, which we had to follow with great precision, as the river was our only guide along the route. Finally, after a journey of five or more hours, we reached Juncal, which consists of a few houses amid the mountain peaks. This was to be our grand lodging for the night.

Some passengers arrived earlier than we did, others later. There were about forty-five of us who were to undertake the journey in a caravan with mules through the most difficult pass of the Cordillera early the next morning. As soon as the coaches arrived, the passengers rushed off to go to bed for the night. We made our way also, but as the others were quicker, they arrived first and so were served first. Not knowing what to do, we went to the one who was to drive the caravan the next day, but we were cautious in our dealings with him, as he inspired us with very little confidence. At first he was somewhat rude, but finally, at our repeated requests, he softened toward us. He told us that on the other side of the mountain, where he pointed with his finger, there were other apartments, better than these, where he and his wife were going to stay, and that if we went there after supper, we would find everything all right.

Shortly afterward, an old shepherd with a kindly appearance, somewhat resembling Saint Joseph, said to me, "I am one of the muleteers appointed to act as guide tomorrow. I am also going to sleep on the other side of the mountain, so you don't have to worry." His kind manner and serious personality inspired us with confidence, and so we went to dinner with more courage and ate the coarse and badly cooked food and hard black bread as if it were the most dainty food, for the air of the village sharpened our appetites in a most extraordinary manner.

At dinner, all spoke of the next day's crossing: some of its great dangers, others of their fear of the mists that can be fatal to those who are crossing the pass. Stories were also told of the frost in some of the passes that freezes the limbs and of the atmosphere that hurts the eyes and causes the skin to bleed.

A delightful description, indeed! Still, amid all this discouragement, I felt safe and happy, for I knew if Our Lord had helped and blessed us so far, He would do so to the end. I also took comfort in the hope of finally having something new to tell you, since after four long voyages, everything appeared quite familiar to me. I felt sorry for Mother Chiara, who heard all this and who I thought might have changed her mind after her departure from Valparaíso. But when I asked her which way she preferred to travel, by land or sea—over the Andes or through the Strait of Magellan—she answered, "A thousand times over the Andes rather than by sea again." So I said to myself, "All is well."

When the meal was over, we took a little air in the bright moonlight, which shone very brilliantly. The mountains appeared to touch the sky and seemed covered with a beautiful blue mantle and raised us to a state of sublime ecstasy. The earth was the same color as the sky, while the mountain passes wore a blue of a darker shade, giving the impression of great clouds saluting their smiling queen. And really, that night the moon in all its splendor seemed to represent the beauty of our Queen, our Mother Mary, "pulchra ut Luna" ["fair as the moon" (Song 6:10)], who had come to console us with her maternal gaze. Those who work in the Lord's vineyard from morning until night are well rewarded if at the close of day, they receive a loving gaze from her who, after God, forms the happiness of the blessed in Heaven.

We wanted to prepare the points for the following day's meditation, but nature had already prepared them for us. Looking at the moon and sky, which seemed to envelop us, I thought I heard the sweet voice of Mary, along with the most melodious voice of our dear Jesus, transporting us into an ecstasy of love. I seemed to see the purity and holiness of Mary and God's delight in her. What a great sweetness, what a great joy in contemplating Mary, and seeing in her our beloved Jesus! But the night was advancing, and we needed to get some rest, though it did not seem like we would need sleep in this fine air. We abandoned ourselves to the care of our heavenly Mother and to her messengers, who are the angels especially appointed to pilgrims. Happy and tranquil, we set out for the shelter on the other side of the mountains.

When we got to a certain point, we lost our breath. A sort of weight pushed down on us, and we could not understand what it was. Then we saw the old shepherd who resembled Saint Joseph running toward us to tell us to hurry, as we had reached the *puna*, a Spanish word meaning lack of air or shortness of breath. We quickened our steps and soon reached a spot where the air was pure and breathable as before. It was indeed a strange phenomenon, this *puna* in the mountains, and if we had stopped there, we might have died of suffocation. But the silver moon still shone, telling us in its silent language that Mary, the Mother of God, was still watching and protecting us with incomparable tenderness.

When we reached the inn, we found what we had never expected to find in these rough mountains: a nice springy bed for each of us with good bedding, which the old man pointed out to us with much satisfaction and pleasure. He told us there was a key, and we could lock ourselves in by barring the door. He told us also not to be afraid, for he would be sleeping in the stable next to the mules' stables if we needed anything—an admirable instance of God's Providence, and we rested quite peacefully. But the night passed in a moment, and at three-thirty, the noise of the shepherds preparing the mules and packing the luggage awoke us suddenly. We felt more tired than the night before, as we had had very rough treatment during our five-hour coach drive. We mustered up courage, however, arose at four A.M., and dressed ourselves in long brown cloaks trimmed and lined with a kind of cheap fur, which had been given to us by some ladies of Chile. We looked like two monks, but we had begun to feel the cold, and these cloaks were of great service to us.

We descended to the first inn, where everyone was having breakfast, and we took our milk and coffee and hard bread as fast as we could, as everything was ready for the journey. We went out into the open and saw two beautiful mules, with new equipment and two comfortable saddles. We thought they were for an opera singer and her companion who were part of the group—but this time we were mistaken, for the nicest mules were for us: orders had been given by the superintendent of the Transandine Company that they should be assigned to us. However, although we were grateful for the favor, we were not so willing to accept it, because it meant that we would be the first to mount the mules, and since we were not experienced, we preferred to see the others do so first in order to learn the art; but we had to give in. The Saint Joseph of the previous evening came forward and bent down with fingers linked together so I could put my foot in his hands and mount the mule. When I refused, the whole company stood around to see what would happen next. The poor shepherd, so good and patient, went into the house and brought me a chair, which I willingly accepted. I then mounted, placing myself in the saddle and putting my feet in the stirrup, and taking the reins, I drew the mule round while the muleteer mounted his mule and moved forward to make way for me. Mother Chiara followed my example, accompanied by another muleteer, who might not have resembled my Saint Joseph but was also very good. All the others mounted their mules with much less trouble and followed us in procession.

The mountain was steep, but the pass was lovely and smooth for more than an hour. It was almost a pleasure to see the long procession that appeared to be climbing with a certain devotion, as the caravan looked like a devout band of pilgrims—so it seemed to me. Taking my beads in my hand, I was about to invite everyone to recite the Rosary in honor of the Queen of Heaven, who had obtained for us such a beautiful day, and everyone would certainly have willingly accepted my invitation, as they seemed quite pleased to have two religious in their group. In their goodness and faith, they were undertaking the dangerous journey cheerfully on account of our presence. My Rosary plan faded away quickly, though, for soon the beaten path had disappeared and we had to forge our own path through heavy snow. Two muleteers went ahead of us, and when they found it passable, they shouted for us to follow their tracks. As soon as we got past one mountain, another appeared. Often, we found ourselves on the brink of precipices several kilometers deep. I tried to keep my mule away from the edge, but the poor thing, knowing that it had an unpracticed traveler in its saddle, kept going straight, no matter how much I pulled it from one side to the other; it would not obey me. When it came too near the edge of a precipice, I shouted and spoke to it in Spanish, but to no effect. The only thing that seemed to bother it was when I attempted to alight.

These terrible precipices almost turned Mother Chiara's head, and no matter how often I told her to sit straight, she lay like a sack of flour on the mule's back, her head resting on the poor animal's neck. Fortunately, the muleteers were better than good, and as in such difficulties one has enough to do to take care of oneself, I could be at ease, knowing she was well cared for.

We were gradually ascending higher and higher, when from afar we heard the shout for all to dismount. What was it? A great chasm caused by the melting snow was blocking the way, and we needed to proceed with great caution. There was general alarm; the men grumbled about the imprudence of leading the caravan along this route, and the women cried quite hopelessly. Mother Chiara remained in deep silence; she had lost her ability to speak. She was certainly now repenting of having chosen the Cordillera instead of the Strait of Magellan for our journey. Her only consolation was that when she raised her head, I looked quiet and happy, as one enjoying a magnificent spectacle. It was truly grand in all its horror. We were at a height. On one side was an immense abyss, and on the other a vast expanse of pure white snow, spread out like a broad and immaculate mantle, while further ahead there were heights awaiting us. But just in front of us was that large crevice, long and deep, that seemed ready to swallow us up and bury us. The muleteers, though not without fear, tried to make some of the mules jump over the crevice, and when they saw that it could be done, they encouraged the passengers to do the same. As I told you, I was at the head of the line, and I was willing to be the first to go forward in order to encourage the others, for honestly, I was not a bit afraid; I was feeling quite calm. My guide had his staff ready, as he thought he would have to carry me across, but I told him I could take longer jumps than the one across the crevice. He showed me the danger very respectfully and then watched me attentively, because he knew by experience that I wouldn't be able to make it on my own. I jumped, expecting it to be easy, but realized too late that, probably on account of the cold and the thin air that sapped my strength, I was like a feather that, however hard it is thrown, will not move unless borne along by the wind. I would have buried myself alive if not for the muleteer, who, like a true St. Joseph, saw the danger, dismounted, stretched his feet across the crevice, and pushed me onto the other bank. Then, with the help of his companion, he jumped to the other side and drew me by the arm after him to safety. The shock made my heart beat so hard that I thought I was going to die. The good muleteer took me aside, and I fell fainting in the snow. I couldn't speak a word, and it was obvious from the frightened looks of the good man that he expected a catastrophe. But this was not God's will. As soon as I was able to speak, I told him to go and help the others; I didn't have to tell him twice, as the need was urgent. I remained alone, stretched on that white bed of snow, and little by little, helped by the pure air, the palpitations ceased, and I was as lively as ever. I arose to find that everyone had crossed the dangerous pass and that the muleteer was waiting for me to mount my mule again.

We resumed our journey and arrived at a higher point, where we had to pass between snowbanks fifteen feet high, which had been cut through by the Transandine Company for the caravan. It was a grand sight to pass through the fortress of snow, but not quite so pleasant for me, for I was afraid of not being able to bear the cold. They told me to keep my goggles on so that the cold and great whiteness of the snow would not injure my sight, but I preferred to see clearly where my mule was going, not trusting my goggles, which I did not find very helpful. Pulling the elastic, I put them sometimes on my forehead, sometimes on my chin, but not over my eyes, except when we stopped and there was no need to keep a close watch. In God's good time we reached the Cumbre, which is the topmost height that can be crossed in the neighborhood of Aconcagua, and here we remained some time.

What a majestic sight, what a charming view! We seemed to see the whole world at a glance. There we saw the boundary line between Chile and Argentina. We had said goodbye to that dear country that had hosted us for a month, and which, although it was unfamiliar to us, had treated us with generosity and exquisite kindness. We wanted to enjoy the sea view, but the fog was descending, and so we were deprived of that enchanting sight. The muleteer made signs to me to mount the mule at once, but I begged him to let me enjoy this sublime and inspired moment of meditation. A little perturbed, he turned and begged me to get into the saddle. The poor man had every reason, for it was past eleven, and within half an hour's time the weather would have proved fatal to us.

About this time, from the other side of the top of the mountain, one of those good employees of the Transandine

Company arrived upon the scene, and after greeting us courteously told us that he had orders from Santiago to come and meet us and to make our journey a little easier if he could. He took my reins and led my mule down the steep mountain by the shortest paths. The descent was steep and stony, and I thought I would fall at every moment. The mule would slip now and then, but this good man encouraged me and told me we had to stay on this path in order to get to a comfortable hotel as soon as possible. We reached it at midday, when the snow was falling heavily and the mountain had entirely disappeared in a thick fog.

The landlady of the hotel received us with a motherly heart and brought us to a table, where lunch was already prepared. We enjoyed it, as it warmed us up after the cold we had experienced. When lunch was over, they called the heads of the different families one by one to write their impressions in a large register kept for that purpose. Our traveling companions had been very upset when they had to cross the crevice, so you can imagine what they wrote. I, however, wrote one of my most beautiful reflections on that passage. Everyone was surprised by what I wrote, and the innkeeper said I was the first person, especially at this dangerous time of the year, to speak positively of this crossing; he was all the more amazed because the writer was not a man. The fact is that I was very pleased and happy to have climbed so high in my life, as an additional motivation to urge myself to ascend to the heights of holy perfection, a mountain much higher than the Cordillera.

Not without reason does the Celestial Divine Spouse call His beloved by the sweet name of Dove: "My dove, my perfect one, is only one" [Song 6:9]. He calls her Dove not only because she should be gentle, meek, and mild, but because she has to fly to the heights of the Lord without tiring, rising continually toward Heaven with perfect detachment from earth, raising herself on silvery-white wings by the purity of her affections and intentions.

About two P.M. the coaches were ready to bring us to the station, Punta de Vacas. We set off up the hills and down the valleys. We traveled along the Mendoza River, by way of a path that was rough and dangerous because of the rocks that seemed ready to fall on us at every instant and because of the breaks of the great river, which looked so deep from above, with such a risk of falling into it.

At seven P.M. we arrived at Punta de Vacas, where we expected to rest quietly, after the shaking of the mule ride and the coaches, but an hour before we arrived, the caravan from Argentina, which the next day was going to cross the Andes, had reached Punta de Vacas and had taken all the accommodations. What were we to do? The bell rang for supper, and we took our places at the table with our luggage beside us on the floor, not knowing where to stow it safely. When the frugal meal was over, I asked the innkeeper to give us a place to rest if possible. He told us very courteously that he had not received any orders regarding us, but that we should not be alarmed, because he would be able to provide us with beds very soon. In the meantime, night was advancing, and the only room in the inn was full of men drinking. At nine P.M. I again begged the innkeeper to give us a room, and he said he would do so immediately. Half an hour later he told me all the beds were taken except one in the hall, which of course I did not accept. So I went back and sat down at the table in the corner of the room with Mother Chiara.

It was now ten P.M., and the men went on drinking; the alcohol was producing its effects, and we heard a lot of commotion, shouting, and singing. I began to feel uneasy; but looking around, I saw an American gentleman from San Francisco who had crossed the Andes with us and, like us, had been unable to get a bed. I asked him to stay close to us, as I was afraid of those men. He was the only one in that whole crowd who inspired me with any confidence. He felt so sorry for us that he talked the innkeeper into giving us a room in which there were two good ladies and a boy, but the boy withdrew to make room for us. We called down hearty blessings on that good man, and fell into our beds exhausted and motionless till the morning. At seven A.M. we were at the station and got on the train. Still traveling along the Mendoza River, we crossed new mountains and valleys, and in the afternoon reached Mendoza, the first and nicest city on the way from Chile.

We were received by the Good Shepherd Sisters, and it was a great relief for us to find a safe religious home after such a journey and nights of fear and danger. We visited the lovely churches of this city and then went to the Jesuits, who encouraged us greatly in our mission to Buenos Aires by the news they gave us. They told us we would have enough work to do there. We visited the Franciscans, who blessed us as Sisters of the Third Order of Saint Francis. Our next visit was to the Slaves of the Sacred Heart of Jesus, a newly founded institute in Córdoba. The Sisters received us with great kindness, and they would have kept us for a few days if we had not already arranged our journey with the Argentine railway company. We were to leave the next night, when we would be crossing the Pampas at great speed for two days, and with very few stops.

The Pampas are beautiful! It is an immense plain, where only now and then one sees a peasant's hut, lost, as it were, in the immensity of the expanse. We saw horses and mules in great numbers, flocks of sheep and goats at pasture in all directions, without a shepherd, in that never-ending country, whose boundaries the owner does not know and does not care to know. Now and then we could see skeletons of animals and unburied carcasses, left there abandoned. But the train flew on without minding anything in the midst of the long thick grass of the virgin prairies, and on December 1 we arrived at the capital of Argentina. Now I must stop, with the promise to write as soon as I have finished my work on this foundation, when I shall return to you and then go elsewhere, as obedience ordains.

Let us, in the meantime, live abandoned to the will of God. I shall work in His vineyard, you helping me with your prayers, in which I place my trust. Prayer, confidence, and total abandonment to God will always be our sure weapons! We are good for nothing, but in God we can do all things. "Omnia possum in Eo qui me confortat" ["I can do all things in him who strengthens me" (Phil 4:13)].

May God bless you and enclose you in His adorable Heart, wherein the throne of peace resides, an anticipated Heaven. Love Jesus greatly, and think of nothing else. Work with great zeal for the glory of God, under the banner of holy obedience. Do not seek rest on this earth, but be ready to die on the battlefield in the company of Jesus, with the assurance that the more you fight, the greater will be your crown, a crown that in eternity no one can take away.

Such is the wish of
Yours affectionately in the Sacred Heart of Jesus,
M. FRANCESCA SAVERIO CABRINI

August 1901, Voyage from Buenos Aires to Genoa

Mother Cabrini clearly enjoys seeing the (mostly Catholic) sights and cultures during her journey from South America to Europe, which she describes in this letter.

A.M.G.SS.C.J.
My Dear Daughters,

We embarked on the 22nd of August, but I have not begun to write until today, the 28th, when we have just left the port of Santos. The day I left Buenos Aires I was not feeling well, and your farewell and that of the children had really overcome me, and I remained in this exhausted state for a good while. Having said goodbye to the three Sisters who were at the farthest end of the bay, I went to my cabin and to bed. My bones were stiff with pain, and I didn't have the strength to move the smallest object. I wanted to put my cabin in order, but I had to leave it as it was, for I could not stand up. Two days later I felt better, well enough to go ashore at Santos, though it was raining. I asked the way to the church, and those whom I questioned wanted to know if I was looking for the *igreja*. I was afraid of being directed to some schismatic church, so I said "No", and went on walking. When I asked others, I got the same answer, so at last I understood that the word meant a Catholic church. Some people accompanied us to the parish church, which they call the Mother Church.

When we arrived at the church, we found Solemn High Mass just beginning, accompanied by drums and trumpets, which took the place of an organ or harmonium, neither of which the church possessed. In the meantime we asked a priest to give us Holy Communion at the Altar of the Blessed Sacrament, and thus comforted by the Food of Angels, we returned to the steamer, sure of a happy and prosperous voyage. It was raining, and we got quite wet. Had it not been for our wish to receive Holy Communion, we would not have gone ashore at all. We had two umbrellas, but when we reached the church, my companion's would not close, so we left it open and no one took the least notice. One good man turned to me and said, "It is our curate who is celebrating Mass; he is very good and we love him very much." He spoke to me in Portuguese, and I understood him fairly well, as it is a language that, one might say, is halfway between Italian and Spanish. I could do nothing else but congratulate him. When we had finished our devotions, we went to the sacristy to ask the curate's blessing. He received us with singular kindness. He wanted to entertain us longer, but we had no time, so we said goodbye and left with his blessing, which seemed like that of a patriarch. I wanted to visit the town, but there was no carriage to be had, so we returned at once to the ship.

The steamer then departed, and in two hours' time we reached Rio de Janeiro. It was about two P.M., and I would have loved to visit the town, but the steamer was anchored a great distance from the land. Also, the sea, as usual in this place, was very rough, so I thought it would be better not to undertake the double journey there and back. However, I did not want to miss the opportunity to receive Holy Communion the next morning. The captain had told me they would remain in port until the following day at two P.M., so the next morning we went ashore as soon as possible. They had offered me the ship's boat, but I would have had to wait until eight A.M. So I decided to hire a boat, trusting to the Providence of God to carry me safely through the agitated waves and over a distance that took half an hour to cross. In the end, we reached land quite safely, and headed toward the first steeple we saw. We lost sight of it, however, as we passed through the narrow streets and between the houses. So we asked for the *igreja*, having learned the word at Santos, and everyone pointed out the way with great kindness.

We entered the first church we saw; it was called the Candelaria. It is beautiful, rich, and kept very clean. The altars are of very fine colored marble. On the high altar there is a splendid statue of Our Lady with the Infant Jesus. This Madonna is called Our Lady of the Candelaria or the Purification. I took pleasure in counting the candlesticks on the high altar, which were grand and in the form of a pyramid, placed at the feet of Our Lady. There were fifty-two of them. Perhaps the number had some meaning, but not speaking the language, I was unable to ask why the candlesticks should be fifty-two in number. As soon as we entered the church, we went to the altar of the Blessed Sacrament, which was along the nave of the church, next to the high altar. Above it hung a majestic, monumental crucifix, under which was a painting of Calvary. Several canons were reciting the Office, and two altar boys were seated near the canons. I called one to tell them that I wanted to receive Holy Communion. He spoke to one of the canons, who answered that the Office would last two hours, during which no one could receive Holy Communion. I could not wait, so I asked the boy to show me the way to another church, which he did very willingly. Saluting the Blessed Sacrament, I was just on the point of leaving when I met a priest and told him I would like to receive Holy Communion, but that I could not wait for two hours, and would he please show me the way to another church? "No, no," he said, "stay here. I am going to say Mass, at which you can receive Holy Communion." In fact, as quickly as he could, he came and celebrated Mass at the second altar of the church, which was dedicated to Our Lady of the Sacred Heart and was very beautiful. As the large and rich pews we had used before did not extend this far, the sacristan came forward with two lovely cushions for us to kneel upon. I was astonished at so much kindness, but it was in keeping with the dignity of the whole place that great courtesy should be shown to visitors. Having made our thanksgiving and had a look around the church, we left, and as my companion and I were now very hungry, I looked for a cafe where we could get refreshments, and then, taking a cab, we visited the town, which is partly built on hills. We went to the part called Saint Anna, as they told us the papal legate resided here, but we met a priest who told us the legate was in Petrópolis. We didn't want to waste time, so we went down, and halfway down the hill, we met the vicar general, who asked right away if we had seen the bishop. "No," I said, "for I did not know he lived here, and I have no time to go back." I gave him my calling card to present to the bishop. He took it very kindly, saying he would present it to the bishop, and that he would ask for a special blessing for the successful continuation of my voyage. I was very sorry that I could not go back, but there was no time. From this grand hill you can see the whole town and the bay. I would have loved to go to Petrópolis, but it was three hours away by rail, so there was no possibility of my going.

Rio de Janeiro is really beautiful! I like its cheerful hills, spacious squares, and pretty gardens. I shall say nothing of the churches, as you have an idea after my description of the Candelaria. The canal that enters the bay of Rio de Janeiro is charming. What beautiful cone-shaped mountains! One of these is called the Sugarloaf because of its shape. These and others formed in such a way that they seem to rain abundance on the country. At Santos you get the same impression, though Santos is not as favored by nature. It is simply a road to São Paulo, a city everyone praises for its beauty. Brazil is certainly richer than Argentina. They say it is not healthy, but I think that only applies to the lower marshy parts of the town, and the rest of it, if it was cleaned up and put in order, would not suffer from contagious diseases. There are some very narrow and dirty streets in Rio de Janeiro, and the water that runs in the gutters is not as clean as the water in the beautiful streets of Paris; it is only good for spreading disease, because it looks like nothing less than guano.

At Buenos Aires the superintendent of the Veloce Company had given us two lovely cabins, one for the Sisters and one for myself, opposite each other and in the best possible location: on the west side of the steamer, where, because of the direction we are traveling in, one never feels the contrary winds. We could always keep our portholes open and always have fresh air. At Santos a large number of new passengers came on board. The steamer was quite full, and there was no more room, but some recommended by the superintendent and others by influential persons managed to get on board, and thus passengers in excess of the proper number were accepted. I was a bit concerned, but our tickets were marked "reserved cabins", so I stayed calm. The day was almost over when I saw the doctor coming toward me. He made a request on behalf of the commander. He said I had every right to refuse the favor he was about to ask, but as it was a very special case, he wanted to know if I would allow a Venetian lady, the wife of a pharmacist of São Paulo, to sleep in the same cabin with the Sisters; she was traveling alone for family reasons, and her husband had asked as a favor that she might be placed near the Sisters. He made the request so courteously that it was impossible to refuse him, and so I consented. And I am not sorry that I did, for the lady is very good, so courteous and refined that her company is a pleasure. One would think she was part of the community—everyone admires her and respects her.

After we left Rio de Janeiro, the sea was very rough, or *bravo*, as the Spaniards say; that is to say, so agitated that one would think it was really angry. At night, especially, it frightened me, as it was the first time I had ever made such a long voyage on such a small steamer as the *Piemonte*. When we left Buenos Aires, we couldn't stop praising it, as it did not make the slightest movement, but ever since it took on board a cargo of twenty thousand sacks of coffee at Santos, it has not given us a moment's peace. It may have been the wind or the cargo, but the fact remains that since that day, the rocking has never ceased, and so momentous was it that one expected the steamer to capsize at any moment. Not being an experienced sailor, I thought my fear was justified, but the next day I asked the captain about it, and all my fear went away. There might be other disasters, he said, but not the capsizing of the boat. The captain said the worst disaster of all was fire, but, he added, even in the case of fire, there were many ways of saving oneself; the boat was built in such a way that it could be separated into three separate parts if such a danger arose.

February 1906, Travels in the American West

Mother Cabrini addresses this letter to Sisters who were studying at the order's teachers college in Rome. She weaves together scenic details of the American West with encouraging words about what it means to be a missionary Sister to inspire her teachers-in-training.

A.M.G.SS.C.J.
February 1906, Chicago
My Dear Daughters,

I was very pleased to receive your letters and wishes for a merry Christmas, though I had hoped that this year, at least, I would be in the Eternal City to spend the holy feast with you, and so be able to reciprocate your happy wishes in person; instead, I must now convey them to you, a hundredfold, in writing. I confess that such noble and kind expressions of feelings on your part have given me great consolation in the deep regret I feel at finding myself still so far from Rome. Duty alone, which the missionary must always put before pleasure, has kept me away from Italy so long, but believe me, as soon as the little business that is detaining me now is finished, I shall not delay my departure a single day.

How many times have I thought I was almost at the end of my current mission in the United States, when I found new work to do, work that I could not have neglected without neglecting the holy interests of the glory of God and the salvation of souls? But now I am in a position to assure you that in a few weeks I shall be with you to rejoice in your virtues, in your progress, and in your loving company.

I wrote to you from the summit of the Rocky Mountains, promising to tell you something about my journey to California, and I do not think you would be disposed to forgive me if I forgot my promise. So I am stealing a little time here and there from my religious work and from business to converse with you.

I think I wrote to you of my work in Denver for the expansion of our orphanage in that city for the daughters of our emigrants. Suffice it to say that with the help of the Sacred Heart, always ready to favor us, I have been able to acquire a beautiful property at the foot of the Rocky Mountains, standing upon a pleasant hill that slopes gently down to the banks of Rocky Mountain Lake. The house, to which we are adding a wing because it is already too small for the thirty orphans we have taken in this first year, is surrounded by trees laden with fruit and is enhanced by clear waters of the lake. To the west stretches the imposing

Rocky Mountain range with its snow-covered peaks; to the east is the beautiful city of Denver. To the south and north are great plains, three-fourths of which are the territory of Colorado.

Meanwhile, as I was sitting in a comfortable carriage of the Santa Fe railway on the way to Los Angeles, my eyes swept over those immense plains, which are scattered with the cottages of our Italian farmers around Denver, but which are uninhabited farther away; there are still immense tracts of virgin soil. My thoughts flew to our emigrants, who land on the Atlantic shores every year in such great numbers, increasing the overcrowding of the already-populous cities of the East, where they encounter great difficulties and little gain. In the West there is still room for millions and millions, and its most fertile soil would offer occupation better suited to them, as well as a field in which to develop their activities and their agrarian knowledge, and to crown their efforts and labors with abundant fruits.

This flood of population must have its course intelligently directed. I know that the Immigration Commission is working on this problem, which is so important for the welfare of our emigrants in the United States. Finding a solution, however, presents great difficulty, not only because of the four thousand miles that separate the Atlantic from the Pacific, but more especially because it is difficult to find good-hearted persons who will occupy themselves with the work and will not exploit the sacred interests of the poor.

Poor emigrants! They are so often exploited by those who pretend to be their protectors. This deception is all the more cruel, because these so-called protectors know well how to cloak their private interests in the mantle of charity and patriotism.

During my journey I saw these dear countrymen of ours engaged in the construction of railways in the most intricate mountain gorges, miles and miles away from any settlement. They are separated for years from their families, far from the Church, deprived of the holy joys that in our own country even the poor peasant has at least on Sundays. In Italy the peasant is able to put down his hoe and put on his best clothes and devote the morning to divine service and hear the words of the priest, who reminds him of the nobility of his origin and of his destiny, and of the value of work consecrated to God. He then has the rest of the day to devote to his family and to honest amusements, and is thus able to resume his work the next morning with a refreshed mind.

Here the hardest labor is reserved for the Italian worker. There are few who look upon him sympathetically, who care for him or remember that he has a heart and soul: they look upon him as merely an ingenious machine for work. It is true that the Italian is respected here because he is sober, honest, faithful, and industrious, but he gives up so much real joy by leaving his native country for foreign lands, without anyone to guide him on the road to true happiness, which does not consist in hoarding heaps of money—money that, due to misfortunes, often cannot even be enjoyed. How much better a little plot of land in his native country would be for him. What great social and philanthropic work could be accomplished by anyone who knew how turn the work of these hands, which is all wasted on foreign countries, to the benefit of our own lovely land. I do not mean to deny that there are advantages in these immense fertile virgin lands. They certainly offer the emigrants work and a comfortable life, but I trust that some really generous souls will arise who will take the interests of the poor to heart, and guide them well and conscientiously when they land on these shores.

I can assure you now that in my journey through our missions, the evidence of the good that our institutions are doing for the emigrants is of the greatest comfort to me. What we, as women, are not allowed to do on a large scale, such as helping solve important social problems, we are doing in our little sphere in every state and in every city where we have opened houses. These houses shelter orphans, the sick, and the poor, and such charitable institutions make it easy for the Sisters of a colony to come into contact with a great number of people, which allows them to do an immense amount of good. Relations between the Sisters and the people they serve are very cordial. The poor people call them "Mother" and "Sister", and they feel the meaning of these words: they know that there are truly maternal hearts that go with these titles. They know that the hearts of the Sisters beat in unison with theirs, and that the Sisters have put aside all thoughts of themselves and made the troubles, interests, and joys of the people they serve their own. All this, however, is not by our own merit; it is the fruit of the love of Christ and of the prodigious fertility of our holy religion, the true friend of the people, the light that guides them in the darkness, the house of refuge, tower of strength, and port of safety.

While I am conversing with you, we have reached Colorado Springs, that aristocratic city of Colorado that rises in the shadow of Pikes Peak, one of the highest summits of these mountains. The weak and consumptive are attracted here by the mildness of the climate, the healthfulness of the surrounding mountains, and the myriad mineral waters that spring up everywhere, fresh, foaming, and sparkling. The Indians were astonished at such an abundance of mineral waters and thought their god Manitou—an Indian word that means "Great Spirit"—lived in these mountains, especially in the one called the Garden of the Gods. On my return I will show you a picture of this natural park, several hundred acres large, in which brightly colored rocks are scattered by the thousands and sculpted by nature into the strangest shapes, now imposing, now grotesque, sometimes austere, sometimes frivolous, presenting the strangest appearances. Not far from here, General Palmer, one of our good benefactors, possesses a private "Garden of the Gods", a real jewel of art—both as regards the palace he has built and the natural beauty of the rocks, which form very high peaks, reflecting the most varied colors. Among the rocks can still be seen the nest of an eagle, which lived here as queen of the mountains for years. But a short time ago its young eaglet was killed, and since that day the noble bird has deserted her nest, naturally to the great regret of the general, who had taken great pride in it.

Leaving Colorado Springs, we reach Trinidad in a few hours. This is an important mining area, especially for coal, where a great number of Italians are employed. Our Sisters visit them regularly, and to these poor people, such a visit is like a ray of sun in the darkness of the bowels of the earth. They speak to them of their daughters, who are under their charge, and of their families, whom they have visited. They remind them of their religious duties, comfort them in the sadness of their miserable conditions, and always leave them happier, or at least more resigned to their poverty. The fatigue of the Sisters in climbing up the steepest mountains is rewarded by the smiles that light up the faces of these poor people on hearing their mother tongue resounding in these dark vaults. Poor miners! Do you want to know what their life is like? Those who work the day shift enter the mines at six o'clock and remain buried there until midday. They come out at twelve o'clock for a short meal and go in again at twelve-thirty and don't leave until five o'clock. They spend half an hour washing themselves and preparing for supper. When they have finished this meal, they throw themselves exhausted on their little beds, to rise again the following morning at the sound of the whistle that calls them to work. On Sundays they smoke and sleep. This is the life they lead, far away from their families and separated from the company of men. They continue without interruption year in and year out, until old age and disability creep over them, or at least until a landslide or explosion or accident of some kind ends the life of the poor worker, who does not even need a grave, being buried in the one in which he has lived all his life.

Oh, if only the voice of religion could reach all these poor people and teach them to sanctify and ennoble such labor, and to render it fruitful for eternity! Thus you see the tremendous responsibility that rests on those who take away the gift of faith from the working classes, for in doing so, they rob them of every hope of the life to come, banishing the love of God from their hearts. Take away the supernatural principles and commands of our holy faith, and what remains but wickedness and the indulgence of every passion? Pray, my good daughters, that the number of missionary workers may be increased, and that they may be truly zealous and goodhearted, because the efforts of such missionaries are capable of stemming materialism and unbelief, which, like a poisonous gas, leak in everywhere, causing immense and irreparable damage.

Pray that all the docile faithful may listen to the voice of the vicar of Jesus Christ, Pope Pius X, who is conscious of these great evils that threaten to shake the foundations of society and proposes to restore everything in Christ. Strengthened by the power of God and assisted by the Holy Spirit, he will not fail to fulfill in the Church the high mission for which God has chosen him; but at the same time, what fatigue he must suffer, what cares, what troubles must torment his heart and preoccupy his mind in such an arduous task. At least let him be comforted by the love and obedience of his children, and let him find in each and every one that co-operation that we are bound by duty to give to him. This co-operation will make the fulfillment of the holy aims of the Pope possible and halt this flood of evil that threatens to inundate the world.

Having left the large manufacturing city of Trinidad, the train enters the heart of the mountain district. As the locomotive struggles to climb, we are able to admire the beauty of the landscape. Every minute the view changes. We behold austere mountains whose peaks are white with pristine snow, hills quite green with pine trees and reddened by the colors of the rock and soil, sharp peaks that seem to touch the sky and on which the eagle alone may rest, plateaus where the hardy goat back from his mountain excursions comes to graze upon the green grass in which they are so rich, and where the slow ox and the proud buffalo graze together quite unconscious of the howl of the white bear resounding in the nearby ravines. Here and there silver streams descend among the rocks and soon become threatening torrents that in rapids and waterfalls, follow their beds of many-colored rocks. No region could deserve the name Colorado more than this enchanting country, these most beautiful natural parks, enriched by nature with a beauty upon which the hand of man could never improve.

In truth, here one exclaims spontaneously: How wonderful is God in His works! But, meanwhile, we have begun to descend the western slope, and turning with a rapid run toward the Pacific, have crossed the border of New Mexico. This country is most interesting. Here the Indians still live in their pueblos, little villages constructed like fortresses on steep and almost inaccessible mountains. It may, indeed, be said that the rock itself forms three sides of the house. The front is hermetically sealed, with neither door nor window, so that one can descend into their little houses only by means of a ladder and an opening in the roof. The Indians of New Mexico seem to be temperate, frugal, industrious, and agricultural, unlike other tribes who are less domestic and primarily hunters. To protect their provisions and the fruits of their labor from their neighbors' greed, their pueblos are built like regular fortresses. From the train, I saw these poor Indians sitting before their huts, in their picturesque clothing, either making small baskets, which they are very good at, or curiously watching this great agent of civilization and commerce pass by—the train—which, however, has not managed to disrupt the primitive simplicity of this people.

When I arrived in Albuquerque, the metropolis of the valley of the Rio Grande, I was able to get closer to them, as they were lined up in double rows under the arches of the station, offering to travelers the products of their industry. Some were selling terracotta pots, daisy arrangements, and ingeniously woven baskets, while others contented themselves with offering pomegranates, topazes of various colors, and other little stones found in the Mexican deserts. The interior of the station contains a beautiful collection of Indian art, and the most skilled of the Indian people weave the famous Navajo blankets.

The Indian races are very numerous and varied. Some of them have a high forehead and aquiline nose, with a proud intelligence shining in their faces, and a close look reveals the hardiness of their race, not to mention their nobility and kindness of heart.... The women [of other tribes] seem very fond of painting their faces in various colors in a way that resembles tattooing.

Their dress is greatly varied, and I will not attempt to describe it, because the illustration I am bringing back with me will give you a better idea of their clothing than my own description could.

Just as I got off the train, some Mexicans and a few Indians crowded around us, delighted to see the Sisters. The Indians were more timid than the others and came forward gradually, offering me their crafts. They were attracted by my shining cross and asked to be allowed to kiss it. While satisfying this innocent desire of theirs, I thought, "How many among these people do not yet know God, and are immersed in the darkest idolatry, superstition, and ignorance, without anyone to help them a little bit, and all for want of missionary workers!" Oh, how the heart of the missionary suffers when she is burning with zeal for the glory of God and the salvation of souls, but is paralyzed by her inability to go everywhere the interests of God call her! These poor souls, in the meantime, fix their eyes curiously on us, and seem to say in their silent language, "Why do you not come and bring the light of your faith to us?" Oh, generous and Christian souls! Why do you not listen to the call of these distant brothers of yours? You do not lack courage, energy, intelligence, or heart. Why do you leave so many beautiful gifts with which the Lord has endowed you hidden and buried, and not employ them for the benefit of those who do not know the true God? Why do you not reflect that these talents of yours, put in the service of the Lord, will produce immense merit on earth and glory in Heaven? Thus spoke the poor Indians of Albuquerque to my heart. These Indians represent to me the numerous and scattered tribes of the West of the United States, and a deep feeling of regret makes my heart bleed at not being able, through lack of assistants, to remain among them at this time and to apply myself to their spiritual and intellectual education. The Missionary Sisters of the Sacred Heart who work day and night in the United States already number more than four hundred, but they are like one stalk of wheat in a boundless field. Oh, may the Sacred Heart grant that for His greater glory and for the salvation of souls redeemed by Him, many generous souls may come forward and enroll themselves in our ranks under the banner of the Sacred Heart! There is room for everybody, for every activity, for every talent, and for every inclination. She who consecrates herself to Jesus as a missionary Sister and is willing to carry His name to the utmost ends of the earth, sacrificing everything she loves and even life itself, is a true heroine in whose heart the flame of love burns brightly. She does not stifle her own heart or put the shining light of intelligence God has given her under a bushel. On the contrary, the flame kindled in her heart becomes a regular volcano of love that embraces everything. That gleam of light becomes a brilliant torch, causing darkness to disappear and wandering souls to find their way. Happy the one who arrives at the tribunal of God followed by a great number of souls saved through her. The voice of God calls many, but not all heed it. For this reason we very often have the sorrow of seeing a great harvest lost for want of workers.

You, my good daughters, in your great mission of education, are the first collaborators in the missionary works of the Sacred Heart, and for this reason you are especially dear to my heart in the great family that Jesus has given me. I have great hope in you. It is not only your native country and religion that have great hope in you, but the whole world. To be a missionary, it is no longer necessary to travel all over the world. Modern transportation and emigration allow people to travel from one country to another as easily as going from their house to their backyard. Every year we see thousands and thousands of our countrymen landing here. We see them in constant contact with heretical, uncivilized, and idolatrous people. If we raise every child who is entrusted to us in our schools in the fear of

God, and if we train these little minds, we educate their hearts and instill in these children the principles of religion and honesty so that they will grow up to be good Christian citizens. Also, is it not likely that these pupils of ours may in turn become teachers themselves, and effective ones at that, because teaching in a familiar way, and by example, is more effective than sterile and abstract instruction? The teacher who educates her pupils in the way I have indicated sows the mustard seed abundantly. This seed, according to the words of our divine Master Himself, will grow to a great height, and the missionary will never know in this life how much fruit it bears for eternity. My good daughters! May your school be a school of not only literature, science, mathematics, and history, but also virtue—solid Christian morality; then you will have rendered a great service not only to religion but also to your country. Moreover, you will greatly contribute to making our country honored and respected by all other nations.

Now we have left New Mexico and have entered Arizona, or, more accurately, the desert. The deserts of Arizona are not at all what you would imagine from their name; they are neither monotonous nor without life. They are vast territories intersected by mountain chains, deep canyons, extinct volcanoes, and various colored peaks and mountains of different imposing shapes, so varied that with a bit of imagination they seem at one moment like castles with turrets and defensive towers, while at other times they look like colossal monuments adorned with an infinite number of columns and marvelous sculptures. The sands of the desert have already proved to be fertile soil for whatever the cultivator may desire to produce, i.e., if he has the courage to dig wells in dry sands and sow vegetables and plant fruit trees. The great heat of the country enables the producer to gather his products in the winter when they are expensive.

We are approaching California, the land of giants in the plant kingdom, where the yuccas and shrubs and grasses assume colossal proportions. Here the cactus, which is called *Cereus giganteus*, reaches a height of sixty feet. But the greatest attraction of this desert is the Petrified Forest and what is called the Grand Canyon of Arizona.

The Petrified Forest, which is an area of about 2,500 square acres, was probably located on the shores of an inland sea, and over time became submerged by the waters and is now covered by the desert sands. Here we find lying on the ground or protruding from the sands innumerable trunks of petrified trees of different sizes, some of them extending to ten feet in diameter. They seem to have been pines or cedars. Water has gradually filled up the cells with silica, manganese, and iron oxide mixed with other such substances, which have given them the beautiful colors that captivate the traveler. Under the action of the heat or cold, these trunks have become fractured so that they look as if they have been sawn by the hand of man into enormous disks. In their natural state these masses of wood do not possess very brilliant colors, but when they are skillfully worked, they justify the name of "jewel forest", an appellation given to this wood because every particle of these trees has been transformed into chalcedony, agate, amethyst, topaz, etc. One of these trees, with its trunk still intact, has fallen across a chasm forty-five feet wide, so that it forms a kind of bridge. Its top and root are buried in the sand, which gives you an idea of its height. You will surely be curious to see a specimen of this beautifully petrified wood, and to satisfy your curiosity I will bring a piece of it on my return.

From this wonder we pass to another still greater, which until now no one has been able to describe: the Grand Canyon of Arizona. I shall not even try to convey its beauties, when gifted writers have found the task beyond their ability. The word "canyon", from the Spanish *cañon*, is often used here to indicate the gigantic gorges, mountains, and precipices, call them what you wish, that the immense rivers of these countries have carved over the centuries in these titanic regions. The Grand Canyon is an intricate system of canyons, more than 6,000 feet deep, 125 miles wide, and 180 miles long. Anyone venturesome enough to look over the edge of the canyon would imagine he was on the top of a very high mountain, instead of on the edge of a deep abyss, upon seeing the stupendous panorama spread before him. It is a labyrinth of immense architectural forms infinitely varied in design. There is no reason to envy the pyramids of Egypt or the majestic mausoleums of the pharaohs, decorated as they are with the most curious ornaments, when nature can produce these marvels, sometimes resembling festoons of lace or veils hanging from the rocks painted in a great palette of colors. Diaphanous tints of marvelous delicacy are also to be seen. The highest mountains that dominate this abyss change color according to the hour of the day, so that the rubies you see now change themselves into emeralds later on, and afterward they become as brilliant as diamonds under the powerful rays of the sun, and like sapphires in the evening. In the presence of such an imposing spectacle, man feels very small. To the eye of the faithful, this is an image, though a faint one, of God.

Down the Grand Canyon, whose ridges are about six thousand feet high, the train descended at a dizzying speed along the sides of the mountains, coasting, as it were, on the brink of precipices, until we arrived at the city of Needles, which is only a few feet above sea level, only to ascend again immediately about three thousand feet. The position of this city, nearly buried between two very high mountains, combined with the nature of the soil, all covered with lava that erupted during past centuries from the neighboring volcanoes, makes Needles one of the hottest places in the world, or at least in the United States. Really, the heat was suffocating. Not being able to endure the flaming heat, which entered through the small windows and even through the cracks or small openings in the train, I tried to shelter myself behind cushions, but in a few minutes they also became so hot they seemed to be on fire.

Needles is on the border of Arizona, and is therefore the gateway of California. If I had judged California by this city, I would have had a bad impression of it. Fortunately for us, the darkness of night soon enveloped this unattractive landscape; and the next day, as soon as the sun rose, the train was running through clusters of orange groves, hedges of eucalyptus, and the most beautiful green meadows and flowerbeds. We were in California.

With good reason, this state is often compared with Italy, and especially with our Riviera, and those who say it should be compared with the Promised Land, flowing with milk and honey, are not mistaken. California is rich in gold, silver, and every precious metal, including the famous mines of tourmaline, a stone that is now coming into style. But one of its main attractions is its incomparable climate. Here it is always spring. The sky is even more beautiful than that of Italy. It only rains two months out of the year. There are hot days, it is true, but in summer the heat is tempered by sea breezes. The nights are very cool. When I left California in the month of December, the hills were already green and the trees were putting forth their new buds. A beneficent fog, loaded with all the smoke and miasma of the city, rises every evening, but during the night it is pushed slowly toward the sea by a current of fresh air that comes from the mountains. In the morning another kind of fog envelops the hills on which the city of Los Angeles stands. The sun takes some time to dissolve it, so that often it does not emerge until ten A.M. This fog, which emanates from the sea, is of a transparent blue, and as it is driven by the sea winds in a direction opposite to that of the evening fog, the atmosphere becomes purified and remains clear and serene for the rest of the day.

As far as the climate is concerned, you know what the products of California are better than I do. Every fruit tree and every plant grows to immense proportions. Here there are gigantic trees in whose trunks chapels are built and arches cut out through which motor vehicles pass to and fro. Here is the celebrated water-lily *Victoria regia*, which you know from the description. Here is to be seen a trunk of *Washingtonia regia* that is hundreds of years old. It is the giant of the forests and fell by some unknown accident. Its immensity is such that a squadron of horsemen can ride over it as if it were a main street, or better still, a parade ground for military display. Here the geraniums grow to such a height that they form hedges that divide the various properties, and sometimes climb to a height of thirty feet and gracefully adorn the trunks of palms that line the streets and adorn the gardens.

The fruit has a special fragrance and flavor. Here, near Los Angeles, lives the celebrated naturalist Burbank, who, adding new wonders to the wonders of nature by his ingenious experiments and graftings, has produced new kinds of fruit and flowers, apricots and plums without stones and grapes without seeds.

To the glory of the Church, I must tell you that the one who showed Mr. Burbank the way to success was Abbot Gregory Mendel, who, half a century ago in his monastery in Austria, began the experiment that has made the name of the naturalist of California famous. What the latter now accomplishes is due to the ingenuity and skill of an intelligent Augustinian monk. From this we see how much we owe the Church as the cultivator of sciences and arts.

As soon as I arrived, I began to look around the town and its suburbs to find suitable grounds for a school and orphanage. There is not a hill or valley that I did not visit, and always with an increasing admiration for God's goodness, which is seen so clearly in this privileged country. Every valley is a natural sanatorium, where by just staying in the open air night and day, one is cured of some particular disease, and there is such a valley for every illness. Those suffering from tuberculosis pitch their tents at the foot of a hill. They sleep and live in these tents, and after some years find themselves stronger and more vigorous than ever before. In other places those who suffer from asthma, nerves, and anemia likewise recover their health. The air acts as both doctor and medicine to all.

Los Angeles had only eleven thousand inhabitants in 1880; now it counts one hundred fifty thousand, and in the winter this number is increased by tourists who come to spend the season here. While I was there, thirty thousand more were added to the population. It is only about sixteen miles from the sea, which is easily reached by an incomparable system of electric trains. The most elegant palaces, not to be found in other states, adorn the streets, while villas and parks extend from the brow of the hills to the plains. There is no house, however small, that does not have a flower garden, and palms give the city an air of elegance. It was precisely on one of these hills that I found a place suitable for our work, and I can really say it was prepared for us by the Sacred Heart, for the palm trees in front of the house hide it so nicely that it seems like a real convent. At the same time we are but a short distance from the town, and at the foot of the hill where our house is situated, the Italian families live, so that the Sisters can reach the mission field in just a few minutes and are quickly able to reach the school that Bishop Conaty is erecting for us.

While I was making the arrangements to buy this property, I had the opportunity to visit the Venice of America, as it is called. This place is situated in a most charming location on the shores of the Pacific Ocean. It is a small city built in the style of Venice. There are artificial canals and bridges, small copies, one might say, of the Queen of the Adriatic, and the canals are navigated by small gondolas.

Stone buildings are few in number, as are brick houses in Los Angeles, but the houses made of wood are of exquisite workmanship. Therefore, except in the main streets, which remind one of Italy, the city consists mainly of tents. There are thousands of them, lined up neatly in such a way as to form streets, and they are as large as a good-sized room, well furnished, and lighted by electricity, and even the richest people leave their palaces at least for a month to enjoy the freedom of the Pacific beaches.

A restful and pleasant excursion was offered to me by Mr. Banning, owner of the famous Santa Catalina Island, who gave me tickets for his steamer. I had heard so much about this pretty island that I could not leave California without being able to tell you something about it. We went recently, on a sunny day, when the sky was cobalt blue and the ocean lived up to its name Pacific. The three-hour trip seemed very short, absorbed as we were in the sight of the ocean and sky. As we approached, only the outline of the rocky island could be seen—about thirty miles in length—but when we entered the bay, the fog gently lifted like the curtain of an immense stage, revealing the enchanting scenery prepared by the hand of God. I thought I was viewing an earthly paradise in a dream. Against the background of a sapphire blue sky rose green mountains dotted here and there with elegant villas, nestled among pines and palms. The air is so clear that the eye cannot gauge distances, and the power of vision seems to increase. In the transparent blue waters, the bottom of the ocean is easily seen, swarming with a myriad of fish, among them the flying fish that suddenly darts into the air like an arrow and then dives into the waves. Seals, imported from the banks of Newfoundland where they are numerous and serve as a major resource for the English, playfully swim among the fish, which are accustomed to their company and seem to pay no attention to their antics—just as they are not frightened by men diving and swimming in their midst. Such is the harmony of nature reigning here. Even more friendly are the aquatic birds, playing around and hovering over the fishermen. Thousands of seagulls live in the bay of Avalon, flying, dipping, or gently rocking on the waves. They roost on masts, on the edges of boats, on rocks. Any object rising above the waters is adorned by their elegant white forms. But a more enchanting sight may be enjoyed by taking a trip in a glass-bottomed boat. I had heard of the undersea gardens of Santa Catalina, and I imagined that through some optical illusion produced by mirrors and lenses, people could see fantastic plants and flowers at the bottom of the ocean, and I did not think it worthwhile to take the trip; but what I saw surpassed all my expectations.

In the bottom of the boat there is an opening with a glass window, through which you can see everything in the sea. We had hardly left land when the sea, which appeared smooth and sandy at the bottom, gradually became full of rocks and then of green mountains. Between these were plains and valleys, all covered with green sea plants, which in some places reached a height of a hundred feet, waving to and fro with the movement of the sea. There was a never-ending variety of aquatic plants, some of which bore purple flowers and different kinds of fruit of delicate tints, fresh like the blossoms of spring, and they were continually moved by the waters as if by a breeze. If the view of a park on land is beautiful, I can assure you that an underwater park is much more so, especially when you see it inhabited by every kind of fish, including the goldfish, and its rocks adorned by shells of the most brilliant colors. After two hours of these wonderful sights, we landed on Moonstone Beach. Moonstones are rough pebbles that are cut and polished and made into various kinds of ornaments. The chalcedony of which these are made must have fallen from some high mountain, who knows how far away. It is beaten by the waves on the beach. Tourists find them, and thus have the opportunity to carry away with them an interesting souvenir of Santa Catalina. I remained there more than twenty-four hours. The island belongs to a rich man, who refused to sell it for five million dollars. He has made it into a holiday resort and a terrestrial paradise for tourists.

The perfect system of electric trains that connects Los Angeles with its suburbs offers foreign visitors a beautiful pleasure trip, which I was able to take through the kindness of friends. Less than four hours after leaving the shores of the Pacific, we reached the top of Mount Lowe, six thousand feet high. Leaving the beach, we passed through vineyards and fields, which reveal the fruitfulness of the soil. There you have only to plant a seed and leave it to the care of the sun and rain, and in the autumn you will get an abundant crop. In less than half an hour, Los Angeles appeared like a majestic queen with her beautiful white palaces scattered through the perennial green of the surrounding hills. Then, between more hills, we reached the aristocratic city of Pasadena, where the millionaires of the United States spend the winter. In the midst of green carpets dotted with flowers and amid the perfume of orange trees, we reached the foot of Sierra Madre. To the inhabitants of California, the word "foothill" suggests the most beautiful and healthy things you can imagine. There, oranges and lemons blossom and ripen without danger of frost, and there one can gather the most delicate vegetables, even in winter. There the sick also recover their health.

From Altadena, which is at the foot of the mountain, you can ascend in a funicular railway to a height of five thousand feet. At this height the most attractive part of the view begins, because once you are there you immediately enjoy the splendid panorama of the open valleys and plains. An electric railway, built with the characteristic daring of the Americans, spreads its lines from peak to peak, suspended over dizzy abysses below, and then climbs the granite rocks, which seem inaccessible, to such a height of six thousand feet. And so one enjoys the whole beauty of the mountains without being a mountaineer. I spent several hours contemplating the splendid sight that one enjoys up there and stretched my vision as far as the ocean, which one can see on clear days.

But I must return to Los Angeles. Our Sisters are already well settled and have begun their work, not only on behalf of the Italians but also for the poor Mexicans, who are numerous here and in great need of help. Evangelical laborers are so few here that the devil, by way of the Protestants, has already sown a great deal of weeds in this beautiful country. I have never seen a city with so many sects, and of the most ridiculous kind. Returning home one evening at six P.M., I had to pass through one of the main streets, when my attention was drawn to a group of women and men prostrate on the ground at the corner of the street, crying and beating their breasts, while one of them preached in a loud voice that they should be sorry for their sins. I was told to wait a minute if I wished to see a wonderful sight.

Then, quite suddenly, they all stood up and clapped their hands and jumped around and danced very joyfully. The preacher assured them that the sins they had been lamenting had been forgiven, and they jumped with joy. This custom is the origin of their name, the Holy Jumpers. There are also the Nazarenes, who profess to live without eating or drinking, and not finding any men who are gullible enough, content themselves with women for ministers. Christian Science holds sway everywhere. Right in the center of the town these people have a big tent on which are written in big letters the words of Holy Scripture referring to the miracle performed by Saint Peter at the door of the Temple, and there they perform their miracles, which are carefully prepared beforehand, of course. There the lame walk and the blind see, in the presence of those foolish enough to allow themselves to be deceived. But a poor lame man who, in good faith, went in the hope of being cured was treated badly on one occasion. The spirit invoked was unwilling to perform the miracle. The minister shouted, "Lord, listen to us because we are holy and innocent, and we follow you closely." But it was of no use. The poor man could not walk, and the minister was so displeased and enraged that had the man not left the tent in a hurry, it would have gone ill with him.

Some of our poor Italians fall into the trap set to catch them. A good knowledge of our faith is necessary everywhere, but especially in these Protestant countries. And this shows us how necessary it is to study the Catechism well. How can a poor emigrant be faithful to a truth he barely knows? How can he practice something of which he has no understanding? The small Catechism contains the greatest doctrines of our holy faith. Scholars who penetrate the

Divine Mysteries like eagles find green pastures in it, while the simple, who are not as eager to speculate, are contented to find the road that leads to eternal life. Take religion away from man, and nothing remains in this life but illusion, trials, and countless afflictions. Where can he find the strength to resign himself to trials and misfortune, if not in the comforting thoughts religion suggests? Where do rebellions and seditions come from, if not from a lack of religion? We are greatly mistaken if we want to contribute to the greatness of our country, each one in her own sphere, but we do not build our edifice on the cornerstone that is Christ and His Church.

Very fortunate you are, my dear daughters, that while you attend to the acquisition of culture that is necessary for yourselves, you do not neglect the study of that highest science, religion. You are even more blessed in that you know how to draw fruit from this study. Therefore, yours is not vain science that puffs itself up, but that which reforms manners, educates the heart, and forms character. Blessed are you for becoming worthy instruments in the hands of God. The Church and society expect great things from you, because your presence alone, your virtues and your teachings, create a salutary environment, and you exude a beneficent influence, educational in the full sense of the word, and you will do an immense amount of good.

Having finished my work in Los Angeles, I returned to Chicago, where I found the hospital progressing very nicely after opening last February. In the past twelve months, 900 patients have been treated and 350 operations performed with splendid results. When I arrived, the famous Dr. Murphy, president of the hospital, asked me what I thought of my children—alluding to the many doctors who work there night and day. I answered that I was delighted. We are not actually dealing with children, but with physicians and surgeons, some of whom are already famous in the medical world; yet you should see how humbly they submit to the regulations I dictated, after carefully studying the local conditions. If discipline is necessary in a school, it is essential in an institution of this kind, where the danger of abuses is great. If I am now able to leave Chicago with a tranquil mind, it is because I know my instructions are being carefully observed.

Regulations are helpful not only to religious but to everyone, because it is human nature to tire, relax, and change plans according to events. To persevere in our good resolutions in spite of difficulties and aversions that may arise strengthens character and assures happy success to individuals and institutions.

And now, my good daughters, after having tried your patience, I greet you warmly, taking comfort in the thought that I will be able see you again soon, and implore for you the choicest blessings of the Sacred Heart.

Yours most affectionately in the Most Sacred Heart of Jesus,

MOTHER FRANCESCA SAVERIO CABRINI

August 26, 1901, Voyage to Genoa, Italy

In this brief letter written to an individual Sister, Mother Cabrini shares a spiritual insight based on the flying fish she saw on her voyage.

A.M.G.SS.C.J.
My Dearest Daughter,

I have never felt so miserable in leaving you as I did this time. As soon as you disappeared from sight I retired to my cabin and went to bed. It was a fever that stayed with me all day Friday, leaving me exhausted. This is the reason you did not get letters from me in Montevideo. Now I am beginning to recuperate and feel the good effects of the sea.

We shall arrive at Santos on Tuesday, so you can imagine how slowly this steamer is going. Patience! I'll use the time as a sea cure, in the hope that the air might strengthen me to work with greater vigor when I arrive and run in the ways of the Lord at a quicker pace. My little companions suffered a little during the first days; now they are good sailors. We are enjoying very good accommodations, and the service is excellent.

It is admirable how well and how quickly they do everything here. They are so good that peace and serenity reign everywhere. That is just the way I like it. Where there is peace, there is God and grace abounds. Love peace, oh my daughters, and make any sacrifice to maintain it. If you do this, I assure you that Jesus will give you the grace to attain perfection and to be blessed in all your undertakings for God and man.

I wonder if this will reach you by the feast of Saint Rose and if we shall catch a fast boat at Santos, but I think this is unlikely. You will have a grand feast day with all the prelates, while we, between one wave and another, will have our celebration with the innocent fish. The fish, our little brothers, teach us a lovely lesson: after flying about, they dive into the sea with immense pleasure, thus showing us that after working gladly in the fulfillment of our duties, we should immerse ourselves in God in the salutary waters of grace and then return to work again with renewed vigor; so now you understand the wise disposition of our *orario*, which has us immerse ourselves in the Sacred Heart of Jesus seven times a day.

I greet you all cordially and ask you to remember me to the children and all the people I know. May the good Jesus bless you. I envelop you tightly in the Sacred Heart of Jesus so that you may learn meekness therein.

Affectionately in the Most Sacred Heart of Jesus,

M. FRANCESCA S. CABRINI

The Voyage She Did Not Take in 1912

In April 1912, Mother Cabrini needed to return to America to raise money for a new hospital in New York. Her community in England purchased a ticket for her, hoping she would visit them on the way. Mother Cabrini decided to travel by a different ship to arrive in America sooner. It is fortunate that she made that choice, or she would have sailed on the final voyage of the RMS Titanic in April 1912.

4. The Spiritual Director

Mother Cabrini asked her religious Sisters, particularly those who were superiors of communities, to write to her regularly because she wanted to know about each Sister's material and spiritual condition. Although she could not respond to every letter she received, she carefully read them all. The following letters were written by Mother Cabrini to different religious Sisters and show the kinds of problems—both practical and spiritual—her Sisters faced, as well as how she chose to respond to them.

* * *

August 8, 1878, Codogno, Italy

This letter was written to a young woman named Chiarina, whom Mother Cabrini calls her first spiritual daughter.

Dearest Chiarina,

The occasion of the upcoming spiritual exercises gives me a pleasurable opportunity to write to you. Even though you have been rather silent, I have not forgotten you; on the contrary, I have you engraved in my heart as the first lily, the beloved child of my brief career as a public-school teacher.

I want you, too, to recall the past, so that you remember me especially when you find yourself all alone with your good God. Yes, pray for me, my Chiarina; pray for me with all your heart.

I want you to know that the spiritual exercises will begin on September 8 at five P.M., and I would like to have you at my side to profit from this lovely occasion; invite Judith Ottobelli too. What consolation would be mine if you two would come! Tell your good Aunt Christina to notify other young ladies so that they can accompany you; do the same among your friends. The good you will thus bring about will be a double advantage for you.

Kindly give my best regards to your reverend pastor and inform him of the spiritual exercises; also tell Rosina that I expect her to come with you. Remember me to Sarini, Marianna, your father, and the entire family. As soon as you know the number of those who are coming, please inform me. I greet you fondly, and in the Heart of Jesus I am

Yours affectionately,
MOTHER SAVERIO OF JESUS

P.S.—Danelli, Passerini, and Asti greet you and want to see you.

June 23, 1888, Codogno, Italy

Mother Cabrini writes to a group of Sisters—apparently all superiors—and explains to them how to undertake the difficult task of correcting their spiritual daughters.

J.M.J.F.
Sister Carmelina, Sister Salesia, Sister Augustine,
My Dearest Daughters,

Do you want to know how to behave when you have to correct Sisters of their defects and it seems likely they will be offended? Here is the way:

Use great charity drawn from the heart of Christ to see to the welfare of your Sister's soul, and then with sweetness, but with a holy freedom, advise and make known the harm and damage that builds up in the soul and the offense given to our Spouse.

If the matter concerns a novice, it is the duty of the novice mistress. She should get to the root of the problem in order to eradicate it. In the case of a professed Sister, it is the duty of the superior assisted by Sister Augustine. In such cases, use a great deal of tact—which the novice mistress does not have to use, because the novice must be well instructed, and this is her time of probation.

In a few days I shall be among you and I shall explain better what is to be done in these circumstances. Meanwhile, do the best you can. Are you afraid I will stay in Rome for a long time? No, my daughters, that is impossible. Even if some important business should detain me here, I would only stay until the middle of April at the latest, but I am sure I shall return before that time. Pray with all your heart that the Sacred Heart will help me in all things.

In the decree, the Holy Father praises our aim to make reparation to the Heart of Jesus. This has given me immense pleasure because it seems that the Sacred Heart wished to approve our desires through His holy vicar and wants to be our all; entrusted to Him, we need have no fear.

Oh, how good the Heart of Jesus is! He will help you in all things, and when it seems that things are not going very well, He will show His power by making everything work out for our good. Everything depends on how we respond to His great mercy and take advantage of the occasions that come our way to show Him our fidelity.

I recommend the Holy Hour on Thursday, to which a plenary indulgence is attached; likewise, on Good Friday, there is a plenary indulgence for whoever makes the hour to Our Lady of Sorrows (or even half an hour) meditating on the Passion of Our Lord. Don't miss these treasures of indulgences, which will whiten the souls of those who receive them with the proper dispositions.

Greet all the Sisters for me, and I hope to see you soon—sooner than you think. May the Heart of Jesus bless and help you to fulfill your duty by the sweet force of His holy love.

Yours affectionately in the Most Sacred Heart of Jesus,
M. FRANC. SAVERIO CABRINI

August 27, 1888, Codogno, Italy

Mother Cabrini gives detailed advice to a Sister who is about to begin a spiritual retreat.

J.M.J.F.
My Dearest Daughter,

Tomorrow evening you will begin the spiritual exercises. Remember that it is a great grace of the Sacred Heart of Jesus to which you must respond and for which you will someday have to render an account. Put your whole soul, empty of all else, into these exercises so that you may receive the imprint of divine grace with all those lights that the most loving Heart of Jesus will deign to bestow upon you. Uproot your small faults and see how they have spoiled that lovely enclosed garden of your soul where your divine Spouse had the right to find fresh and fragrant flowers.

I shall pray for you and I shall have others pray too so that you may give me the consolation at the end of the exercises of knowing that you are transformed and disposed toward a true life of perfection. But what perfection? That of Saint John Berchmans, who disdained extraordinary things but performed ordinary things in an extraordinary manner. There it is in one sentence: what I want from you this year as I also wanted it from your Sisters here, who, it seems, wish to satisfy my desire. Don't lose yourselves in ethereal things or in what you feel or hear, but settle down to what is practical and solid. Examine yourselves carefully on the Holy Rule, the horarium, and punctiliousness in carrying out all the pious practices of the Institute. Seek not to make grand resolutions, but rather make many small ones, knowing that with diligence in small things, you will arrive at grand service to the adorable Heart of Jesus.

I am enclosing our horarium. You may keep the one you made, but see that it is scrupulously followed. During the time of spiritual reading, read the Holy Rule, but pause frequently to call the attention of the Sisters to what has not been observed. Let them write their small resolutions in their little books. The small resolutions will be a method of life that each one shall follow to better observe the Holy Rule of the Institute. Take Saint John Berchmans for a model, my daughters. Read this letter to the Sisters so that they may benefit from it.

Give my respects to the retreat master and tell him that I hope he will transform you into true and perfect religious—and that I entrust to his prayers the seventy who made the retreat, so that they may preserve the fruit of the retreat they made so well.

I began this letter on Friday as soon as the retreat ended. I had to stop, and there was no way I could pick up the pen again. I was sick but am now feeling better. Better late than never.

I am sorry about Sister Michelina. Have her examined by a doctor, and later, we shall see; meanwhile, make the retreat in great silence.

About the school: if they don't pay you for the teachers, the students will have to pay. Perhaps you can find one of our graduates who is attending teacher's college, but for now, do not think of anything else but your soul and that of the Sisters. Woe to you if you do not become perfect religious, for the Heart of Jesus wants it. May He bless you, enlighten you, help you. I give you a little remembrance for all: humility, obedience, silence, diligence. I am putting down my pen, but in spirit I am in your midst.

Yours affectionately in the Most Sacred Heart of Jesus,
M. FRANC. SAVERIO CABRINI

June 6, 1889, New York

In this letter, Mother Cabrini demonstrates her willingness to perform that very unpleasant spiritual work of mercy: correcting others in their mistakes.

J.M.J.F.
My Dearest Daughters,

I regret having to say this, but I am not at all pleased with you, because in following your self-love, you have all fallen so low. Instead of desiring to be corrected, you dislike it and wish that no one would ever notice your defects.

You are so full of desires and wish to do your own will where the assignment of places and roles is concerned. My dear daughters, do you think this is any way for religious to live? I do not even recognize you as good Christians, because the good Christian knows that he must be humble and submit to authority. Think, then, what a religious, a spouse of Christ who is committed by her vows to deny her self-will and do God's will through her superiors, ought to do. She should not even permit a thought or desire to the contrary.

She who desires to follow her own will places herself on the road to perdition, for only by denying it is salvation assured. Consider, then, the state of your souls, and let anyone who feels proud and quarrelsome quickly uproot these weeds from her soul, for on my return I want to be consoled by all of you.

In the meantime, since you are not doing very well, I shall reject other offers for the extension of our good works. If I have to engage in important affairs with subjects deprived of fundamental and solid virtues, I feel I am building on sand—something I cannot do in good conscience. Let each one look to herself as the cause of this decision of mine; let no one think that one is more culpable than another. This would be a thought, suggested by hidden pride, that could lead to ruin. Let us hope that in the future, you will not wound the Heart of Jesus and that of your mother but console her as she has a right to expect you to.

Warm yourselves with the love of the Sacred Heart; let those who feel cold humble themselves, for only in this way will they rise in spirit from earth to Heaven and there find the true flame of love worthy of a true and good religious.

Make a triduum for my intentions. I do not cease to pray for each one of you, because I want all of you to be truly holy. May the Sacred Heart of Jesus bless you!

Yours affectionately in the Sacred Heart of Jesus,

M. FRANC. SAVERIO CABRINI

August 6, 1892, New Orleans

A Sister complains that her prayer life has become dry, and Mother Cabrini gives an interesting response.

J.M.J.F.
My Dearest Mother Virginia,

I rejoice with you over the high degree of holiness to which God is calling you with the gift of great aridity. Courage, my daughter; it is in battle that the valor of a soldier is proved, and so it must be with a true missionary. If only I, too, were worthy to suffer like you; instead, Jesus always treats me like a child.

Let us walk along the path God chooses; it is enough for the goal to be the same. Certainly it is far better not to have consolation and pleasure during these brief days of life; thus we can resemble our beloved Jesus all the more.

While you offer up this tribulation, pray for me, and you will obtain more graces for me in one day of desolation than in a thousand of celestial joy. Offer your aridity for my intentions because there are ever so many things I have at heart.

Write to me soon, for I desire your letters. May Jesus bless you and enclose you in His Divine Heart to make you what I desire you to be.

Affectionately yours in the Most Sacred Heart of Jesus,
M. FRANC. SAVERIO CABRINI

Genoa, Italy, November 15, 1893

Mother Cabrini writes to a Sister, Mother Ignatius, who has apparently accused herself of many faults.

To Mother Ignatius, My Dearest Daughter:

Once the disciples asked Jesus if He would call down fire upon those who were behaving badly, and He answered that they did not know what spirit they belonged to. Likewise, you know his response to the accusers of the adulteress; and to you, daughter, what shall I say?

Are you holy, charitable, docile, mortified, obedient, pure, etc., etc.? If you are not, you wish to be so, and that is sufficient for me. Grace will be given to you in accordance with your good intentions, and you will become a saint. Meanwhile, aim at the beautiful virtue of the Sacred Heart that attracts you most, and with kind words help those who seem to be living badly; Jesus will note down such charity in letters of gold. Conquer that which you call stubbornness, cleave the mountain, enter the cleft, and you will meet Jesus. Have courage; work assiduously.

With reference to your relatives, I don't think you do yourself justice, since you have always shown yourself to be detached. It should have sufficed to have shown me the letter. I know the case, and none of the Sisters were involved. Content yourself to let the matter drop; as your mother says, it is not worth talking about.

May Jesus bless you and help you in all things so that you can serve Him with the fidelity that you know He expects from you. Pray for me, and according to my intention, offer some sacrifice to our good Jesus.

The Sisters wish to be remembered to you, and they commend themselves to your prayers. They believe you to be a saint established in humility; make sure that this is true.

Aff. in the Most Sacred Heart of Jesus,
M. FRANC. SAVERIO CABRINI

February 8, 1894, Rome

It is difficult to be certain, but it appears that a Sister had humbly admitted her faults to Mother Cabrini, and this letter is Mother's reply.

J.M.J.F.
My Dearest Daughter,

Your letter was very consoling. I discovered in it those traces of humility that speak of present grace, of the ardent wishes of a soul who desires to place herself on the trail blazed by our dear Lord in perfect self-denial. With all my heart, I therefore grant you permission to make the eight-day retreat, confident that with your present dispositions, you will make it with the great profit you are obliged to gain from it; otherwise, you take the risk of being reproached, one day, for squandering the great graces that the good Jesus has bestowed on you for your spiritual advancement.

When we detest our sins with humility by blaming only ourselves, not seeing the defects of others but only our own, then grace is prepared for us in such abundance that our immersion in it is a foretaste of Paradise. This will make us sweet and charitable, of great comfort, and a good example to all our Sisters. Isn't this wonderful? Don't you want to experience it? Yes, grace has already set out to enter you, and after the retreat, everyone will have to admire a change in you that is astounding. I shall accompany you with my poor prayers, so proceed with courage under the protection of the Blessed Mother, who will cover you with her precious mantle.

After the retreat, try to pay that terrible debt as quickly as possible, so that on my arrival not only is it settled, but there is something left over. I give you this obedience; if you have faith and you are no longer what you are now, you shall work miracles.

Make the spiritual reading on Holy Week beginning with the chapter on "The Dangers in Which an Imperfect Religious Finds Herself", continue until the chapter on

"Silence", and if possible, read to the end. Use Pinamonti for meditation and follow the order that has been marked. Enclosed is the *orario*.

Perform as many penances as you wish, keeping Christian discretion in mind; for example, one hour of wearing a coarse garment, a Miserere of the discipline, five minutes of prostration on the ground, but not more than five, otherwise the blood will go to your head. As for meals, try to eat in community even if you have stomach problems, which are often a ruse of the devil to tempt us to ask for special treatment. Our dear Saint John Berchmans used to say, "My greatest penance is community life."

By the time this letter reaches you, I shall have visited the tomb of your patron saint, where I will pray that you will conquer yourself and become like a lamb. I did this with Ribadneira, whom I supported with great patience without ever telling her that she was dishonoring the Institute with her foolishness. Charity, oh yes, charity must be the fruit of your retreat, a product of true humility.

I want Sister Tomasina to remain at Manresa until further notice. There you will have a good opportunity to put your true reform into practice and to give an example of charity; in this way you will obtain great graces for the house and the Institute. May the good Jesus bless you and enclose you as a meek, white dove in His Sacred Heart, from which you will never depart.

Affectionately yours in the Most Sacred Heart of Jesus,
M. FRANC. SAVERIO CABRINI

Letter (undated)

Mother Cabrini encourages an ailing Sister who complains of being distracted by her imagination.

J.M.J.F.
My Dearest Daughter,

You have recovered and I am so glad. May the Heart of Jesus give you so much health that you can glorify Him greatly in your dear Institute by sanctifying your every act, even the most trivial.

Courage, my dear daughter; do not worry about what passes through your imagination, which is still of the world. Withdraw your gaze, shut the window, and enter into your cell, the Heart of Jesus, where all is peace, joy and sweetness. Your guardian angel is doing very well and knows how to help me in various circumstances; get along with him very well, as well as with the angel of the Institute who resides in this house.

You told me the other day that Christmas is the day of your consecration, but I do not know which one; however, on Christmas morning, renew your vows and promises, the sweet ties that bind you to God, and by this new promise intend to make reparation for all the infidelity of your past life so that your holocaust will be perfect.

Take care of yourself as much as you can; for obedience's sake, use all that is necessary and useful. Send greetings to your father and mother, but don't mention anything, and the same thing holds true for your sister; then tell my guardian angel all the things you would like to have said. Does this make you happy? Pray for me and believe me always.

Affectionately yours in the Most Sacred Heart of Jesus,
M. FRANCESCA S. CABRINI

Letter (undated)

Mother Cabrini tries to help a Sister forgive the failings of her Sisters and also encourage them.

J.M.J.F.
My Dearest Daughter,

By the time you receive this, Mother Umilia will already have apologized to you for her mistake, but I caution you to treat her kindly; otherwise, you will harm her soul. I knew that this would happen after I heard that you had sent Battistina away. She was really the only one who kept the place clean and orderly; therefore, the disorder and the lack of help have upset her, and even though I see that the fault is serious, I cannot say anything more to you than to be compassionate with her.

Next time, when changes are under discussion, do not impose your will on them, but seek their advice. In this way you will gain much, and you can speak to the nuns without offending them. I have tried this method with Sisters who had a difficult personality, and I have found it very satisfactory; at other times, when I was austere and strict, I achieved nothing. It is no use; we are Missionary Sisters of the Sacred Heart, and we must imitate the meekness of this adorable Heart in order to gain souls.

So, courage! Know how to swallow bitter pills with joy and how to offer them for the welfare of the Institute and the sanctification of religious. Try to be cheerful, and always speak kindly; do not be categorical. When you see that a Sister is sad or keeping at a distance, try to cheer her up. Conquer yourself in all things; for now, you have some lovely opportunities to advance in perfection; offer the bitter pills for my intention sometimes.

As I told you before, we have solemnly celebrated the centenary of Blessed Alacoque at Codogno and Milan. The crowds were tremendous during the three-day celebration, and the priests, in particular, were so enthusiastic that they conceived a great desire to see the Beata canonized. They want us to obtain the first-class miracle needed for canonization. I did not hesitate. I prepared a novena to be said three times in a row and a list of miracles that the Beata could obtain from the Sacred Heart of Jesus. We have already begun the novena with great confidence, and now I am sending it to you. Send copies to the houses quickly, and urge them to make the novena with fervor, adding the practice of virtue to it. We also have holy priests praying for this purpose.

Invite Fr. Massi or Fr. Ciampi to be the extraordinary confessor instead of Fr. Cardella. Mother Michelina knows Fr. Ciampi's address; of course it is understood that you must get the requisite permission. Treat Mother Michelina with kindness and gain her confidence because it is now more important than ever for you to direct her and the others.

May 15, 1895, New Orleans

A sister has misplaced her crucifix, and Mother Cabrini turns it into a spiritual lesson.

A.M.G.SS.C.J.
My Dearest Daughter,

You lost your cross? Then you are the most unhappy person in the world because the one who has no cross is not a follower of Jesus Christ; so I wish you a very long and very large cross full of thorns, which you will carry as a precious jewel with a smile on your lips and without a word of complaint about its weight.

In fact, she who loves Jesus with a pure and tender love is so intimately united with Him that she no longer feels the burden of anything; and what is more, when she sees the benefits she gains from the unitive way and the pleasure it gives Jesus, she desires and asks for more.

But let us thank God that you have lost only a material cross, which you can certainly replace if you go to the store behind the cardinal vicar's office. The price is 150 lire.

And our Blessed Mother? Seek to imitate her closely: be pure, free from worldly things, immaculate, and a lover of sacrifice so that she will not escape from you again.

Were you insured against damages? It is necessary to insure the furniture for the highest possible amount because there is always risk where you have boys.

I know the house is well insured. I have been in New Orleans for twelve days, and I shall leave on the twenty-fourth for Panama on a liner that will bring me to Limón, a distance of sixteen hours from Colón. The captain of this liner is a good Catholic, a saint. When I asked him which liner I should take, he said: "Take my liner, and have as many Sisters as you wish. You can travel for free, since I consider this good luck for me." And not satisfied with all this, he is figuring out a way to have me taken directly to Colón. See how often the good Jesus treats us with His gifts. I will come on Saturday to give the holy habit to three postulants, very dear young ladies who have done very well and who are pleasing to the archbishop. They are three angels.

I need about one hundred Sisters here because they are needed in so many places and I have difficulty deciding what place I should take. I don't have time to see them all. If I can't decide now, I will do it on my return from Panama. Pray that Jesus may inspire me about which ones to accept.

I am happy to hear that Msgr. Tedeschi is thinking about giving us some help. If he is thinking, something surely will be done, and you won't know anything about it until it is done. You know how he is: he doesn't say a word until he is sure. Pray and you will obtain all you desire from Jesus. Jesus never says no to His faithful spouses; He refuses nothing; have great faith.

Fr. Dubon was with Fr. Antonio Legeano, the one I always recommended to you since he did so much for us, but from your correspondence, it seems that you have neglected him. I hope the young teachers have used sound judgment; the students who read bad books should not be allowed to pass. I respect those who are serious and know that they have a soul to save.

Try to do your best in all things. If you do not touch the money in the bank, it is better; but if you really need the money, then use it. I cannot send you anything more since this liner and that of Panama are not safe. On the twenty-second, we shall transport the remains of our Mother Battistina to a chapel that was donated. It was Mother Battistina herself who provided it. During her lifetime she knew how to do a great deal for her Institute.

Greet the Sisters for me and tell them I am anxious to have the consolation of knowing that they love Jesus and want to console His Divine Heart.

May Jesus bless you and help you do everything in a holy manner. This is the desire of

Affectionately yours in the Most Sacred Heart of Jesus,
M. FRANC. SAVERIO CABRINI

September 15, 1896, Genoa, Italy

Mother Cabrini sandwiches a serious criticism that this Sister has lost her authority over other Sisters in between practical news, apparently to lessen the blow.

A.M.G.SS.C.J.
My Dearest Daughter,

As soon as I arrived in Italy, I had to run down to Rome in a hurry, since the Bank of the Holy Spirit, where we kept our money, failed. I had to take care of this important matter, and from there I had to go to Genoa to look for certain important documents and then return to Rome, leaving even the spiritual exercises that a large group of Sisters are making. A pack of letters from America is at Codogno, and so I cannot receive the news I greatly desire. Patience! By the end of the month I shall be free; just now, I am busy from morning till night, but thank God, all is going well. The Heart of Jesus is seeing to it.

Then I am thinking of coming to New York within two months because I am not too pleased with you. It seems to me that you are losing your spirit, and that is the worst thing that can happen. If we loosen up a bit and relax, the Heart of Jesus will withdraw, and then what will we do? You, who used to know how to trust greatly in Jesus and even work miracles, now seem to have lost that ability to trust in God; you need help and really can't do without it.

Meanwhile you are losing your authority over the Sisters, who are scandalized by the change in you and understand that you are no longer only for Jesus and for the Holy Souls who were your only helpers. Now that you have made the spiritual exercises, you must be once again the person who can do everything only with Jesus. Is this so? Then you will also have the grace of eliminating the disorder in Brooklyn.

Meanwhile, I will try something: I am enclosing a letter that will induce her [an unnamed Sister] to come to Italy gladly. If you have already removed her from there, let it go and burn the enclosed letter. If she is still in Brooklyn, seal it and send it. Send her along with an American postulant who has a good spirit and can teach English, for we have need of one here. If you think she needs a different companion, then send the superior of 14th Street, who I see does not have the health for that place.

In a short time you will have the new legate, Msgr. Martinelli, the superior general of the Augustinians and a good friend of Msgr. Corrigan and the Irish. This is for your information. I have seen him and have recommended you to him. I have given him our addresses, and perhaps he will come to visit you. Prepare the scapulars of Our Lady of Good Counsel, and he can delegate authority to any priest to invest you with them. Prepare a feast for him.

What I say in the letter to the Pallottines is true, but it isn't true that they are talking about you; rather, the archbishop of New York is complaining loudly about you because he says that two or three vicars have gone to him saying that you do not observe the diocesan rules when you go around the parishes, and he hopes that I will impose this upon you; so know what is going on and be conscious of the fact that they have their eyes on you.

Send me all you have at your disposal, for I have need of it. Greet all my good daughters, even those who are a little unfaithful to grace.

I place you all in the Sacred Heart of Jesus so that He will unite you with Himself as true and faithful spouses and make you holy. May Jesus bless you.

Affectionately yours in the Most Sacred Heart of Jesus,
M. FRANC. SAVERIO CABRINI

October 12, 1896, Rome

In this letter, Mother Cabrini has stern words for a Sister who has allowed the Sisters under her to become openly critical of one another.

A.M.G.SS.C.J.
My Dearest Daughter,

Since I had come to Rome for only three days, I left all the American letters at Codogno, as well as those that were coming in daily. Seeing that I was delayed, I sent for the mail. In reading the letters from New York, I was grieved to see that so many novices who should be like angels have judged, criticized, and condemned the professed nuns.

I am horrified that even you have fallen into the immaturity of believing the gossip of others. Humble yourself profoundly before God and return to your pristine spirit that pleased me so much because it seemed that you would not complain or listen to complaints. So you have lost your prestige, as I told you in the previous letter. In the future, from now on, use great charity with all but do not listen to gossip about your Sisters.

Give a stiff penance to anyone who accuses one or another of the Sisters; make no distinction, because my daughters, whether good or bad, holy or not, are all very dear to me. I don't want the bad ones to be criticized, but to be corrected by you and by the superior.

The superiors must be respected, and the assistants must realize that their greatest duty is that of obedience in order to give a good example, for example is stronger than words. The assistant must never think that she is the mayor or the judge of her superior. Be careful about this.

Assign Mother Margaret as the assistant at 14th Street. You remain united with God; trust in the Sacred Heart and the Holy Souls without ever relying on the Sisters, and then you will have the blessings you enjoyed before. When you are holy, the necessary means to pay all your debts will come, and you will even have enough to undertake new things.

I felt Gabriella's departure deeply. Her mother had told me that she would leave her there for a few years to gain some devotion and detach herself from those young men she was worried about. I am sorry for Gabriella because in the end, she was good. If you had been your usual self, you would have helped her to be steadfast, but instead you let yourself be influenced and so contributed to her downfall.

Poor girl! If she ever returns, accept her and help her, always with charity and never listening to those who speak for or against her. When you see Gabriella, give her my regards and tell her that after she had done well for two years, I had hoped that she would be more faithful to Jesus, who loves her so much. Tell her to be good and keep herself pure for Jesus.

I hear from Codogno that a telegram has arrived announcing the arrival of the Sisters. I shall be at Genoa to meet them. This, then, will remove the obstacles to peace and good order there; but instead, I assure you that if you do not do as I have told you, conditions will be as they were before, and possibly worse. Others will criticize and judge.

Therefore, I recommend humility, charity, and silence. On your part, do not give long conferences; a few words said gently and sweetly will suffice. I would like the nuns to continue praying during their work; great will be the harvest of grace from this practice. Forbid them to talk in the streets; in the house, see that they obey the Rule perfectly.

When you send me a letter, take care to write clearly. Your last letters were truly confusing. Then when I received four at once, each contradicted the previous letter. This grieved me no end since it showed a decadence of spirit. It was no longer you who were piloting the ship, but those whom I had not meant to steer it. Be careful, please.

It is a good thing that I found so much to console me in Italy; otherwise, the news from New York would have crushed me. Do not waste any more time talking, but work instead, because we are missionaries for this purpose; secondly, don't pay attention to those who deceive you with praise and compliments. Rebuke those who have this habit because it leads to no good.

I would like you to have Fr. Saponara for a confessor; otherwise, look for a Franciscan of good spirit. If Fr. Ferretti continues, it will be better. Become saints, and abandon all frivolity; be solid, serious, and always smiling. Use few words and much mortification. This is what I want.

May Jesus bless you and help you to put the garden that you have disrupted in order. Trust in Jesus and Mary.

Always your affectionate mother in the Most Sacred Heart of Jesus,

M. FRANC. SAVERIO CABRINI

March 7, 1897, Rome

Mother Cabrini reminds this Sister that she needs to correct the Sisters under her to create peace and eradicate pride in the community.

A.M.G.SS.C.J.
My Dearest Daughter,

The news you gave me of Quenay consoled me greatly. By acting directly, you have avoided much disturbance. How grateful we must be to the Sacred Heart for having solved this difficulty for us.

I am glad about what you told me about the superior. Now I can rest more secure. The Sisters also wrote to me about it, stating that they found everything well regulated and in such a good spirit that it was like being on retreat. The superior has written to tell me how holy they are and how edified she is. Let us hope that Jesus will bless this mutual charity.

Although Sister Diomira is not very conscious of it, you should have corrected her when she spoke badly of the house she left. The correction will make her more cautious, especially since she desires to make profession; likewise with the new arrivals. You know it is customary to warn them at the station not to bring news of their house or of the world. When I accompanied them, I always spoke to them upon their arrival. Now it is your job to go meet them and to advise them like a good mother.

You should also have corrected Mother Clement for her levity rather than going to the superior. She should never have done that, and it is your duty to prevent it. You realize that such levity is incompatible with our Institute. What you have not done so far, you will do now; next time it happens, remedy the situation before writing to me about it. I expect this from you on account of the position you hold.

New Orleans has been a matter of serious concern to me on account of the arrival of the new archbishop. I fear that Mother Ignatius, with her great pride, will succeed in compromising herself. It seems that she has reached the point where she was at my arrival, when she made Fr. Cardella believe that she was the only capable person and the only nun whom Mother General trusted, etc.; therefore, call her to your house. It will be necessary to give Mother Ignatius a rude awakening so that she will move without hesitation. You may tell her that Mother General is thinking about organizing the hospital in Chicago and wishes to send her there. This is probable as soon as I can get to it; then keep your eyes on her and do not permit any innovation. Please do this in a hurry before something happens. If she goes, things will be much quieter in that house. The proud always do damage because the grace of Heaven cannot fall on them.

Greet all the Sisters for me and ask them to pray for my intentions. Make the necessary arrangements for the two retreats and the list of Sisters attending each. I will surely be there by that time. Find out from Chicago how that house will maintain itself; until I know that, I cannot make any decision. May Jesus bless you and help you to do all things well.

Affectionately in the Most Sacred Heart of Jesus,
M. FRANCESCA S. CABRINI

November 24, 1897, Codogno, Italy

This Sister receives a strong rebuke for a lack of charity.

A.M.G.SS.C.J.
My Dearest Daughter,

I feel so badly about Mother Alacoque, and I hope you have not aggravated her condition with your cold and uncharitable heart. I hope she recovers soon; as soon as you can, remove her from the place where you put her and send her to New York with Mother Stefanina if she is in such a state that you cannot use her. If she is still downcast, send her with Mother Vincent.

If you do not put an end to your serious failings in charity, you are placing yourself in opposition to the meek and humble heart of Christ; consequently, you create such thorns for me that wound me deeply. I don't care how bad they are, you must not treat them badly but always persuade them with kindness. If I had treated you, with your defects, as you are treating others, where would you be? Instead, I merely ask you to humble yourself profoundly before God and remain in humility. Woe to us, my daughter, if we do not use discretion in the direction of souls! We shall ruin instead of saving them. And then, when we are dealing with professed nuns, we have to be even more circumspect since they are bound to the Institute, and we must keep them on their feet.

Well then, it is better to begin late than never. Start a new life now, a life full of charity toward your Sisters; if you don't know how, ask the adorable Heart of Jesus, Who is charity itself. He will not only teach you but will impress charity on your heart in accordance with your good will. Do this sincerely, for I shall be in your midst soon, and I will expect you not only to console me but to remove all traces of bitterness. Will you do it? I am sure you will because you have always shown a good heart where your mother was concerned.

If candidates ask for admission and they seem suitable for our Institute, accept them if they are under twenty-five years of age and give them a trial. I would like to accept the proposal of the Irish institute, but I cannot say anything now. If they are not in a hurry, I would like to wait a while before making a decision. I also liked the other proposal about the Rosary, but you have not mentioned it lately. When you are questioned about these matters, make sure that they have a plan or description of the project that you can send me.

I wish you all a Merry Christmas. Prepare a nice soft bed for the Christ Child. Hurry to become the true consolers of the Heart of Jesus. I send my greetings to all the benefactors and to the students, who I hope will console me on my arrival.

May Jesus bless you and all; may He grant you courage and generosity in giving yourselves to the love of Christ, our Spouse.

Affectionately in the Most Sacred Heart of Jesus,
M. FRANCESCA S. CABRINI

May 8, 1902, Rome

This Sister, on the other hand, receives a pardon and encouragement for whatever wrong she had committed.

A.M.G.SS.C.J.
My Dearest Daughter,

Come, come into the arms of the mother whom the Sacred Heart of Jesus has given you in religion. Come and do not be afraid, for Jesus accepts penitent souls that return to Him. Come and we shall forget the past. Think only of being a good, observant religious, a true spouse of Christ, Who has chosen you and Who now favors you with a loving call to His arms in order to enclose you in His Sacred Heart.

Come, my daughter, come quickly, because I long to give you the embrace of pardon. Yes, my beloved daughter, I not only pardon you, but I shall forget everything, and that love that I had for you before is still there; do not be afraid. Thank the Sacred Heart for having blessed you so. The good Jesus will bless you and bring you here, your place of peace.

With love I greet you; make sure I can embrace you for the feast of Pentecost. Mother Virginia will have someone accompany you. Believe me that I am and always will be

Yours affectionately in the Most Sacred Heart of Jesus,
M. FRANC. SAVERIO CABRINI

October 1, 1902, New York

In this letter, Mother Cabrini gently encourages a Sister.

A.M.G.SS.C.J.
My Dearest Daughter,

For now it is better that you stay out because I too am on the go. Since you have been out, I have already been in three places. Always let me know where you are, and I will let you know if it is convenient to come before I go to Denver.

Your letters consoled me very much since I saw that grace was deeply rooting itself within your heart. Continue in generosity and you will see that after a long and constant practice of solid virtue, you will find that you are a true spouse of Christ and all your wild imaginations will cease. The

Heart of Jesus will never allow Himself to be outdone. Run toward Him and don't allow any difficulty to come between you, but always approach Him with great simplicity.

As far as silence is concerned, if you behaved like a hermit for a month, either in a spirit of penance or for the exercise of virtue, your reward would be great, and I would see graces pouring down from Heaven. For your comfort: a few excerpts from your letters have served as an impetus toward the conversion of those you had harmed. Stay closely united with God and keep watch over yourself. Greet Sister Michelina for me and tell her to become a lover of silence.

May the good Jesus bless you and favor your steps.

Affectionately in the Most Sacred Heart of Jesus,

M. FRANCESCA S. CABRINI

November 14, 1902, Denver

This Sister apparently wrote to Mother Cabrini that she was afraid she was losing her soul, and Mother Cabrini responds with encouragement.

A.M.G.SS.C.J.
My Dearest Daughter,

Please take Sister Caroline of Brooklyn and Sister Giovannina Curtarelli to be naturalized. They are the names I have given you for the property in Maryland. You haven't told me anything more about those three houses. Take care that you don't lose them; also see whether the Immigrant Bank is disposed to lend us the capital minus $15,000. Start the negotiations at once.

Do not be astonished at my fears, for they are reasonable and are part of our Rule. When a Sister tells me, as you have told me, that you are in danger of losing your soul, without giving me any explanation, I surely have cause to fear. A good mother is obliged to worry, but I am not obliged to remove you from there unless you give me good reason to. Be as simple as a child with your mother, as you used to be, and then all will be crystal clear. I will feel better and you will be more tranquil.

I hear that Dr. Levy is sick. I am so sorry. If he dies without becoming a Catholic, I will have to say that you are not a zealous missionary, for over such a long time, a good religious should have succeeded at least in this; otherwise, what are we doing for them? Even as a token of gratitude we are obliged to procure eternal life for them. Go to see him with Mother Gertrude and Mother Cherubina and say many nice things to him for me and tell him that I am praying for his recovery.

Yesterday Mass was celebrated in our house for the first time, and we also had our hour of adoration. The bishop will come for the inauguration on Monday. I saw the highest mountains in the United States, among them Pikes Peak. I really like Colorado, and I hope we strike gold here. I have already received gifts of precious minerals. Soon I will go to Chicago but haven't decided on the date. It is not cold here, and I feel fine. If everything goes well, I may need some money; so when I send you a telegram, please send the money insured; on the other hand, I may not need it at all.

May the good Jesus bless you. Write soon.

Affectionately in the Most Sacred Heart of Jesus,

M. FRANCESCA S. CABRINI

December 20, 1902, Chicago

Mother Cabrini gently jokes with a Sister who is ill.

A.M.G.SS.C.J.
My Dearest Daughter,

What got into you that you got sick at such a busy time? Well, this time I forgive you, but don't do it again without the permission of obedience. As soon as you are well and able to move, go the hospital for a few days. I shall arrive there the second day after Christmas so that you can spend a day with me either at the hospital or at the villa.

If the Sisters are good, they will deport themselves as true religious during your absence, for perfect observance is worth more than austerity. As Saint John Berchmans used to say, "My greatest penance is community life", and you know what a great saint he is. I wish that all my beloved daughters would imitate him. Take good care of yourself until you are well because I want to find you in excellent health.

I prayed and had others pray for you, but I did not write because I was afraid my letter would not find you in Brooklyn. May the new year see not the defects but the virtues of the Sisters, in which they must grow daily in order to please the Heart of Jesus. Let Mother Teofila fill in for you during your absence.

May the good Jesus bless you and all the Sisters, and may He make you holy and defend you from all harm.

Affectionately in the Most Sacred Heart of Jesus,
M. FRANCESCA S. CABRINI

May 7, 1903, Chicago

In this letter, Mother Cabrini detects an old bad habit in the Sister and offers advice.

My Dearest Daughter,

From your descriptions I very much like Seattle and would love to open an orphanage there. I hope you will not disappoint me, for it seems to be the key to many other missions. The fact that it must be on a small scale is good, since that is what suits us at the moment. Take this matter seriously and begin at once; the rest will follow.

Your last letter displeased me very much because in it I noticed signs of your old malady, of which I think you don't want to be cured. I believe that you have good will even though you don't show it. Angry people who have good will and a heart beg people not to approach them so that they won't bite them; but you frequently send out your bites across the states, giving vent to your passions. See what a naughty daughter you are? While I was writing to you, you were writing to me, but not with the same sentiments of joy that I was nurturing for you.

Read the chapter on modesty and see if Juliana acted contrary to it. All this serves to make you humble, which is the only medicine that can cure you. Yes, humble yourself beneath the feet of all your Sisters. This must be your tonic, and then you will become a good patient. All your other qualities are worthless without humility, which brings the blessings of God.

I said not to worry about the box any longer; you have told me, and that is sufficient. This does not cancel any of the assignments I have given you and that you will carry out with humility in punishment for your pride. I want you to be as simple as a child because Jesus wants it too, but how long must I wait, my child? Remember that only the humble deserve to work in the field of the Lord, so become the good servant of Christ and consider all your Sisters as being better than you are. During the month of May, honor Mary with humility so as to prepare yourself to honor Jesus with the humility you have acquired. Silence and conquered vanity will greatly help you achieve this end.

Tomorrow I will see Archbishop Riordan here, but I am not expecting much. For now, think about Seattle, which I like very much. Greet your companion for me and treat her as if I were at your side; otherwise, I'll come in during the night to pull your ears. May the good Jesus bless and help you.

Affectionately in the Heart of Jesus,
M. FRANCESCA S. CABRINI

January 8, 1904, Seattle

Mother Cabrini tells a complaining Sister that she cares for her and gives her spiritual encouragement.

A.M.G.SS.C.J.
My Dearest Daughter,

Soon after mailing my letter I received yours, full of sad, sad complaints. How can you imagine that I am not pleased with you? I don't believe you have any reason for thinking that. You have always been a good, true daughter of the Institute and have always made sacrifices whenever there was a need. When it became necessary to admonish you, you always received advice with simplicity and humility. You have always deported yourself in such a manner that I could never complain about you, and, what is more, thinking about you has always been a sweet relief and consolation. In the future you must never hurt me again by thinking that I don't care for you, and when I am delayed in responding, you must realize that it is the business of the missions that prevents me.

You know that I find myself way up north, but I haven't reached the Pole yet and I wish to do so. There is a territory that used to be part of the Orient and is now a possession of the United States that is calling us. Italians are there as well as Eskimos, whom we could evangelize. For that mission we need participants who are very mortified and unselfish because they will have to endure many privations, including intense cold. Who among you would like to go? I am waiting for applications from all over; so far I have received forty, out of which I have selected five.

Try to inspire the Sisters to the practice of generosity and sacrifice to answer this call. Work hard for vocations and offer retreats in order to attract them.

I am sorry about the death of Bishop Sala. Who will replace him? Perhaps Brera? Then we will have to brace ourselves for another trial, but let us leave everything to the Sacred Heart of Jesus. He knows how to do all things well.

By the time you receive this, you will have already celebrated your feast day, that of the Holy Name of Jesus. May Jesus be Jesus to you and save you from all harm, and may He make you victorious in every difficulty and in the tribulations that are inevitable in this vale of tears. May He be Jesus to you by making you a great missionary who will save souls and be a comfort to His Divine Heart. May the good Jesus bless and accompany you always.

Affectionately in the Most Sacred Heart of Jesus,
M. FRANCESCA S. CABRINI

August 13, 1904, Chicago

Mother Cabrini reminds a superior how to correct the Sisters who serve under her.

A.M.G.SS.C.J.
My Dearest Daughter,

I don't know how much time those you listed for profession have put in. If they are really good and have been in for more than a year and a half, they can be admitted. It is useless to admit those who have no spirit. They make their profession when they have acquired religious spirit, for the Institute needs subjects of whom it can be sure. Consult Mother Caroline, Mother Gertrude, and Mother Mistress. If you don't work fast, you will not have enough time to prepare everything you need. Those who are left behind can make their profession before I leave America. I cannot possibly leave without straightening out this Chicago affair.

If Mother Antonietta has made the retreat, let me know by telegram; I may send for her. I am glad you had a nice feast day. I remembered you were Filomena when I read your letter. This does not mean that I don't think of you and pray for you.

You tell me the Sisters are so holy, but I still have your previous letter in which you almost excommunicated them. Don't look for compliments but for the virtue that each one possesses. When the occasion arises, correct them with holy freedom. This is the best gift you can give them, even if they don't realize it.

Prepare for the retreat with good dispositions because after that, I want you all to be saints. You too must not talk during retreat. May the good Jesus bless you and all. Pray for

Affectionately yours in the Most Sacred Heart of Jesus,
M. FRANCESCA S. CABRINI

August 23, 1904, Chicago

Here is another letter in which Mother Cabrini advises a superior on how to guide her Sisters.

A.M.G.SS.C.J.
My Dearest Daughter,

Tell Mother Andreina to give the rest of the money to Concetta after deducting the cost of a round trip ticket to Chicago, where we sent her because she said that her brother or relative wanted to kill her.

Work hard, my daughter, to cultivate the spirit of the Sisters who are making the retreat. It is the greatest act of charity you can make. Make them know their defects that make them unworthy to be called true daughters of the Institute; inspire them to walk the way of observance and perfect submission.

Be careful to send only a few of them to the superior, so that she will have some time for herself and her reform. A superior always has more need than the others do of becoming a daughter of the Institute who conforms to the Rule and the desires of the Mother General, who is God's representative in your midst. Don't focus on the poor woman herself, but on the authority she represents.

Tell everyone to take a daily walk in Hell with Saint Teresa [of Ávila] to see where their chair has been placed, because if they go there during life, they will not go after death.

Pay my respects to the retreat master and tell him I hope he will make them holy and true Missionaries of the Sacred Heart. Tell him that we have Fr. Van der Eer here, and I am most pleased with him because he is working with a strong spirit as if he had always been with us. Pray that I finish and can come by the end of the month. I send a special blessing to each one of you, because I want you all to become holy, and especially the superior.

May the good Jesus help you.

Affectionately in the Most Sacred Heart of Jesus,

M. FRANCESCA S. CABRINI

August 27, 1904, Chicago

Mother Cabrini confronts a Sister for excusing her own faults in the past, but she commends that Sister for being willing to admit her mistakes now.

A.M.G.SS.C.J.
My Dearest Daughter,

Let us thank the good Lord for having enlightened you and given you the grace of conversion. Now you can say that you are a true daughter of the Institute and can occupy the place that obedience has assigned to you. Perhaps you did not know that when a local superior is not in conformity with the sentiments of Mother General, she ceases to have the authority of a superior. But you have experienced this, since your work did not have the blessing of God. A local superior should frequently ask Mother General to admonish her about her defects, and having been admonished, she should be grateful for this favor and promise to be careful not to harm the work of the Lord but to help it.

Instead, I have on hand many of your letters full of excuses and at times even insolence, especially when I advised you to guard your heart. Now that you are well disposed, I will repeat the admonishment: Guard your heart and treat everyone the same. Don't permit others to compliment you or give you gifts or gaze at you, which will also teach them to observe their vow of chastity. Observe all the rules, especially that of silence, in particular the rigorous silence and meditation that no one must fail to make at the appointed hour, for that has a special blessing from God.

You ask me if you did wrong to talk to Mother Joseph, and I tell you that you did wrong every time you failed to do so. How can she be a good religious if you fail to inculcate conformity to the Institute in her? The fault is with the others: you are responsible for every fault that you don't correct, and you will have to give an account of it to the Mother of God; but blessed be the Heart of Jesus, Who has shown you mercy. Be faithful from now on.

Pray that I can be there for the first of September. Today matters have taken a turn for the better. Have everything ready. May the good Jesus bless you and all.

Affectionately in the Most Sacred Heart of Jesus,
M. FRANCESCA S. CABRINI

February 5, 1905, New Orleans

Mother Cabrini reminds a Sister of the virtues inscribed on the order's banner and how they can be helpful in examining one's conscience.

A.M.G.SS.C.J.
My Dearest Daughter,

On the banner of the Missionary Sisters of the Sacred Heart of Jesus is inscribed IMITATION OF CHRIST—SELF-ABNEGATION—DETACHMENT FROM SELF AND CREATURES—UNION WITH GOD—OBEDIENCE—CHASTITY—POVERTY. No one is compelled to follow this banner; that is the reason why ample time is given to make one's choice. If, however, this banner is chosen, no one is permitted to tarnish it; on the contrary, everyone is obliged to honor and defend it with holiness of life and perfect observance of every rule and tradition.

Let each one examine her conscience on how she observes the rules and traditions, whether or not she loves the Institute as her family, and whether she shows this love by her actions, humility, and obedience to her lawful superiors, who represent God Himself.

So let all foolishness cease! Let each one attend to herself in obedience and simplicity, for without these virtues, no one can conquer her own spiritual enemies; but let all this be done by love and not by force. Our good Jesus does not want any force to be used in His family of the Sacred Heart.

Do you love this family of the Sacred Heart? If so, proceed with courage; eradicate your disorders and soon you will be holy. If not, it would be a useless waste of time, because you would harm not only yourselves but also your Sisters, and you would never become holy. Don't waste any more time, my dearest daughters, in vain fantasy; castles in the air will never enrich you. With a drop of humility and love of God, you will remedy all things. I forgive you with all my heart.

I want you to make sacrifices as you used to do, with great enthusiasm and generosity, so that you may continue until death in humility, simplicity, and true obedience to your superiors. For penance, receive Holy Communion for my intention.

May the good Jesus bless and keep you close to His Sacred Heart.

Affectionately in the Most Sacred Heart of Jesus,
M. FRANCESCA S. CABRINI

September 27, 1914, New York

In this letter, Mother Cabrini shows her relief that a Sister is safe despite being endangered by wartime violence.

A.M.G.SS.C.J.
My Dearest Daughter,

May God bless you for the great consolation your unexpected letter brought me. Imagine! I thought that you were in the midst of the fray and under the bombs; instead, I hear that you are there as calm as can be. I am really very happy. Oh, the Heart of Jesus of Montmartre, in Whom I have the greatest confidence and to Whom I entrusted you, will defend you and all of Paris, I hope. The vow of the French people at that famous shrine cannot be anything but blessed. I am pleased with the precautionary measures taken by the ambassador to send a group of children and Sisters to Genoa. Thus you can act more freely and with less fear.

In the middle of my worry, I was inspired by a certain sense of security, knowing that you are courageous, and courage is all that is needed in those circumstances. I wish you could divide yourself in two and be in London at the same time. They are so fearful that I don't know what they will do.

Write frequently and tell me everything. Send me a letter every week, since that is the greatest gift you could give me.

Take the children of all the wounded soldiers regardless of social status because this is a time to help everyone, rich and poor. You have room; use all of it. Providence will not fail you but will be with you in abundance. Greet the small communities for me, be brave, and Heaven will save you. Write to London and to Rome and encourage everybody. I would love to be with you. Patience! In London they have the Belgians in the house, and I am glad to hear of the good they are doing.

I had not been able to sleep for two weeks, thinking about you; then your letter came and I am able to sleep once more, so write to me. May Jesus bless you and help you in all things.

Affectionately in the Most Sacred Heart of Jesus,
M. FRANCESCA S. CABRINI

P.S.—Keep your hearts and your hopes fixed on Montmartre. That Divine Heart will look down and save you.

296

New York (undated)

Mother Cabrini encourages this Sister to remain detached and focused on the Lord, as well as advising her to forgive those who have hurt her in the past.

A.M.G.SS.C.J.
My Dearest Daughter,

The perfect detachment from all creatures and from yourself that you now possess with great value for your soul is a sure sign of present grace; therefore, be at peace. The time to make a more minute confession is when you have the chance to go to a good Jesuit, and the superior of Codogno will help you find the opportunity.

I needed consolation and comfort, and you have given it to me. Stay humble, distrust yourself, and trust greatly in the adorable Heart of Jesus in order to have the gift of perseverance; then you will gradually arrive at that perfection to which your Beloved once called you and now is calling you again. I always pray for you, and I hope you do the same for me.

I'm glad that you are continuing to keep the registers for the country children. See that the number keeps on increasing, but look out for situations that may spoil your heart. Be strong of spirit and have no concern for human opinions when it comes to breaking away from even the smallest of these. Do not think about the people who once co-operated in your ruin. Try to forget them, because the devil is very clever and tries to make us return to our old affections that wound the Heart of Jesus.

When it comes to perfection, keep in mind that charity begins with one's self. Keep yourself safe and be sure that you will become the grand missionary of the world.

It is said that two-thirds of the conversions made by Saint Francis Xavier were really made by Saint Teresa [of Ávila], and yet she never talked to anyone; but she knew how to pray, suffer, and love our beloved Jesus. That accounts for the two-thirds. And you, with your love for Jesus, your generosity, and your prayers, be the support of all the missions and win many associates for the country boys.

Write to me often. May Jesus bless you and make you taste the sweetness of a soul intimately united with Him. This I wish and implore for you with all my heart.

Affectionately in the Most Sacred Heart of Jesus,

M. FRANCESCA S. CABRINI

P.S.—It would be good for Sister Agatha to go to Codogno for a few days, so send her with the Sisters who are going for the retreat at Easter. In this way she can rest a little, regain her strength, and continue to walk in the way of holiness.

5. The Mystic

Saint Frances Cabrini was a powerhouse of apostolic activity. She founded schools, orphanages, and religious communities as she traveled all over the world. What has often been forgotten, however, is the source of her boundless energy: the many hours she spent in prayer with God. For her, prayer was the heart of the missionary life and the very lifeblood of Christ's saving work in the world. Without prayer, nothing we accomplish is worthwhile. Throughout her life—as shown in the following diary entries—God used Mother Cabrini's openness in prayer to provide her with solutions to seemingly unsolvable problems and to grant her deep peace despite worldly opposition and during life-threatening situations.

Few people realize that Jesus Christ and the Blessed Virgin Mary even appeared to her in visions, not only to console her, but also to encourage her as she built up her religious order. The following excerpts from her journals show us how a true saint converses with the Lord and give us an insight into how a spiritual bride speaks with the Bridegroom of her heart.

* * *

Journal entry during a retreat, November 29, 1878

Mother Cabrini made this retreat to prepare for the Memorial of Saint Francis Xavier—her own patron saint and the patron of missionaries—and for the Solemnity of the Immaculate Conception. This retreat occurred almost exactly two years before she founded the Missionaries of the Sacred Heart. During that retreat, Mother Cabrini made the following private vow to the Lord that would quietly drive all of her subsequent apostolic work.

So far in these spiritual exercises, O Lord, your mercy presses me to desire to suffer all things for your love, O my Jesus, and in imitation of your life, which was a continual martyrdom of pure suffering. You make me long to be humbled in your love, and you show me the way to do it. Yet in so many circumstances, it is as if I lack the courage to put your holy inspirations into practice.

O afflicted Heart of Jesus, for the abandonment you felt in the Garden of Gethsemane, for the horror you felt when you were covered with all my sins to the point of sweating blood, ah, help me, give me courage, that I might overcome all the obstacles that make me less dear to you.

Yes, yes, O Jesus, so worthy of love, allow me to stay here on the Mount of Olives with the sleeping disciples.

My Jesus, I yearn to embrace you, to hold you to my breast, and to dry the precious drops of that blood, which make me hope for salvation and the highest perfection.

Lord, unite me closely with you. Let my bond to you never loosen, O my Love, O Heart of my heart, O Life of my life, O gentlest, most lovable sweetness of my soul.

As you have inspired me, O my Lord, and as you have long asked of me, here I am to offer myself to you as a victim, both today and for the rest of my days, in union with your painful agony in the Garden, for the sake of all the poor dying souls throughout the world in every hour, so that, contrite and sorrowful for their sins, they might breathe their last within your loving arms.

O my Jesus, I will even turn this offering into a vow, as soon as my superiors grant me permission. O my sweet, immaculate Mother, wrap me in the mantle of your protection now and forever, and be pleased to accept the vow that I will renew perpetually on the day of your feast [of the Immaculate Conception], according to your intention, in order to merit your constant devotion, your protection of my needs, and your assistance in death.

Jesus and Mary, beside you, my soul will be at peace! Amen.

From a journal entry during the Spiritual Exercises, October 21, 1882

Mother Cabrini went on a spiritual retreat two years after she founded the Missionaries. She noted in her journal that all of life, even its dullest moments, should become a prayer.

1. I have a great need of the Spiritual Exercises, and I feel an intense hunger for the word of God, which shakes me and lifts me up from my dust.

2. Yet the Lord is always there, ready to console and comfort His most unworthy bride with the holy Spiritual Exercises. I thank you endlessly, O great God, who show me so much kindness by sending such mercy.

3. These Exercises could be the last mercy that God offers me, and woe to me if I do not take advantage of them to prepare the whole treasury of the religious virtues. I could die, and it might be soon, or even very soon, both because of the uncertainty of life and because of my own feeble health, which at every moment puts before my eyes the grave that is waiting for me. Ah, my merciful God, have pity on me; before I die, enrich me with all the virtues

that you desire in me, as you have made me feel so keenly. Speak, O Lord, speak. I am listening, and I want to follow your footsteps.

Lead me along the road that most pleases you. As long as I am doing your will and giving you the most beautiful proofs of my burning love, I am rich enough.

. . .

5. The Sacrament of Penance is one of the greatest treasures because of the humility that it carries with it, requiring us to manifest our sins. Oh, how precious it is when we humble ourselves before God! A single act of humility is worth more than the practice of the most impressive virtues. Humility is truth; it puts us in our true state, for indeed, what are we compared to God?

6. As a Salesian Missionary of the Sacred Heart of Jesus, my heart should burn exclusively with zeal for the salvation of souls.

7. Zeal is a great charity indeed, but only when it is tempered by a kind and gentle love—the love of the Heart of Jesus Christ.

8. Kind words move even the most hardened of souls, leading them to repentance. I must always be gentle in speech.

9. When our words are not heard, let us run to prayer and tell the Heart of Jesus to touch the hearts of His creatures himself. Oh, how much better a job He will do than us!

10. Even in our most ordinary actions, in every kind of work, with every movement, let us be sure to pray to the Heart of Jesus on behalf of sinners.

11. As we are sewing, let us imagine that with every stitch, we are pricking the hearts of sinners, to shake them and help them reform.

12. May we keep the practice of the presence of God always active in our spirits. Let us see Him in every object

that comes into our view, reflecting on the omnipotence, wisdom, and goodness of our lovable Jesus, just like those dovelike saints who were so in love with Him.[1]

13. Even a blade of grass should speak to us of Jesus and serve as a reproach to us, since the grass is so much more ready than we are to do even the least desire of God—we who have vowed our wills to our most lovable Bridegroom.

From a journal entry during a retreat, December 8, 1903, Seattle

By 1903, the Missionary Sisters of the Sacred Heart had expanded their reach to South America and to almost every corner of the United States through schools and orphanages. Mother Cabrini was the superior of several hundred Sisters, and her private retreat notes show that she was constantly including them in her prayers, asking God how best to lead them. What follows is a short exhortation on prayer addressed to her Sisters, written during a retreat on the Feast of the Immaculate Conception. For her, prayer, not work, is the true source of Christian strength.

Prayer is the mysterious ladder of Jacob, rising up from earth to heaven. The delegated angels ascend and descend to come to our aid, communicating to God our vows, our tears, and our sighs, and then they descend from that highest Throne with a return of grace and mercy for us. Yes, prayer opens up the heavens, shuts up Hell, unsprings the dungeons of Purgatory, unlocks the treasury of heaven, stops the scorn of God, calms His anger, makes Him meek and merciful toward His creatures. Prayer draws heavenly

[1] Mother Cabrini is probably referring to the early virgin martyrs: Agnes, Lucy, Agatha, Cecilia, Felicity, Perpetua, and Anastasia.

blessings to the earth, changes human destiny, makes nations happy and prosperous, and supports the families of religious orders. With prayer, the Missionary of the Sacred Heart can do good for all and thus faithfully carry out her mission. Never let the fervor of your prayer go slack, because it is the most loving Heart of your Jesus who awaits you in His love, calling you to Himself from the earliest hours of the morning. He Himself entices you, invites you, draws you gently to His altar, where you pray with devotion and draw out His graces. So prayer, you see, is an immense treasure for you. Its riches are without number, its jewels beyond price, its daisies impossibly radiant. Gather them all, and let not one of them fall from your hand. Treasure them.

Journal entry during a retreat, November 1, 1910 (All Saints' Day)

Here, a sixty-year-old Mother Cabrini reflects on the central place of humility in the spiritual life. For her, all our good works will collapse if we lack humility.

1. In order to build a temple in your own heart and to be united there with Christ, in God, you must silence all enemies, that is, your own passions, putting them all underfoot with one decisive victory.

2. The first step toward an interior life is victory over your own passions. You must not grant any favor they ask of you, for it is written that God cannot live in a heart enslaved to the passions.

3. Reason, faith, and the example of the saints all demonstrate that you cannot reach a true spiritual life except by fighting strenuously against the lower will. This need for combat holds true for everyone, without exception, though

the combat will be more or less painful according to the abundance of grace [received by the person] and the strength of the passions.

4. The most indispensable virtue for developing the interior life is humility. God Himself in the Sacred Scriptures tells us that He detests pride and those enslaved to it—that He resists and humbles the proud while gladly exalting the humble and revealing Himself to them.

5. Humility is the foundation of faith. And since faith, that beautiful daughter of God, is the cornerstone of our whole holy religion, the basis of Christian discipline, and the principle of eternal salvation, it is clear that humility is of incomparable value and excellence.

6. Humility is also the firm and enduring foundation of all the other virtues. Just as pride is the chief of all the vices, so humility is the root of all the virtues. Humility sows virtues in our hearts, cultivates them, and conserves them. She is the mother, the nurturer, the linking thread, the anchor, the support, and the bond of all the virtues.

7. The religious sister who accumulates virtues without humility acts like someone throwing dust into the wind, because when humility wanes, all the virtues that were gathered around it fall to ruin; all good works are nothing if they are not seasoned and perfected by humility.

Miscellaneous notes (undated)

In this extraordinary piece of writing, Mother Cabrini, who was famously discreet about her own interior life, recounts the visionary experiences of an anonymous "soul" in prayer. Although she labels them merely "thoughts from a mysterious book that left an impression on me," the mystic relating these visions is identified several times as the founder of the Missionary Sisters of the Sacred

Heart—that is, as Mother Cabrini herself. Throughout these revelations, which include visions of the Blessed Virgin Mary and of Jesus Christ, with his Sacred Heart visible to Mother Cabrini, there is one persistent theme: the encouragement she received from heaven regarding her mission. Remember that each time the following passages mention "a soul" or a "a servant of God", Mother Cabrini is speaking of herself.

1. Dressed in a dazzling pink gown, with an equally dazzling blue mantle, Mary Most Holy opened her arms in the gentlest show of joy, drawing her trusting daughter to her breast. This fortunate soul claims that no image she has ever seen, not even the most beautiful, captures the lovely and lovable features she beheld in that vision of the Blessed Virgin.

2. One day, a soul was troubled, not knowing whether to accept a certain work for the greater glory of God, since she was afraid of putting those under her in too much danger. Then in the depths of her bitterness, she passionately begged the Lord, who was exposed there on the altar, to grant her a clear guiding light, when suddenly she saw the blessed Host transform into a great light and come to rest on top of a globe, representing the world. The globe began spinning before her eyes, and the Lord showed her, with vivid intimacy, the vast expanse of the places where she would go to bring His work and give Him glory.

She could not yet make out the names of these far-off places, however, because they were written in foreign letters, in a language she did not know at all. Nevertheless, she was eager to carry out all that was being offered to her.

3. Still, she wavered inside, seeing herself as totally incapable and lacking the true spirit required for such an apostolate. Then the Blessed Virgin appeared to her again, with

the Holy Child in her arms. In one hand, she held the world on a looped string, playing with it as though it were a ball. She said to her daughter: "What are you afraid of? Don't you see that everything is in my hands and that I can do whatever I want with the whole earth? If I help you," she continued, "what will you have to fear?"

This soul was deeply consoled and energized by such a great future.

4. Two other times, the Lord showed her the crown He had prepared for her, should she take up this work, which was so dear to His kind and merciful Heart.

5. Once, a servant of God was meditating on the life of the Blessed Virgin Mary when there entered into her mind profound, sublime images of the ways she must imitate her Mother in attitude and action, both for her own sake and for the sake of those under her authority. She felt herself inspired to undertake not only a few great works, but also another lesser one that until then had repulsed her, since it had seemed to her like an act of mere material charity.

But then there appeared a bright light, which made her understand all the spiritual good she could glean from this work of mercy. The light also instilled in her the precepts she would need to pass on and instill into those under her for this exercise of charity, in order to protect their souls from harm.

6. A soul was once afraid to set out on a long voyage and spend many days at sea, also wavering in her doubt over whether the Lord was really pleased with the work she was about to undertake. Then there appeared to her the Most Sacred Heart of Jesus, beautiful and majestic, in a garment of splendid white, who placed a hand on His most adorable Heart and showed her the initials of His Most Holy Name, which was painted there with His bright Blood. Interiorly but vividly, He said to this soul, "Go, because in this Holy

Name, in which you have so much faith, your voyage and your work will be blessed."

She was greatly encouraged by this, and she received Communion with fervent thanksgiving, feeling inspired to perform many beautiful acts of holy love.

. . . .

10. All through this year, this soul had an extremely vivid sense of the presence of God—of her own nothingness and God's enormity—sometimes feeling as though she were melting in her love for her Jesus.

. . . .

12. Once, a soul was very disturbed by certain people who wanted to disrupt a work she had undertaken for the glory of God. They went as far as to make horrible threats and to intimidate her. The good Lord consoled her several times in her deep pain. On one occasion, He showed her a great light shaped like a triangle. In the center was His eye, serene and encouraging. Suddenly from this gentlest of lights came a voice: "It is I; do not be afraid. I will guard you and defend you in everything." After this, the vision disappeared, leaving the soul greatly strengthened in her suffering.

13. Another time, the twelve Apostles appeared to her and, one after another, consoled her in her grief, encouraging her toward greater perfection. This vision left such an impression on her that, even for a long time afterwards, she said she would still be able to tell which Apostle was which simply by his appearance, if she were to see them all again.

14. On a different occasion, she saw herself transported by her guardian angel into a vast field of light, where she spied the gates of Paradise, which were also made out of a resplendent light. She knew that in order to get to these gates, she would need to fly over some clouds of extraordinary beauty, without setting foot on the ground, but she

could not see any road.... She understood that arriving at these blessed doors would mean detaching herself perfectly from everything, purifying the affections of her heart more and more, suffering willingly, and conforming herself in everything to the most holy will of God. She would have liked to explain all she had witnessed, but she could only repeat with Paul, "I have seen what no eye has seen" (cf. 1 Cor 2:9). Having grasped things that the human mind cannot conceive, she could merely say that she felt inspired to make every sacrifice for the love of her dear Jesus.

....

19. A servant of God used to say that the Sacred Heart was her spiritual director and the Blessed Virgin Mary was her teacher. When a holy priest warned her that this seemed quite prideful, she stopped. Even in her inner life, she tried to convince herself of what this priest said, focusing instead on her unworthiness and great wretchedness.

About six months later, while she was deep in prayer and reflecting on how she should go about receiving the Pardon of Assisi, the Sacred Heart appeared to her, wearing a brilliant white garment and radiating gentleness. He said to her, "Why do you no longer call me your Director? This name pleased me so much."

"My Jesus," the soul replied, "you know well how terrible I am, full of misery, unworthy even to be in the presence of your tabernacle!"

Jesus answered, "And yet my riches are yours. I will always help you, giving you my grace and my treasures wherever you go. Trust in me, have great love for my Heart, and teach this love to your disciples."

The same day, she saw the Blessed Virgin Mary in a dazzling gown and a sky blue mantle, with a gorgeous crown on her head, her hands held wide apart. She said, "I am your mother, the Mother of Graces. I always want to be called your teacher. Come to me with great confidence, not only for your needs but also for the needs of those who depend on you. I will teach you how to serve well the Most Sacred Heart of Jesus."

Receiving all these graces, the soul was profoundly humbled, since the heavenly light revealed her own poverty all the more clearly. Yet at the same time, she felt greatly inspired and energized, as if relieved of the pain that certain people were causing her in those days.

20. Once, a servant of God was sick and thus taken away from all her great tasks. She accepted her time of bed rest as a holy retreat, a time of union with God and God alone.

As she was praying one day, in a state somewhere between sleep and consciousness, she saw Jesus, who drew near to her and, with the gentlest expression, said, "Now I want to show you how much goodness there is in just a single one of my hairs.[2] Come with me." Placing her on His shoulder, He carried her over a little cloud and brought her all the way to the gates of Paradise, where, with great wisdom, He pointed out the coat of arms that hung above them.

It consisted of a palm and a beautiful lily, wonderfully intertwined, with two keys at the center. Over the palm, sketched lightly, was a waving whip, and over the coat of arms stood an angel with a sword, to hold back anyone who tried to enter the gates without bearing the mark of the crest.

Beholding this symbol, she had the clear sense that it was the crest with which every member of her Institute must be

[2] Sisters Imelda Cipolla and Maria Regina Canale, the editors of Mother Cabrini's collection of letters in Italian, recognize how unusual this expression is, yet insist that it is indeed what the saint has written: "Uno dei miei capegli" (a poetic plural of *capello*, "hair"). It is a curious phrase but apparently what our Lord said to her.

marked: the lily of great purity and candor, required of all those souls who have given themselves over to the Mission; and the palm of absolute sacrifice, which makes them true victims of the Sacred Heart, in accordance with their Institute, to such a degree that some will even be blessed with martyrdom. The lightly drawn whip indicated penance, showing that the sweetest and most beautiful penance of a religious sister is the perfect observance of the Holy Rule and the perfection of her holy vows.

The marvelous archway was made of solid gold adorned with precious gems, reflecting all the most beautiful colors.

The gates were built of a great, compact light, impenetrable to anyone who does not yet have the gifts of a glorious [i.e., resurrected] body.

Above the arch, she could see the beginnings of a great vault—this, too, made of light—which reflected yet another marvelous light that came from the center of that blessed place, though she could not see the light itself.

Then Jesus told her, "I will communicate all this to the sisters of the Institute, so that they might know the important obligations that will lead them to beatitude. You, too, will benefit from it in your own mission, moving the hearts of many people and guiding them to the perfect observance of the Commandments, for these have been so wounded and neglected."

6. The Saint

The following short excerpts from Frances' letters are spiritual gems that she shared with different Sisters, generally in the middle of long letters discussing practical matters. Her insights on the value of suffering, prayer, virtue, and love of God are applicable to anyone, anywhere.

* * *

Remain Calm in Times of Suffering

November 19, 1883, Codogno, Italy

That you should not feel well from time to time is understandable because you are the spouse of a tortured and suffering Christ, Who is pleased to try His beloved spouses; but that you are depressed and unhappy at times—externally, of course—this must never be. You must be a calm sufferer, like a soul truly abandoned to the Sacred Heart of Jesus, so now take the iron tonic; I trust it will benefit both body and soul, converting you into a missionary of iron.

The Consolation Found in Jesus' Love

May 2, 1885, Codogno, Italy

You must not weep in the midst of your pains but always console yourself with the thought that Jesus loves you very dearly when He draws you to His cross. You know very well what that great saint used to say: To suffer or to die! And you should repeat, it is better to suffer than to die, because in suffering what is pleasing to God lies our first and true mission, by which our soul is purified and we can obtain graces for sinners. Don't worry too much about your lack of confidence in the superior; banish that thought as much as you can. What you cannot tell the superior, you can write and tell me. So why be disturbed?

Trust in Jesus

June 14, 1890, Codogno, Italy

May Jesus be Jesus to you! His Name brings life, health, grace, peace, and joy because it is a salutary name. When it is invoked, demons flee, angels draw near, and graces flow copiously in proportion to the confidence with which it is invoked. Here, then, is my wish, which I am sure will please you: that you may constantly invoke Him with boundless confidence. Jesus has often complained of the enormous weight of the graces that He cannot bestow because of lack of confidence; you, at least, be faithful to Him with great trust. May Jesus be Jesus to you!

Draw Close to the Sacred Heart

September 3, 1890, Codogno, Italy

Cast yourselves into the arms of God, enclose yourselves in the Sacred Heart of Jesus, ask Him to work freely in your souls, and promise Him never to complain or say no to anything He asks of you. Do not exaggerate by making things seem large when they are really small, for all earthly things are small in comparison with God's love. You have the good fortune of making the retreat with a saint, a person imbued with the spirit of perfection whose words will be drawn from the Sacred Heart of Jesus.

The Mount of Calvary

March 28, 1891, Rome

Remember well—I repeat—that Calvary is the mountain of true lovers and that the true lovers of Jesus are always glad, happy, and content, with never a cloud on their horizon. Thus they can always exclaim, "Alleluia! Alleluia! Alleluia!" Yes, alleluia! Today we have risen with Christ. Study the properties of His glorified Body and make them your own.

Mary, Our Mother

September 8, 1891, Voyage from Le Havre, France, to New York

What an admirable model we have in Mary. The child Mary is but three years old, and yet she abandons father, mother, country, and friends—indeed, everything—and flies to God with the swift wings of a dove. She takes refuge in the Temple, a figure of our convents. She, this privileged Virgin, accomplishes, in the Temple of God, all that she had vowed to God from her birth. Mary sees herself rich in grace and fears nothing, and still she flees from the world and retires. Her profound humility is like a thick veil that she uses to hide herself and her gifts. She seeks solitude and silence, a solitary dove, because she desires to unite herself intimately with Him Who is her only love. Mary will certainly have exclaimed, "How lovely is your dwelling place, my God and my all! My soul yearns and pines for You; my heart and my flesh exult in You, O my God and my life! O my God, You are my inheritance, You are my glory, my joy, my crown!"[1] How promptly Mary answered the divine call—and we? How have we responded to the call of God? How do we respond to the grace of God now? What are our virtues? How is our conduct? What are our efforts, our generosity? Mary knew her mission and accomplished it. And what do we do? We also understand what our mission is; obedience shows the way. But do we follow it faithfully? Perhaps we allow ourselves to be carried away by self-love, our corrupted nature, human respect, pride, lukewarmness. Oh daughters, do not waste time. Let us follow faithfully in the footsteps of Mary, our sweet Mother. Let us conquer ourselves, whatever the cost, and we shall have joy in our hearts and peace in our souls! Let us strive, oh daughters, to conquer ourselves, and Mary will cover us with her mantle of virtues; then we shall not have any trouble in making our journey. Let humility, daughters, humility and great charity, detachment from everything, from ourselves, accompany us everywhere.

Jesus Wants Your Heart

February 24, 1892, Granada, Spain

Oh, yes, my daughters, may our Jesus really be our all so that our hearts may never incline this way or that toward creatures. Creatures without Jesus can in no way help us; on the contrary, they can harm us if we bestow on them the affection of our hearts, of which Jesus is very jealous.

[1] Mother Cabrini quotes from multiple psalms in this passage.

Jesus wants all your heart. How many times have you felt sad, troubled, melancholy, and disturbed without knowing the reason?... Enter into the silence of your soul and examine your tendencies and sentiments. You will always find that the cause is your detachment from the fountain of life, your Jesus, and your attachment to yourselves and creatures. These things seem trivial to us—like little things—but they are really apostasies, and Jesus is offended and leaves us to struggle alone.

Listen to the Voice of Christ

October 18, 1892, Rome

Listen to the voice of Christ that spoke so clearly to you and that still speaks. Follow Him faithfully in the way of perfection at the cost of any sacrifice. Let self-love scream, but you remain firm. Be humble, very humble, but at the same time joyful and serene. She who easily loses her peace of mind is not humble. She may be endowed with a good character—which is of no value for eternity—but she will never possess humility.

Put on a Mantle of Charity

January 16, 1893, Genoa

Put on a very broad mantle of charity, a mantle twice the size of your cloak, and you will see that you can establish peace everywhere—the only thing I really want—because where there is peace, there is God; where there is no peace, there is Hell with its demons. Strive at all costs to bring peace to everyone; in this way they will love Jesus more and will console His Divine Heart.

Live by Faith in Jesus

May 15, 1893, Codogno, Italy

Jesus is good, He is always with us, around us, and within us and never abandons us for an instant, even though the darkness of our spirit hides Him from view. How lovely it is to live by faith! And the best time to exercise faith is precisely the time of desolation. What is more, everything that is done merely out of faith is done more purely and with greater merit.

A Model of Perfection

December 1894, Genoa

I am sending you a model so that you will not deviate from the way of perfection. Place the memory of this picture in the sanctuary of your heart; dearly love the interior life, which flourishes in silence, in prayer, and in suffering. Everything is passing now, but that which comes afterward lasts for eternity. May the powerful Holy Name of Jesus give you grace in abundance as well as all the virtues of a good religious, the perfect spouse of Jesus. With the cross is Mary, who wants to help and protect you; trust in her, and everything will go smoothly for you.

Rise Again from Your Defects

April 15, 1895, New York

If every day you rise again from your defects, if every day you make new resolutions and say, "Today I begin again," then you have risen again. Yes, you have not only been raised with Christ, but, like doves, you are living in the sacred clefts of the living stone, Jesus Christ your Spouse. Do not regret the effort involved in conquering self, in mastering your pride; submit to obedience like faithful virgins, not caring who gives the command or what it is.

Honoring the Sacred Heart in June

June 1, 1895, Voyage from New Orleans to Panama

Today, a beautiful and sublime spectacle is offered to the spiritual sight of the soul.... The dear month of June is at hand, in which all of us, united into one heart far and wide and animated by the same faith and trust, will honor the Sacred Heart of Jesus, in order to procure for Him all the glory we can with the fidelity that belongs to loving hearts, to make reparation for so much ingratitude, which He lamented to His beloved Margaret [Mary Alacoque]. This is the month of love, and love ought to transform us all.... But what are the necessary means for achieving this blessed transformation? The first is to approach the Sacred Heart of Jesus in a spirit of humility and confidence; the second is to let grace work in us, following its impulses with fidelity and constancy. In prayer and in the pouring out of our souls, the good Jesus, through the goodness of His Divine Heart, makes known to us our ugliness and our misery. But we should not fly away frightened by the knowledge we receive of ourselves; we should rather humble ourselves and beg God to free us from our misery. Let us not be discouraged at seeing ourselves so far from the perfection of holy love, because Jesus desires to grant it to us, to help us in our own efforts. It is enough if we have recourse to Him with a sincere desire to respond to His graces and to entrust ourselves entirely to His love. Let us throw ourselves into the blessed flames of the Most Sacred

Heart of Jesus, and let that holy fire penetrate into the very center of our spirit, so that it may destroy, purify, renew, and sanctify all our thoughts, affections, sentiments, intentions, and desires. What have we to fear if the Most Sacred Heart of Jesus protects us? And what may we not hope for, if we entrust ourselves to the Heart of such a compassionate and powerful Advocate? Let us fix our gaze on the wound of the Sacred Heart of Jesus. We shall read in characters of blood the height and depth of the love that He bears us, and we shall always feel comforted, wherever we are, in hoping for everything from His infinite goodness. Very often our prayers are imperfect and deserve to be rejected by God; but the loving Heart of Jesus corrects them and turns them toward better ends, and He Himself asks, on our behalf, for that which He sees will be for our greater good, and compassionately covers our unworthiness with His merits.

Transformed by the Love of God

June 26, 1896, Buenos Aires

Oh, how the love of God can transform a soul! I hope to find you all transformed so that I can enjoy the peace of Paradise in your midst. If we are not already in Paradise, we are in an antechamber, and the Heart of Jesus is always the center of Heaven. If we want Him, He is always at our disposal.

The Power of Prayer

August 1896, Voyage from Buenos Aires to Barcelona

Prayer is powerful! It fills the earth with mercy and makes the divine clemency pass from generation to generation;

from age to age, wonderful works have been achieved through prayer. We are the dust of the earth, and our days are like the grass. Man is here on a pilgrimage, and shortly will be no more, but the mercy and clemency obtained through the power of prayer will always produce generous and salutary effects in people.

Be Sealed with the Name of Jesus

January 16, 1897, Italy

Tomorrow then, tell Jesus to place His name as a seal on your arm, lips, and forehead so that from now on you will no longer work, but He will work in you. "I can do all things in him who strengthens me" [Phil 4:13], and even more, for it will be He who works through you. The holy picture I am enclosing must be your model: you think of Jesus and Jesus will think of you; so do everything with calmness, ardor, and zeal and be calm and serene always.

The Sweetness of the Name of Jesus

January 5, 1899, New York

Jesus! Jesus! Oh, what sweetness there is in pronouncing this adorable name, at whose sound the demons fly. The name of Jesus is unction, sweetness, and strength; these qualities Jesus must give to you, His Gesuina, on your feast day so that you will be a true and holy missionary. Always remember that although everyone has the obligation to become a saint, you have it in a special way since you bear the name of Jesus, and I had no other intention than that when I gave it to you. In your difficulties it is sufficient for you to say "Jesus", and He will make them vanish. Love,

love your Jesus and remain in His Sacred Heart. Enclosed in it, it will be easy to attain the perfection of our state that I wish for you with all my heart.

Placing Total Confidence in God

September 2, 1899, Voyage from New York to Le Havre, France

Do continual violence to yourselves, ever mindful of the words, "Omnia possum in Eo qui me confortat" ["I can do all things in him who strengthens me" (Phil 4:13)]. Have great confidence in God; let your confidence grow greater every day. You are poor creatures, and so you must lean on the Creator. You are weak and miserable; hence you must rely on the divine omnipotence. Yes, my daughters, lean on your Beloved, because the soul that abandons itself to the Most Adorable Heart of Jesus in everything it does is not only sustained but even carried forward by Jesus Himself.

Mary, the Immaculate Conception

December 8, 1900, Voyage from Genoa to Buenos Aires

This morning, before the break of dawn, the glimmering rays foretold that a bright light would arise to illuminate us with its splendor and raise our souls to noble and higher sentiments. So I could sleep no longer. It was the precious dawn of the day of the Immaculate Conception, and it seemed to me that the gentlest dove, our most pure Mother, had turned her gaze of special predilection to greet us amid these wild waves, and with her voice, which carries away one's heart, invited us to rise and praise her and to place ourselves securely under the mantle of her maternal protection. Thinking of our dear Mother, I forgot all about fatigue. Going quickly to the chapel, we heard the first Mass. At the second, we received Holy Communion in company with Maria Santissima, and so where we could attain no merit for ourselves, it was gained for us by her who is called the Immaculate, whose mantle is beauty and loveliness. Oh, how beautiful is Mary Immaculate! God Himself created her worthy of Himself, all beautiful, all pure, all noble, all glorious! Oh, how beautiful is our Mother! The three Divine Persons love her singular majestic beauty. Mary is the greatest and the most glorious work that came from the hand of the Omnipotent, after the most holy humanity of Jesus. Mary, among all the pure creatures, is the closest and most perfect image of God; the arm of God, the wisdom of God, the goodness of God are reflected with visible splendor in this privileged creature. She alone renders more glory to God than all the angels and saints combined, and the radiance of her virginal purity exceeds the purity of all the angels. "Tota pulchra es, Maria, et macula originalis non est in Te" ["You are all-beautiful, Mary, and the stain of original sin is not in you," from the fourth-century hymn, Tota pulchra es]. How beautiful is Mary! How lovable! This most noble creature is the manifestation of God on earth. Through her, God will be known, adored, loved, and blessed in the world, and thus she is, in a special way, the Mother of the Missionaries of the Sacred Heart, who have as their purpose the sublime mission of instructing her people in the knowledge and love of our divine Redeemer, Who, in the infinite goodness of His Divine Heart, has deigned to call us to so sublime a vocation. What shall we fear, daughters, if Mary Immaculate, the pure dove of God, is our Mother, our refuge, our hope, the cause of our joy? Dear daughters, let us put all our faith, our hope, and our joy in God as their principal cause, and in Mary as their secondary cause; in God as the source of all good, all graces, and in Mary as the salutary aqueduct through which we derive the most pure waters of His divine goodness and mercy.

Be Conformed to the Will of God

December 12, 1914, New York

I hear someone in the corner saying, "Oh, Mother, how can we have peace while our passions seem to foment a rebellion within us?" Don't be afraid; with good will you will make much progress on the way of perfection. Begin today to conform yourselves to the holy will of God and accept everything that happens to you as coming from His hand. Then you will begin to enjoy that peace, tranquility, and joy that the saints experienced here on earth.

SOURCES

Primary Sources

Cabrini, Saint Frances. *The Letters of Saint Frances Cabrini*. Trans. Sr. Ursula Infante, M.S.C. Missionary Sisters of the Sacred Heart of Jesus, 1970.

———. *Lettere di S. Francesca Saverio Cabrini*. Àncora, 1968.

———. *Pensieri e propositi*. Centro Cabriniano, 1982.

———. *Travels of Mother Frances Xavier Cabrini*. Missionary Sisters of the Sacred Heart of Jesus, 1944.

Secondary Sources

Maynard, Theodore. *Too Small a World*. Ignatius Press, 2024.

Saverio de Maria, M.S.C., Mother. *Mother Frances Xavier Cabrini*. Translated by Rose Basile Green, Ph.D. Missionary Sisters of the Sacred Heart of Jesus, 1984.

Sullivan, Mary Louise, M.S.C., Sister. *Mother Cabrini: "Italian Immigrant of the Century"*. Center for Migration Studies, 1992.

Online Resources

Located in America, the Saint Frances Cabrini Collection, or Cabriniana Collection, of Villanova University (formerly owned by Cabrini University) is an archive of information about Saint Frances Cabrini and the Missionary Sisters of the Sacred Heart. The collection contains letters, diaries, reports, clippings, personal items, books, and other resource information, both in Italian and in English. An online database can also be accessed at https://saintfrancescabrini.contentdm.oclc.org/digital/.

Based in Italy, the website of the Missionary Sisters of the Sacred Heart, which includes information about Mother Cabrini, can be found at https://www.cabriniworld.org/.

ACKNOWLEDGMENTS

The author wishes to thank the Missionary Sisters of the Sacred Heart for granting permission to share the letters and journals of Mother Frances Cabrini, once again, with the world.

The author also wishes to thank Anne Schwelm, former curator of the Cabriniana Collection of Cabrini University, for her assistance in research, as well as her insights into the life and spirituality of Mother Cabrini; Thomas Jacobi, associate editor at Ignatius Press, for his vision in bringing Cabrini's letters to a new generation of Catholics, as well as his gifts as a speaker and translator of Italian; Abigail Tardiff, copyeditor, for her masterful editing of these letters to help modern readers better appreciate Cabrini's talents as a writer and her insights as a saint; and all the staff at Ignatius Press for their professionalism and hard work in bringing the words of Mother Cabrini back into print, allowing her to inspire a new generation of the faithful.